The INFO WORLD

Test Center Software Buyer's Guide

1991 Edition

With introduction by Michael Miller
Editor-in-Chief, *InfoWorld*

IDG Books Worldwide
San Mateo, California 94402

InfoWorld Test Center Software Buyer's Guide
Edited by Michael McCarthy, Editor-in-Chief
and Jeremy Judson, Associate Book Editor
Interior design by Michael McCarthy, Mark Houts and Michael Fox
Composed by Michael Fox

Published by
IDG Books Worldwide
155 Bovet Road, Suite 730
San Mateo, CA 94402
(415) 358-1250

ISBN 1-878058-11-8

Printed in the United States of America

10 9 8 7 6 5 4 3 2 1

Distributed in the United States by IDG Books Worldwide.
Distributed in Canada by Macmillan of Canada, a Division of Canada Publishing Corporation.
Distributed in the United Kingdom and Ireland by Computer Bookshops.
For information on translations and availability in other countries, contact IDG Books Worldwide.
For sales inquiries and special prices for bulk quantities, write to the address above or call IDG Books Worldwide at (415) 358-1250.

Dedicated to the hard-working staff of the *InfoWorld* Reviews Department and the *InfoWorld* Test Center, who week after week create the best reviews in the business.

Thanks to Jo Rainie Rodgers and her staff, who converted the reviews to PC-readable format. Many thanks to Jonathan Sacks for his support and tireless inspiration.

Special thanks to William Murphy, without whom this book would not have been possible.

InfoWorld Test Center Software Buyer's Guide

TABLE OF CONTENTS

Chapter 4 - Spreadsheets

Six spreadsheet packages that rule the number-crunching hill

Lotus 1-2-3 Version 2.2 PlanPerfect
Lotus 1-2-3 Version 3.0 Quattro Pro
Microsoft Excel   SuperCalc 5

Chapter 5 - Professional Desktop Publishing
Testing the best for professional results

PageMaker3 for the IBM PC and Macintosh
Quark XPress (Macintosh)
Ventura Publisher (IBM PC)

Chapter 6 - Publish or Perish

Six affordable DTP packages for the nondesigner.

Avagio	GEM Desktop Publisher
Express Publisher	PFS: First Publisher
Finesse	Publish It

Chapter 7 - Relational (Multifile) Databases
Top DOS databases for the right mix of power and convenience.

Clarion Professional Developer	Informix-SQL
DataEase	Paradox 3
dBASE IV	R:BASE 3
dBXL	Smartware II Database
FoxPro	

Introduction

By Michael J. Miller
Editor-in-Chief, *InfoWorld*

The key to successful computing is choosing the right tools for the job. In most cases, this means picking the application software that has all the features that you need to get a task done, and that also will let you perform that task easily.

At *InfoWorld,* the weekly newspaper for PC professonals, we've been evaluating hardware and software for more than a decade — since before there even was an IBM PC. We've seen software change dramatically over time, as new programs and new versions of existing programs have become both more powerful and easier to use. Programs that were the best in their class five years ago would be no more than also-rans today.

In this book we've collected our most recent reviews in the most popular software categories: word processing, spreadsheets, relational databases, and desktop publishing, with a bonus chapter on Windows 3. All these reviews reflect our unique method for evaluating computer software — a complex process that involves a reader survey, a large testing facility, and outside reviewers who are experts in particular software topics.

We begin each product comparison by surveying 1,000 of our readers who buy programs in a particular category. Our readers know a lot about needs in different software categories, because they spend, on average, nearly $250,00 a year buying hardware and software for their organizations — businesses, government, and universities. From the reader survey we get information on the programs our readers want evaluated, how they intend to use these programs, and how importantly they weight various features. From the survey we select the products for testing and then develop a comprehensive test plan that looks at each aspect of the program.

All of the software is tested in two different ways. The programs are examined by technicians at the *InfoWorld* Test Center, a multimillion test facility in Menlo Park, California, which performs objective tests, looking at features, speed, and compatibility. At the same time the programs are put through their paces by one or members of the *InfoWorld* Review Board, a 40-member board of people who are experts in how particular product areas are used in real businesses. (For example, our word processing reviewer has been responsible for specifying word processing software for a major university, our spreadsheet reviewer heads the planning department of a large bank, and our desktop pub-

1

lishing reviewers set up desktop publishing systems using PCs and Macintoshes). The Review Board looks at the objective features, but places special emphasis on how these programs would be used in the real world. Finally, one of our reviews editors is responsible for pulling together all of the information and forming a consensus opinion that results in a score for each aspect of the product.

These scores are then given various weightings, as determined by the reader survey, and totaled together to come up with the bottom-line score. The results form the *InfoWorld* Report Card. Since those weights are an average, we've left room for you to insert your own weightings so you can put more emphasis on the aspects of a program that are most useful to you and generate your own, personalized bottom-line score for each product.

The process may be complex, but we feel it helps us produce the most accurate, fair reviews — and reviews that accurately portray the needs of the people who use these packages most heavily.

Remember that the passage of time, and the efforts of vendors to improve their products, can change some issues and facts in these reviews, such as list prices, system requirements, technical support quality, and cited defects. So before deciding to buy anything, double-check important elements.

While reading this book, I urge you to keep in mind your own particular needs. For instance, we may give a mail merge feature in a word processing review fairly heavy weighting, but that doesn't matter if you don't need this feature yourself. You may be more interested in footnotes and tables of contents, or have a stronger need for graphics capabilities. If you keep your own needs in mind, we believe you'll find this book to be very helpful in selecting the software package that is just right for you.

CHAPTER ONE

Evolution of a Test Center

BY LAUREN BLACK
INFOWORLD TEST CENTER DIRECTOR

With responsibility for billions of dollars in strategic purchases, corporate PC buyers face an almost daunting array of hard choices and complex decisions. It is a source of considerable pride here at *InfoWorld* that for the past decade, these volume buyers have relied on us for the information and analysis that makes their jobs easier.

Now, in this book, we offer the same comprehensive product coverage to consumers and small business people, who have just as strong a need to make smart PC purchasing investments.

It was our commitment to informing and understanding America's volume buyers of microcomputer products that led us to build the most advanced microcomputer testing laboratory in the business, and give our readers the most reliable product reviews possible.

Our Test Center now tests and evaluates some 1,000 products each year as part of *InfoWorld's* weekly product comparison and review coverage. Since 1987, we have invested more than $4 million to develop and run our state-of-the-art testing facility, located in our Menlo Park, California, headquarters. In our 4,000 square feet lab, seven expert technology teams are responsible for covering all PC, Macintosh, and networking product categories. Teams comprised of two Test Center evaluators specialize in computers (including boards and monitors), database software, Macintosh systems and software, spreadsheets, local area networks, desktop publishing, and word processing. In addition, a team dedicated to test development works to continually refine the Test Center's methodology.

While the technology expertise behind *InfoWorld's* product reviews is at the Test Center, the entire process involves other key players, including *InfoWorld* subscribers, the *InfoWorld* Independent Review Board, and our reviews editors.

Our Independent Review Board is made up of a 40 person panel of expert PC users who are employed in business, academia, and government jobs. To ensure that our reviews are accurate, fair and balanced, we have established a unique "checks and balances" system that, from start to finish, lasts up to 16 weeks for each published product comparison.

A Tough Test

To select and test more than 1,000 PC products a year, we start with our readers. Here's the countdown for our recent comparison of word processing programs:

Week 1-3: Four months prior to the scheduled word processing product comparison, the Test Center staff selects 1,000 *InfoWorld* readers who have word processing purchasing authority to participate in a Product Evaluation Survey.

Week 4-7: Completed surveys begin arriving at the Test Center. Respondents identify which word processing products they use, which they'd like to see reviewed, a ranking of important features/benefits, and more. Once surveys are in, *InfoWorld* reviews editors and the Test Center staff are back in business. The Center's research specialist tabulates and analyzes survey data and identifies the top ten products for reviews. Next, the test development team develops a battery of tests and establishes a weighted scoring system. At the same time, *InfoWorld* reviews editors contact software vendors to obtain two copies of products — one for the Test Center, one for the Review Board.

Week 8-9: Products testing begins. The assigned Test Center team puts the 10 products through benchmarking tests to evaluate product performance, compatibility, power, and other key benchmarks. Raw testing data is documented. Data is forwarded to a Review Board member.

Week 10-14: Over the next five weeks, the Review Board member puts the ten products to the test by using them in actual business environments — similar to the way our readers would use the products. Word processing software packages will be compared in ease of use, documentation, and real-world application benefits. The next challenge is to document how the ten software products performed, on a day-to-day basis. The Review Board member drafts the product comparison feature, combining their application-specific appraisals with the Test Center's benchmarking data.

Week 15-16: The product comparison is forwarded to an *InfoWorld* reviews editor for final check-off to ensure Test Center numbers and Review Board observations are in sync. Following final approval, the word processing comparison goes to print.

Each year our test development team reevaluates its benchmarks, methodology, and focus. We believe it is the only way to have our reviews reflect what PC buyers need to know. The most significant change in our testing process has been our move beyond benchmark testing. While performance, speed, and other important benchmarks serve as a starting point, they are no longer the core of our review process.

A good example of our solutions approach is evident in the way we evaluate network software products. In a recent product comparison, we had network operating systems such as NetWare and LAN Manager running various business applications on an active, 24-node network. In contrast, other PC testing labs test network software products by running them on a six-node system — too little traffic to see any real benefits or problems.

While many other high technology publications rely on freelance technology writers to evaluate products and submit reviews, we look only to the Test Center, with its 100 PC units, 2,500 software applications library, and staff of 15 full-time, trained PC specialists. This enables us to deliver consistent product comparison and evaluations year after year. The same team that evaluated 386-based PCs last year will put this year's new offerings through the wringer. By developing this centralized, team approach, we ensure that all product reviews are thorough, fair, consistent — and useful — straight across the board, 1,000 times a year.

CHAPTER TWO

How We Test and Score Software

InfoWorld's readers are in the business of buying, managing, supporting, and using personal computer use in businesses, government agencies, and universities across the country. They are no-nonsense about their computer needs: They want power and convenience, expandability and a future growth path, solid suppliers, well-designed and well-made hardware and software, and they don't want to pay gold-plated prices for it. They turn to InfoWorld for knowledgeable, in-depth, no-nonsense reviews that don't flinch at calling a spade a spade.

InfoWorld delivers those reviews by being consistent, explicit, and realistic.

By consistent we mean we always use the same tests and scoring criteria on all products that are alike and aimed at the same market. That way you can directly compare any two reviews we publish of, say, low-end desktop publishing packages, even if the two reviews were done months apart, tested by different technicians, and written by different reviewers.

By explicit we mean that we spell out our procedures and our requirements, and the basis for our judgements, in enough detail that you, the buyer, can second-guess us. We don't ask you to take our judgements on faith. We know a lot about computers, but you are the world's leading expert on your own needs. If you don't agree with our assumptions or our weightings, you have the information you need to change them to suit yourself.

Being realistic in our tests and judgements is hardest of all. Every user's needs, budget, expectations, plans, and constraints are different. To strike a balance, we survey InfoWorld's readers. Each week a detailed, multi-page questionnaire is sent to 1,000 *InfoWorld* readers who are knowledgeable in particular product areas. From these surveys we decide what kinds of tests to run, how to judge the results, and how much weight to give various features.

The InfoWorld Report Card

The fruit of this labor is the InfoWorld Report Card you find in this book. In it, we rate each product in several categories. The Performance category is broken into subcategories that vary depending on the kind of product being tested. You'll find details on how we test and score performance for each software category at the end of the individual chapters. In word processing, for example, we look at basic editing, plus advanced features like style sheets and graphics handling. In spreadsheets we rate formulas, capacity, speed of calculation, and the ability to graph data.

In all performance testing, we use computers that would be considered fairly middle-of-the-road by the typical user in that product category. For example, in word processing we use 8-MHz AT compatibles, because word processing doesn't usually need a lot of processing power — except for the Windows and OS/2 word processors, we can't even get off the ground on such a modest system, so we test them on 386s.

The remaining categories have the same requirements for all software products. Following are details on these scoring areas. In a few product types, we add or change requirements: relational databases, for example, have more extensive and detailed error-handling requirements. Details on these cases are given in the individual chapters.

Documentation:

Documentation scores reflect the quantity and quality of both printed and on-line information. At a minimum, documentation should describe the product and how to use it. We rate as satisfactory documentation that offers a basic printed tutorial, a reference section (or card), and a full index. Bonus points are awarded for a quick-start guide, good on-line tutorial and help programs, useful quick-reference materials, a written tutorial, and error messages that clearly explain problems or offer suggestions on how to resolve them. We also look for clear writing, in-depth information conveniently arranged and readily accessible, good examples, and useful quick-reference material. Poor organization, missing information, or an incomplete index lower the score.

Ease of Learning:

Scores depend on the user interface and the intuitive design of the products. Other factors that influence this score include the complexity of the program and the quality of documentation and tutorials. To earn a satisfactory score, a program typically must be learnable by novices (exception: the relational databases, which are not intended for novices). Clear documentation, tutorials, sample files, and other materials designed to aid the learning process are pluses.

Ease of Use:

Like ease of learning, ease of use is in large part a function of the program's design. It evaluates how easy the average user would find the program to use once the basics have been mastered. Command shortcuts and an easy-to-follow menu system are two features that can simplify the use of a program.

Error Handling:

To earn a satisfactory score in error handling, a program must prompt you to save files and shouldn't do anything to corrupt data or make it easy for you to lose information. It should offer basic protection against data loss and system crashes (i.e., disk full errors, open drive door, etc.), and have basic error messages.

Bonus points are awarded to products that offer more extensive or helpful error messages, an undo command which lets you "undo" an editing action such as deleting a block of text or placement of graphics, and automatic save or timed backup.

Support:

Support is divided into two areas: support policies and technical support. In scoring support policies, we begin with a satisfactory score and award bonuses for product usability warranty (a written policy that if the product does not do what the documentation says it will, the vendor will fix the problem or refund your money), money-back guarantees, a toll-free support line, corporate extended support plans, support hours longer than 10 hours per day, fax support, and electronic bulletin board support. We subtract points when vendors provide no technical support or limit their support to 30 or 90 days.

To judge technical support, we make multiple anonymous calls to the vendor over the course of several days, asking questions about problems we run into while installing and using the product. We base our score on the quality of service we actually receive, and on the availability of knowledgeable technicians.

Value:

Value scores reflect the price vs. the performance, ease of learning, ease of use, and other features of each package tested, taking into account the competition and the intended market.

CHAPTER THREE

Word Processing: Treasures Abound

Word Processors get more graphical and sport even more features

By John Lombardi, Contributing Editor

The hot word processing marketplace has become incandescent in recent months with the appearance of several new-generation DOS and Microsoft Windows products that raise the ante for state-of-the-art word processing.

The 8 office/professional word processors reviewed here illustrate this quantum leap in sophistication. Two these products — Samna Ami Professional, and Microsoft Word for Windows — exploit the new graphical tools provided to Windows-compatible products.

The other six products — IBM DisplayWrite, Microsoft Word, Ashton-Tate's MultiMate, Software Publishing's OfficeWriter, Word-Perfect, and WordStar — offer various levels of text-based professional word processing with graphical capabilities. A few of these text-based models stem from Wang emulations, and still appeal to users with that background.

The differences between these graphical and text-based groups of word processors are both stylistic and substantive. Obviously, the Windows interface differs from what we consider a "traditional" word processor look and feel. The use of icons, mixed graphics and text on the same screen, extensive mouse control, and WYSIWYG editing — all characteristics of the Windows environment — go far to improve ease of learning and use.

In addition, the new graphical products each bring, to a greater or lesser degree, publishing and page-makeup concepts to the word processing desktop. This blade is double-edged, however: For users familiar with a desktop publishing environment, page-layout concepts are second nature; but for those used to typewriter-style word processing, many of the new methods require an adjustment of perspective and understanding. (See sidebar, "Word Processing, Desktop Publishing Use Different Tackle to Catch the Big Fish," in this chapter.) Concepts such as frames (on-screen movable boxes containing text and/or graphics) can take time to grasp. Nonetheless, for many applications the Windows-based products are clearly superior in ease of use, especially for documents requiring complex formatting, multiple fonts, and mixed text and graphics.

These advances in capacity and visual elegance come at a price. While basic program prices have not accelerated substantially — they are hovering just under $500 list and significantly less through retail — the requirements for a minimally acceptable hardware platform have skyrocketed. To run the three new Windows products, you'll need at least a very fast 286 machine; a graphics monitor (VGA is best, but color is not required); a minimum of 1 megabyte of RAM (more is better); and, of course, a mouse (while you can run Windows without one, with one it's much easier).

While we have seen great advances in graphics inclusion, tables and macros have also become major new features for competitive enhancement among these products. Previously we accepted tables built with decimal tab stops, but now many products offer a spreadsheet-like table mode that constructs a mini-spreadsheet inside the word processing programs, complete with rows and columns, calculations by row or column, and formulas. These table objects make the manipulation of tabular material much easier and offer a variety of advantages for importing data from common spreadsheet programs such as Lotus 1-2-3 and Excel. Cell sizes adjust automatically according to font sizes and the amount of text in each. Once you've used automatic tables, you won't want to settle for less.

Macros, once simple keystroke capture facilities, now come with virtually full programming language capabilities. These make some of the word processors truly effective as programming environments for complex word and number management tasks. Very sophisticated automated systems can be built with these tools when combined with the powerful mail merge and forms management capabilities of some products.

All this increased sophistication has also increased the demands on your expertise and training. While the new graphically based products are significantly easier to learn and use, the effective exploitation of their capabilities requires study and experimentation. At an advanced level of expertise, both WordPerfect 5.1 or Word for Windows will

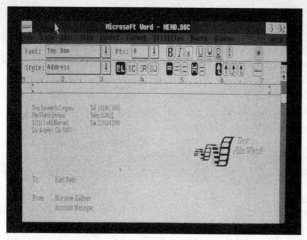

Word for Windows - *Graphical interfaces have added pizzaz to the once staid Word Processor.*

require about the same amount of preparation and training, even though their approaches to text preparation are significantly different.

In short, as the new decade gets under way we are entering yet another era in word processing on microcomputers. As the hardware required to support the graphically based products declines in price, we should expect to see fewer text-based products excelling in the professional word processing class, although the huge installed base of products such as WordPerfect, Microsoft Word, and DisplayWrite will slow the transition to Windows-based products.

In this comparison, we have taken another step in our approach to reviewing word processing. In the past, our methodology focused much more directly on in-depth discussions and analysis of the features than on the actual process involved with document production and use of the product. We have enhanced and in some cases over-hauled our testing criteria to incorporate more of a "hands-on" analysis of the myriad components now common to high-end word processing. The features are still taken into consideration, but as an integral part of accomplishing a task. While you will not read lengthy iterations of features sets within the body of each product's write-up, we have constructed a comprehensive features chart for your reference.

This current crop of programs clearly indicates a fundamental change in the word processing world. The two Windows products fall into the new mode of windowing, layout-oriented word publishing. The remaining are DOS programs which share a character-based inter-face with graphics preview capabilities that vary in sophistication.

EXECUTIVE SUMMARY

As the evaluations indicate, four of these packages are head and shoulders above their competition: Ami Professional and Microsoft Word for Windows are the two top graphics-based packages; while Microsoft Word 5.0 and WordPerfect 5.1 are the two top character-based packages. Among the Windows programs, the edge goes to **Microsoft Word for Windows**, primarily because it has a stronger set of office/professional word processing features combined with strong layout and graphics tools. **Ami Professional** comes in at a very close second, but is stronger in layout and graphics than Winword.

Within the DOS character-based group, the winner remains **WordPerfect 5.1**, although **Microsoft Word 5.0** is a very close competitor. If you use style sheets extensively, Microsoft Word is better.

The two look-alike Wang emulators, **OfficeWriter** and **MultiMate**, do not meet the standards set by WordPerfect or Word, although both serve a form-letter/mail-merge office environment quite well. We prefer OfficeWriter for its better handling of fonts and proportionally spaced text.

WordStar 5.5 shows its age, although it has a simply wonderful page preview, and a number of features common to WordStar 2000 Plus have been incorporated into it. WordStar offers a less effective environment for heavy-duty word processing in spite of its reasonable collection of features, add-on support programs, and optimization for touch-typists.

The least effective product in this group is **DisplayWrite 4**, Version 2, whose clunky interface and limited features place it at the bottom of the heap.

Can any character-based program survive the competition with Ami Professional or Word for Windows? We think so, at least for a while. Windows-based products require a fast 286 or 386 with lots of memory, graphics displays, and ideally laser printers. Without this minimal hardware platform, much of the utility of these packages is lost in slow response and primitive printing. Until the minimum hardware requirements decline in price and become more commonplace, WordPerfect 5.1 and Word 5.0 should continue to enjoy widespread popularity.

INTRODUCTION

Ami Professional

Ami Professional is a full-featured Microsoft Windows-based word processor, with full WYSIWYG editing and extensive graphics capabilities. The strongest competitor for Microsoft Word for Windows and WordPerfect, Ami Pro sports most of the tools required for office word processing: It easily handles graphics mixed with text, imports a host of text and graphics formats effortlessly, and does other office chores such as mail merge with ease and power. It also comes in a scaled-down executive version called just Ami.

Microsoft's Word for Windows

Microsoft's Word for Windows (also known as "Winword") offers an elegant user interface and a powerful set of features that do almost everything we expect of a high-end program with ease and effectiveness. Though Ami Professional, its most formidable competitor, outdoes Winword in graphics capabilities, Word for Windows is the best overall of the new breed of graphical word processors, utilizing many of Word's advantages (such as style sheets) and boasting an interface reminiscent of Macintosh Word. Discounting the interface differences, only WordPerfect can win in a feature-for-feature showdown.

WordPerfect

WordPerfect, by far the best-selling word processor, has built its reputation by offering an effective working environment, endless features, continuous updates, and vastly superior customer support. While still the features champion of word processors, WordPerfect's user interface does not cannot compete with the new Windows-based products, especially Word for Windows. The latest update to WordPerfect, Version 5.1, adds equation editing, table generation, label support, spreadsheet imports, context-sensitive help, and automation of mail merging. Furthermore, technical support hours have been expanded to 24 hours per day and weekend support has been added.

Microsoft Word 5.0

Microsoft Word 5.0, one of the finest character-based word processing programs in the business, is the closest competitor with to the market leader WordPerfect, but now lags somewhat behind its Windows-based namesake in features and WYSIWYG flexibility. Overall, however, it is a fine choice for the vast majority of office word processing chores.

WordStar

The classic word processing program for microcomputers, WordStar no longer represents the state of the art but certainly offers a full

Report Card
Office/Professional Word Processors
Part One

	InfoWorld weighting	Your weighting	Ami Professional Version 1.1	DisplayWrite 4 Version 2
Price			$495	$495
Performance				
Basic editing	(60)	( )	Excellent	Poor
Spelling checking	(60)	( )	Excellent	Good
Mail merge	(20)	( )	Excellent	Very Good
Layout	(60)	( )	Excellent	Satisfactory
Graphics	(50)	( )	Excellent	Poor
Outlining	(20)	( )	Satisfactory	Satisfactory
TOC & indexing	(20)	( )	Very Good	N/A
Style sheets	(20)	( )	Very Good	N/A
Font support	(60)	( )	Excellent	Poor
Footnoting	(25)	( )	Good	Good
Macros	(25)	( )	Excellent	Satisfactory
Printer support	(60)	( )	Very Good	Poor
Compatibility	(60)	( )	Excellent	Good
Speed	(50)	( )	Satisfactory	Satisfactory
Documentation	(75)	( )	Good	Good
Ease of learning	(75)	( )	Very Good	Good
Ease of use	(130)	( )	Very Good	Satisfactory
Error handling	(40)	( )	Very Good	Satisfactory
Support policies	(2)	( )	Very Good	Good
Technical support	(20)	( )	Very Good	Very Good
Value	(50)	( )	Excellent	Satisfactory
Final score			**8.3**	**4.7**

Use your own weightings to calculate your score

InfoWorld reviews only finished, production versions of products, never betatest versions.
   Products receive ratings ranging from unacceptable to excellent in various categories.
Scores are derived by multiplying the weighting (in parentheses) of each criterion by its rating, where:
Excellent = 1.0 — Outstanding in all areas.
Very Good = 0.75 — Meets all essential criteria and offers significant advantages.
Good = 0.625 — Meets essential criteria and includes some special features.
Satisfactory = 0.5 — Meets essential criteria.

Microsoft Word Version 5.0	MultiMate Version 4.0	OfficeWriter Version 6.1	Word for Windows Version 1.0
$450	$565	$495	$495
Excellent	Satisfactory	Good	Excellent
Good	Good	Very Good	Good
Very Good	Very Good	Very Good	Excellent
Very Good	Satisfactory	Good	Excellent
Very Good	Very Good	Good	Very Good
Excellent	Satisfactory	Satisfactory	Excellent
Very Good	Good	Good	Very Good
Very Good	N/A	N/A	Very Good
Good	Good	Good	Excellent
Good	Very Good	Good	Excellent
Very Good	Satisfactory	Satisfactory	Excellent
Excellent	Very Good	Excellent	Excellent
Good	Excellent	Very Good	Excellent
Excellent	Satisfactory	Good	Good
Excellent	Good	Good	Very Good
Very Good	Good	Good	Very Good
Very Good	Good	Good	Excellent
Very Good	Good	Good	Good
Very Good	Very Good	Good	Very Good
Very Good	Satisfactory	Very Good	Very Good
Excellent	Good	Good	Excellent
8.0	6.2	6.4	8.7

Poor = 0.25 — Falls short in essential areas.
Unacceptable or N/A = 0.0 — Fails to meet minimum standards or lacks this feature.
Scores are summed, divided by 100, and rounded down to one decimal place to yield the final
score out of a maximum possible score of 10 (plus bonus). Products rated within 0.2 points
of one another differ little. Weightings represent average relative importance to InfoWorld
readers involved in purchasing and using that product category. You can customize the report
card to your company's needs by using your own weightings to calculate the final score.

Report Card
Office/Professional Word Processors
Part Two

	InfoWorld weighting	Your weighting	WordPerfect Version 5.1	WordStar Version 5.5
Price			$495	$495
Performance				
Basic editing	(60)	( )	Excellent	Good
Spelling checking	(60)	( )	Excellent	Very Good
Mail merge	(20)	( )	Excellent	Very Good
Layout	(60)	( )	Very Good	Good
Graphics	(50)	( )	Very Good	Poor
Outlining	(20)	( )	Satisfactory	Good
TOC & indexing	(20)	( )	Excellent	Good
Style sheets	(20)	( )	Good	Satisfactory
Font support	(60)	( )	Very Good	Very Good
Footnoting	(25)	( )	Excellent	Very Good
Macros	(25)	( )	Excellent	Satisfactory
Printer support	(60)	( )	Excellent	Excellent
Compatibility	(60)	( )	Very Good	Very Good
Speed	(50)	( )	Very Good	Good
Documentation	(75)	( )	Excellent	Good
Ease of learning	(75)	( )	Very Good	Good
Ease of use	(130)	( )	Very Good	Good
Error handling	(40)	( )	Excellent	Good
Support policies	(20)	( )	Excellent	Very Good
Technical support	(20)	( )	Excellent	Poor
Value	(50)	( )	Excellent	Good
Final score			8.6	6.4

Use your own weightings to calculate your score

complement of features. Somewhat less powerful than Word 5.0 or WordPerfect 5.1, WordStar 5.5 ranks above Officewriter and MultiMate, and easily ahead of DisplayWrite. There are a number of stand-alone modules in WordStar, many of which were borrowed from WordStar 2000 Plus, such as a telecommunications program, graphics, and outlining. While effective in their own right, they are not fully integrated with the basic word processor.

MultiMate

MultiMate in Version 4 underwent a significant upgrade that will be very meaningful to the considerable following of this word processing veteran, but to few others. While MultiMate is a strong performer when producing office correspondence and mail merge, it does not have the brilliance or capabilities of the leading text-based office/professional word processors such as WordPerfect or Microsoft Word. This new version adds some interesting new features uncommon in other products, such as a full-featured grammar checker and support for electronic mail. It is somewhat more powerful than DisplayWrite, and equal to OfficeWriter 6.0. Nevertheless, this word processor does its job well and is sturdy and faithful. MultiMate's Wang-emulation roots continue to serve that audience well.

DisplayWrite 4

Something of a dinosaur amidst these classy powerhouses, Display-Write 4 continues a venerable IBM tradition in word processing with its page-oriented, character-based system, and currently ranks at the bottom of this category in performance and functionality. Nevertheless, it is a competent text engine for IBM-standardized organizations.

OfficeWriter 6.1

Following much the same style as MultiMate and DisplayWrite, OfficeWriter 6.1 provides a reasonable selection of features within a smoothly functioning but highly structured user interface. About as powerful as MultiMate, but more effective with fonts and graphics, OfficeWriter 6.1 is a solid office product. OfficeWriter is now published by Software Publishing Corp., makers of Professional Write (our highest-rated executive word processor).

Performance:
BASIC EDITING

Ami Professional 1.1: *EXCELLENT*

Ami's search and replace can look for attributes such as boldface, italic, and whole or partial words. Tabs can be right, left, center, and decimal, inserted by pointing and clicking on a ruler. Paragraph alignment includes left, right, center, or justified. A variable puts in the time and date of last revision or today's date, and full document tracking is available. Hyphenation is effective.

DisplayWrite 4, Version 2: *POOR*

Search and replace is easy to use, but you must identify the case of the word for which you're looking. Tabs can be center, left, right, and decimal, although you cannot generate leader dots (which we consider standard). Date and time stamping appears in footers and headers only. Hyphenation does not occur during editing sessions, but only as a separate operation while paginating or checking spelling. Overall, a limited set of editing features.

Microsoft Word 5.0: *EXCELLENT*

Word is especially adept at creating and cutting and pasting columns, and its hyphenation options are handy. Search and replace is full-featured, including support for mid-word caps. Left, right, center, and decimal tabs are easily set, and time and date stamping is fully supported. You can generate leader dots with tabs. Selected text can be fully, left, right, and center justified.

Microsoft Word for Windows 1.0: *EXCELLENT*

Winword's search-and-replace facility is fully featured, allowing whole word and upper/lower case matching and replacement confirmation. Tabs are excellent and simple to apply to paragraphs or the document, and columns can be cut and pasted. Date and time stamping is easy to use. Hyphenation works automatically. Editing is WYSIWYG at several levels.

MultiMate 4.0: *SATISFACTORY*

MultiMate's search and replace is somewhat minimal, finding words if you know the case they are in. Left and decimal tabs only work if you define them before you type in the text. Leader dots can be created. Paragraphs can be formatted left, centered, or justified, but not right. There is a good date and time stamping for documents.

OfficeWriter 6.1: *GOOD*

OfficeWriter's tabs aren't as complete as we'd like, with only left and decimal stops, and existing text does not adjust to new tabs. Columns can be copied or moved. The search-and-replace function is reasonably quick. Hyphenation is dictionary-based.

WordPerfect 5.1: *EXCELLENT*

WordPerfect's basic editing capabilities are extensive — with easy management of text columns, painless hyphenation, thorough search and replace, and a complete set of tabs (including center, left, right, and decimal). The program supports date and time stamping and revision marking.

WordStar 5.5: *GOOD*

Search and replace offers options to prompt, auto-replace, and maintain case. Tabs are handled through embedded rulers and can be defined as left or decimal, but no right or centered tabs are permitted. WordStar supports columnar cut and paste. Paragraph styles can be applied from predefined styles, but there is no way to center or right-justify blocks of text. Autohyphenation is the default and easy to turn off.

Performance:
SPELLING CHECKING/THESAURUS

Ami Professional 1.1: *EXCELLENT*

While a little slow in operation, the spelling function is very well implemented and designed. Some of the suggested word choices are odd. The thesaurus includes good definitions. Global replacements can be made. Although not quite as good as WordPerfect's spelling checker/thesaurus combo, this is still one of the best spelling checkers we've seen.

DisplayWrite 4, Version 2: *GOOD*

DisplayWrite's spelling checker suffices for most needs and allows word, page, and full-document spelling checking. Suggestions are reasonable, and there is a synonym finder.

Microsoft Word 5.0: *GOOD*

The spelling checker offers suggestions and normally maintains capitalization and punctuation. The thesaurus works well.

Microsoft Word for Windows 1.0: *GOOD*

The spelling checker is easy to use but not flawless; we found a few some words that it missed. Also, you cannot can't do global replacements. You can begin spelling checking from anywhere in the file, and suggestions can be made to appear automatically. The thesaurus works well.

MultiMate 4.0: *GOOD*

MultiMate's spelling checker works reasonably well, although it flags hyphenated words as misspellings and is somewhat awkward to operate. There is also a thesaurus and an excellent, elaborate grammar checker (Grammatik IV), which boosts the score.

OfficeWriter 6.1: *VERY GOOD*
The spelling checker works well and offers nice suggestions. You can specify global replacements, with capitalization maintained. OfficeWriter includes a complete thesaurus.

WordPerfect 5.1: *EXCELLENT*
Spelling checking takes place quickly and effectively, and the program offers with many suggestions. There is also a full thesaurus. The best of the group.

WordStar 5.5: *VERY GOOD*
The WordStar spelling checker is fast and easy to use. It performs global replacements, word counts, and offers a good list of guesses for unrecognized words. There is a useful thesaurus.

Performance:
MAIL MERGE

Ami Professional 1.1: *EXCELLENT*
Ami Pro data files can include imports from many database programs. Producing merged form letters or mailing labels takes little effort with a merge to screen, merge to print, or merge to file for further editing. Programming functions are numerous.

DisplayWrite 4, Version 2: *VERY GOOD*
Mail merging is one of DisplayWrite's strong suits. The program lets you manage complex selection criteria, and the program it supports a large range of external data file types. While the system for creating data files and template documents appears clumsy, the features available are quite extensive.

Microsoft Word 5.0: *VERY GOOD*
Forms management and mailing-label capabilities include variables, formatting, and selection criteria. Word accepts standard ASCII files produced by many database and spreadsheet programs.

Microsoft Word for Windows 1.0: *EXCELLENT*
Mail merging in Word for Windows has myriad programming constructs available for complex merge tasks. It can handle labels, form letters, fill-in forms, and some external files. The program can call macros in its merge function, permitting exceedingly powerful automated functions.

MultiMate 4.0: *VERY GOOD*
As an office-oriented product, MultiMate has strong merge capabilities, accepts many external data file formats, and can select records for inclusion in a merge. It creates labels with ease.

OfficeWriter 6.1: *VERY GOOD*

The facilities for document assembly and list management are handled by a traditional mail merge feature, with conditional selections, mailing labels, and a fine forms management tool called Inform.

WordPerfect 5.1: *EXCELLENT*

Mail merge includes a utility that converts data files into the WordPerfect merge format. This update also lets you set up a merge automatically. The merge permits selections and conditionals that use the same fields and functions as the macro programming language. It handles labels effortlessly.

WordStar 5.5: *VERY GOOD*

WordStar's mail merge feature is reasonably powerful, with multiple selections and conditionals. It uses standard ASCII-delimited files, and complicated form letter applications are possible and easy to produce.

Performance:
LAYOUT

Ami Professional 1.1: *EXCELLENT*

Layout tools are extensive and complex, using a frame-based system to include graphics. You have full WYSIWYG control over the document a non-WYSIWYG mode is also available for quick text entry. Text can be wrapped around graphics and lines can be drawn virtually anywhere on the screen. Tables and charts (generated from a spreadsheet or other data) can be drawn on-screen and automatically laid out. You can easily create multiple columns.

DisplayWrite 4, Version 2: *SATISFACTORY*

While layout is primitive in comparison with the other systems in this summary, DisplayWrite does support column balancing. Editing changes require explicit repagination, and paragraphs have only left and full justification.

Microsoft Word 5.0: *EXCELLENT VERY GOOD*

Word supports multiple columns and table generation, and layout tools in general cover most needs. The page preview offers a good view of final copy. You have fine control over the layout of documents, although you cannot edit in a WYSIWYG mode.

Microsoft Word for Windows 1.0: *EXCELLENT*

Layout options work with great ease, in part due to the icons provided for justification, styles, margins, and spacing. Spacing is displayed on a special ruler at the top of the screen, or you can use a dialog box. Everything appears on-screen as it will in print, which makes layout a snap. As with Ami Pro, a special draft mode for entering large amounts of text will avoid slower operations in the layout modes. Table generation is easy and completely WYSIWYG.

MultiMate 4.0: *SATISFACTORY*
MultiMate offers relatively primitive layout through the insertion of format rulers. You can underline, boldface, and indent with relative ease and you can apply fonts. However, in general, formatting for anything but the most standard layouts is cumbersome.

OfficeWriter 6.1: *GOOD*
Document formatting uses codes and a format line. Adding boldfacing, indents, margins, and spacing is relatively straightforward. OfficeWriter explicitly paginates to wrap columns correctly and automat-ically balance them.

WordPerfect 5.1: *VERY GOOD*
WordPerfect formats through codes in the text. Formatting can be applied to blocked paragraphs or sections of text. WordPerfect also features automatic table generation (done in frames), which is very useful. For a text-based product lacking WYSIWYG editing, none one does layout better.

WordStar 5.5: *GOOD*
WordStar uses embedded codes to handle layout tasks and has added a paragraph style capability that can be applied to generate new formatting characteristics. However, the program's use of dot commands and other embedded codes is clumsy at best for highly formatted document designs. But the preview function, is dynamite (except for the bug we found; see Error Handling) and shows a variety of single and multipage document layouts. This feature enhances the layout score.

Performance:
GRAPHICS

Ami Professional 1.1: *EXCELLENT*
One of the best of its class in working with graphics and formatting layouts that include graphic images, Ami Pro offers great freedom in the placement and sizing of graphic images. You can perform free-form drawing with curved lines, circles, boxes, and a set of somewhat primitive (but useful) clip-art images which is included. TIFF (scanned) files can also be edited.

DisplayWrite 4, Version 2: *POOR*
DisplayWrite includes no graphics support beyond simple line drawing.

Microsoft Word 5.0: *Very Good*
In Word, graphics are imported through a tag line that you insert in the text stream; it calls the illustration at print or preview time. Graphics can be placed across columns.

Microsoft Word for Windows 1.0: *Very Good*
WYSIWYG graphics imported from various supported file formats can be sized, rotated, or clipped, although there are no editing tools. Ami Professional has more extensive graphics support and editing capabilities, however.

MultiMate 4.0: *Very Good*
MultiMate supports many graphics formats. White space is created manually. Graphics, which can cross columns, can be captured from a screen and cut, rotated, expanded, and edited.

Officewriter 6.1: *Good*
OfficeWriter imports a range of graphics formats, which it will display in a preview. You can scale, crop, and resize graphics. Tags for graphics objects open up white space but do not support text wraps.

WordPerfect 5.1: *Very Good*
Boxes serve as frames for imported graphics, which can be sized, rotated, and cropped. There is a screen-capture program and a conversion program for a wide range of graphics formats. Graphics boxes can run across columns, and the program flows text around boxes. Boxes also contain a powerful tables capability. WordPerfect's graphics support is the best available for character-based word processing.

WordStar 5.5: *Poor*
WordStar's graphics are handled through Inset, an add-on screen-capture and editing program. WordStar puts a graphic image into the text with a tag but does not create white space. This cumbersome method lags behind the current standard set by top competitors.

Performance:
OUTLINING

Ami Professional 1.1: *Very Good*
Ami Professional's paragraph numbering schemes have multiple levels but not true electronic outlining with collapsed text under headings. The style-sheet templates include a preformatted outline style.

DisplayWrite 4, Version 2: *Satisfactory*
Outlining is fast and easy with automatic definition of outline levels. You can revise the original outline and change levels, but it does not collapse or expand text.

Microsoft Word 5.0: *EXCELLENT*

The complete outlining function supports multiple levels with the option to collapse or expand text and full formatting control along with numbering options. Outlines can be sorted.

Microsoft Word for Windows 1.0: *EXCELLENT*

This program automatically generates outlines based on the structure of the style sheet for the document. You can move or change levels, and they collapse and expand in true electronic outlining form.

MultiMate 4.0: *SATISFACTORY*

MultiMate's outlining feature involves flagging paragraphs for automatic numbering. It will not collapse or expand text or shuffle outline segments automatically.

OfficeWriter 6.1 : *SATISFACTORY*

Outlining uses outline tab markers that establish levels and permit variable numbering systems. The program does not collapse or expand different outline levels.

WordPerfect 5.1: *SATISFACTORY*

WordPerfect supports up to eight levels of outlining. While sections of an outline can be moved and automatically renumbered, text cannot be collapsed or expanded.

WordStar 5.5: *GOOD*

Multiple-level true electronic outlining is supported by an add-on product, PC-Outline. Which, unfortunately, does not support WordStar formatting (other than through an import). While the outliner is useful, the incompatibility limits the otherwise higher score.

Performance:
TABLE OF CONTENTS AND INDEXING

Ami Professional 1.1: *VERY GOOD*

Tables of contents have three levels and use styles defined in the document. While somewhat less powerful than multiple-level functions, they are very easy to use. Though not as feature-laden as Word for Windows in Ami Pro when you mark a word for indexing and then generate your index, every page number where the word occurs is listed (Winword does not do this). Indexing is automatic but words cannot be tagged for indexing in draft mode, forcing you to use the slower layout mode for creating indexes. Also, index generation does not support words with punctuation marks. These nuisances lower the score of otherwise excellent indexing.

DisplayWrite 4, Version 2: *N/A*

DisplayWrite does not support indexing or tables of contents. You can purchase a separate add-on module for table-of-contents support.

Microsoft Word 5.0: *VERY GOOD*

Tables of contents can be generated with invisible codes or through automatic capturing of outline levels. A good indexing facility supports additional lists; as with Word for Windows, a concordance indexing macro is available on request.

Microsoft Word for Windows 1.0: *VERY GOOD*

Word for Windows automatically creates a table of contents from a formatted document, taking the levels from the document's structure. Indexing is fully supported; concordance indexing is available in a special macro available on request. There are many indexing options.

MultiMate 4.0: *GOOD*

The table of contents feature works by manually assigning tags to each heading; and tabs define the various levels. Automatic indexing is supported.

OfficeWriter 6.1: *GOOD*

OfficeWriter's table of contents can be generated from either outline tabs or section markers. The program will handle various indenting and leader options. Indexes are performed done with concordance lists, after the document is explicitly paginated.

WordPerfect 5.1: *EXCELLENT*

By marking text, you can generate a table of contents with leading characters before page numbers. The table of contents can be placed anywhere in the document and edited or formatted. WordPerfect also supports multiple indexes and lists.

WordStar 5.5: *GOOD*

We found the table of contents and indexing feature difficult to use with WordStar's dot command structure. While you can achieve multi-level tables of contents, the process is needlessly tedious.

Performance:
STYLE SHEETS

Ami Professional 1.1: *VERY GOOD*

Styles are easy to define and to implement. Ami Pro uses a complex system of style storage for documents as well as paragraphs. Most styles can be implemented with a click of the mouse. You have control over all attributes, including hyphenation, margins, columns, lines, and fonts. A number of predesigned styles are included with Ami Pro.

DisplayWrite 4, Version 2: *N/A*
According to our criteria, DisplayWrite does not support style sheets.

Microsoft Word 5.0: *VERY GOOD*
Word 5.0's style sheets blazed the trail in word processing style-sheet standards, and they continue to lead the pack. These fully featured, and multilevel capabilities can be maintained in glossaries and are easily applied to paragraphs. Word's style sheets are the best we've seen yet.

Microsoft Word for Windows 1.0: *VERY GOOD*
Following a Microsoft Word tradition, Word for Windows style sheets have complete flexibility, can be derived from preformatted text, and are easy to apply and change. Styles can be applied to virtually anything quickly and efficiently. This is top-notch style-sheet support.

MultiMate 4.0: *N/A*
Style sheets are not supported in MultiMate.

OfficeWriter 6.1: *N/A*
Style sheets are not supported in OfficeWriter.

WordPerfect 5.1: *VERY GOOD*
Style sheets are extensive and can include a variety of information about formatting, fonts, and other information, but they are not quite as sophisticated as those in Word for Windows or Word 5.0. Still, the support is strong.

WordStar 5.5: *SATISFACTORY*
WordStar supports simple paragraph styles, but little more.

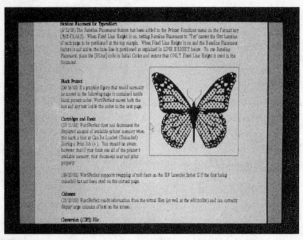

WordPerfect's *preview mode shows document components, including graphics, very realistically.*

Performance:
FONT SUPPORT

Ami Professional 1.1: *EXCELLENT*
Font support is thorough and complete, as with most Windows products. Ami Pro supports a variety of soft fonts as well as printer fonts that look great both on-screen and in print. A nicety is that you can see the various fonts and font sizes in the font selection window. In the draft mode, various font styles appear in different customizable colors. In the layout mode, fonts look better than in Winword.

DisplayWrite 4, Version 2: *POOR*
A reasonable set of fonts come with DisplayWrite, although you can't change font pitch in the middle of the line or use text columns with proportionally spaced text. Soft fonts are not supported. Because of the font inflexibility and lack of soft font support, we must limit the rating.

Microsoft Word 5.0: *VERY GOOD*
Font support is extensive, including soft fonts, although the menus for selection are somewhat confusing. Word 5.0 can apply fonts to paragraphs through styles or to any selected text.

Microsoft Word for Windows 1.0: *EXCELLENT*
Fonts are WYSIWYG and managed by Windows. Fonts can be applied easily through styles or to selected text; you don't have to access a special menu to choose fonts (as you do with Ami Professional).

MultiMate 4.0: *GOOD*
While MultiMate supports soft fonts, its system for previewing and preparing documents using proportionally spaced fonts is clumsy and limited.

OfficeWriter 6.1: *GOOD*
While generally strong in font management and the use of soft fonts, OfficeWriter can't automatically adjust line height for proportionally spaced fonts.

WordPerfect 5.1: *VERY GOOD*
WordPerfect has extensive font support with automatic downloading, and handles soft fonts with ease.

WordStar 5.5: *VERY GOOD*
Full font support for laser printers and complete editing of printer drivers is supported. Fonts display in preview.

Performance:
FOOTNOTING

Ami Professional 1.1: *VERY GOOD*
Footnotes can be placed at the end of the page or the end of the document, but not both. Entering and numbering is easy and effective, and styles can be applied to footnotes.

DisplayWrite 4, Version 2: *GOOD*
DisplayWrite supports footnotes or endnotes (but not both in the same document), and supports a footnote library.

Microsoft Word 5.0: *GOOD*
Footnote/endnote support is standard, with notes printing either at the bottom of the page or at the end of the document.

Microsoft Word for Windows 1.0: *EXCELLENT*
Footnotes and endnotes, which can both be in a document simultaneously, also support cross-referencing.

MultiMate 4.0: *VERY GOOD*
MultiMate supports footnotes and endnotes in documents, with automatic numbering and other options.

OfficeWriter 6.1: *GOOD*
Footnotes work well and can be placed either at the bottom of the page or the end of the document. You can change a document's footnoting format.

WordPerfect 5.1: *EXCELLENT*
Footnotes, endnotes, and annotations can all be entered in the same document with separate formatting and numbering.

WordStar 5.5: *VERY GOOD*
Endnotes, annotations, and footnotes can be entered in the same document. Cross-referencing is not available.

Performance:
MACROS

Ami Professional 1.1: *EXCELLENT*
An extensive macro capability includes elaborate programming constructs, but the free manual must be ordered separately.

DisplayWrite 4, Version 2: *SATISFACTORY*
Macros are available but support keystroke automation only.

Microsoft Word 5.0: *VERY GOOD*
Macros are reasonably extensive and include not only keystrokes but complex programming structures; and macros can be nested.

Microsoft Word for Windows 1.0: *EXCELLENT*
Macros use a complete programming language based on Quick Basic, complete with block structures, variables, types, and other intricate programming features. Unfortunately, the excellent free macro manual must be ordered separately (although it is free, and there is an on-line chapter shipped with Winword for macro information).

MultiMate 4.0: *SATISFACTORY*
Macros are provided to automate keystrokes only.

OfficeWriter 6.1: *SATISFACTORY*
While macros are available in OfficeWriter, they automate keystrokes only. Macros can also be used outside of OfficeWriter, such as for DOS commands.

WordPerfect 5.1: *EXCELLENT*
The macro language is very powerful, with myriad programming constructs, variables, and block structures.

WordStar 5.5: *SATISFACTORY*
WordStar has keystroke macros but no programming constructs.

Performance:
PRINTER SUPPORT

Ami Professional 1.1: *VERY GOOD*
Ami Professional supports all printers carried by Windows, which is an extensive list. It fully supports printing on most types of laser (including Postscript), dot-matrix, and ink-jet printers.

DisplayWrite 4, Version 2: *POOR*
This product now supports many non-IBM printers but no Postscript printers. For the non-IBM printers supported, not all printer features are implemented.

Microsoft Word 5.0: *EXCELLENT*
This program offers printer support for a long list of printers and has a printer editor for creating or modifying drivers.

Microsoft Word for Windows 1.0: *EXCELLENT*
Top-notch printer support is provided through Windows, and additional drivers are included that boost the score.

MultiMate 4.0: *VERY GOOD*
MultiMate supports a long list of printers, including laser printers and Postscript printers.

OfficeWriter 6.1: *EXCELLENT*
The long list of supported printers includes HP and Postscript laser printers; OfficeWriter also provides a printer driver editor.

WordPerfect 5.1: *EXCELLENT*
The printer support for this program is extensive and endlessly expanding.

WordStar 5.5: *EXCELLENT*
WordStar printer support is superior, with the capability to customize printer tables and create new ones.

Performance:
COMPATIBILITY

Ami Professional 1.1: *EXCELLENT*
This program has a wide range of common import and export formats for both text and graphics. While Ami Pro supports one-way links using DDE (Window's dynamic data exchange), Word for Windows' hot-links are two-way.

DisplayWrite 4, Version 2: *GOOD*
DisplayWrite imports a large number of database files and DCA or ASCII text files.

Microsoft Word 5.0: *GOOD*
Compatibility includes ASCII and DCA/RFT plus a large number of graphics file formats.

Microsoft Word for Windows 1.0: *EXCELLENT*
Word for Windows features a slew of text-file import filters and strong graphic file conversions, many of them automatic.

MultiMate 4.0: *EXCELLENT*
Excellent word processor and graphics conversion routines translate numerous common formats for both import and export.

OfficeWriter 6.1: *EXCELLENT*
The program has a long list of file conversions and compatible graphics formats.

WordPerfect 5.1: *EXCELLENT*
With its conversion program for most major text, spreadsheet, and graphics file formats, WordPerfect has quite good support for software programs.

WordStar 5.5: *EXCELLENT*

Text file imports and exports cover most common word processing formats and a few graphics formats.

Performance:
SPEED

Ami Professional 1.1: *SATISFACTORY*

Ami Pro is no speed demon. Limited by Windows somewhat, the layout mode is cumbersome for entering text; draft works much better. Manual scrolling was especially slow. A fast system withlots of memory is almost a must; on the 386 platform, Ami Pro was acceptable. Overall, its speeds are not poor, but they trail behind most in this group.

DisplayWrite 4, Version 2: *SATISFACTORY*

DisplayWrite, while acceptably fast, was one of the slower programs we tested. It was not as sluggish overall as Ami Professional, but it still was in the lower end.

Microsoft Word 5.0: *EXCELLENT*

Microsoft Word was this comparison's jet-stream performer in speed. It blazed through virtually all of the tests (importing a DCA/RFT file being the one exception), meeting or beating all the other packages reviewed here.

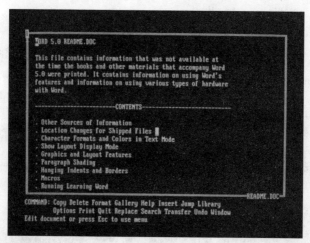

Microsoft Word's *familiar character-based screen features a full set of commands at the screen bottom.*

Microsoft Word for Windows 1.0: *GOOD*
Microsoft Word for Windows did better than its closest competitor, Ami Professional. Winword was actually remarkably fast in manually scrolling through a document, yet it was quite slow in global searching and replacing. Still, considering its Windows overhead, it was quite fast.

MultiMate 4.0: *SATISFACTORY*
MultiMate was on the lower end of the speed tests, turning in several sluggish results. Times were not out of line, however.

OfficeWriter 6.1: *GOOD*
OfficeWriter was about average in speed, coming in with reasonable scores on most tests. It was especially fast in saving a file and in global searching and replacing. It was slow in a few other operations, such as manually scrolling through a document.

WordPerfect 5.1: *VERY GOOD*
WordPerfect was very fast in most tests; the only faster package overall was Microsoft Word. You won't experience any sluggishness with this product.

WordStar 5.5: *GOOD*
WordStar speed results were mixed, with several very fast scores (exporting an ASCII document, loading a document, and appending a file), but with some slower scores on other procedures (importing a DCA/RFT file, jumping from the top to the bottom of a document). Overall, WordStar was quick.

DOCUMENTATION

Ami Professional 1.1: *EXCELLENT*
Documentation is generally good, but the macro manual must be obtained by mail. The manuals cover the program fully, though some descriptions tend to be a little sketchy. There is good indexed and context-sensitive on-line help, and error messages are adequate.

DisplayWrite 4, Version 2: *GOOD*
The documentation you get with DisplayWrite is reasonably complete, covering most features and problems you might encounter. The index is quite well put together.

Microsoft Word 5.0: *EXCELLENT*
Word 5.0's manuals are full of examples and complete explanations, and the indexes are full and complete.

Microsoft Word for Windows 1.0: *Very Good*

The six manuals are well written, have clear explanations, and sport good examples. The main manual is in hardbacked – a bit unusual but effective. The macro programming reference manual, while a fine work, is only available separately.

MultiMate 4.0: *Good*

Although comprehensive and well-written in general, the documentation is difficult to follow when its explaining fonts and proportionally spaced printing.

OfficeWriter 6.1: *Good*

The training manual and reference manuals are both necessary for a clear understanding of the program. The useful printer manual describes how to edit printer files.

WordPerfect 5.1: *Excellent*

The main alphabetical reference manual features every command with examples, hints, and other information needed to understand its use. Documentation is plentiful, and includes a generous quantity of tutorial help.

WordStar 5.5: *Good*

WordStar's documentation includes separately presented material for the add-on packages, but a common index. Most of the documentation is quite well written.

EASE OF LEARNING

Ami Professional 1.1: Very *Good*

Ami Pro is very easy for Windows users, and certainly easy for users of the Ami Executive, but less easy for those unfamiliar with a graphical environment. The style sheet system extensive, takes getting used to, even for word processing afficionados. The WYSIWYG environment eases the learning curve considerably, however, and virtually anyone can be up and running within an hour.

DisplayWrite 4, Version 2: *Good*

This version of DisplayWrite includes elaborate context-sensitive help screens which that greatly enhance ease of learning. While some functions are cumbersome to operate, they are not hard to learn.

Microsoft Word 5.0: *Very Good*

Learning Microsoft Word is facilitated by the great documentation and a fine tutorial, although the sheer complexity of the program may take getting used to for the uninitiated.

Microsoft Word for Windows 1.0: *VERY GOOD*

Winword is very easy to learn for standard office documents, but mastery of all the program's features will take considerably longer. Learning will be easier for those accustomed to a graphical interface, but the operation is surprisingly intuitive for the novice, especially with niceties such as font selection placed directly on-screen. Tackling the sheer complexity and wealth of features can be a formidable undertaking, but Winword does everything in its power to ease the task.

MultiMate 4.0: *GOOD*

MultiMate is easy to learn for simple documents, but more difficult for complex ones and those using fonts on laser printers. Allow a few hours to get up and running.

OfficeWriter 6.1: *GOOD*

Learning OfficeWriter is easy for simple office correspondence. More complicated applications using Inform or the mail merge are more difficult to learn. The help system, book tutorial, and other learning aids help significantly.

WordPerfect 5.1: *VERY GOOD*

The drop-down menus, mouse support, and indexed and context-sensitive on-line help will permit most users to produce standard office correspondence quickly, although more complicated tasks will take longer. While WordPerfect's blank opening screen can be a little intimidating – as can its complexity and huge features list – almost as soon as you dive into the program you realize that it is very intuitive, and learning to use it is actually quite easy.

WordStar 5.5: *GOOD*

WordStar is somewhat hard to learn because of its user interface. It has a "touch-typing" orientation, optimized for the fast typist. While the commands are not necessarily intuitive at first, they quickly become innate with use. The good tutorial helps.

EASE OF USE

Ami Professional 1.1: *VERY GOOD*

The graphical interface, substantial customizing capability, user-selectable icons, multiple editable text views, and shortcut keys contribute to ease of use. Word for Windows is just a tad easier to use, due to the immediate accessibility of fonts. The extensive customization and style-sheet capabilities in Ami Pro also lend ease of use a hand.

DisplayWrite 4, Version 2: *SATISFACTORY*

Good menus and extensive help screens facilitate ease of use, but most functions require selection from a menu. DisplayWrite does not go out of its way to make things easier for the accomplished user in search of shortcuts.

Microsoft Word 5.0: *VERY GOOD*

The complete set of speed keys, complex macros with conditionals and control statements, on-line help, and excellent manuals all combine to make Word easy for experienced user.

Microsoft Word for Windows 1.0: *EXCELLENT*

As you learn the product and the graphical environment, Word for Windows becomes extremely easy to use thanks to the multiple views, speed keys, on-line help, and the graphical environment. Winword can be substantially customized, to the point of changing the menus. This interface is a remarkable hybrid of PC Word and Mac Word, in many cases exploiting the best of both worlds.

MultiMate 4.0: *GOOD*

MultiMate is reasonably easy to use once you're up to speed, but its clumsy structure, need to repaginate under some circumstances, and limitations on using the preview feature and proportionally spaced fonts complicate the management of complex tasks.

OfficeWriter 6.1: *GOOD*

Because of the need to paginate documents explicitly, the clumsy operation of some menus, and the highly structured and inflexible format, OfficeWriter does not get substantially easier to use with experience. Yet it is basically easy to use, and most accomplished users are quite comfortable with its interface.

WordPerfect 5.1: *VERY GOOD*

WordPerfect's flexibility makes the program very easy to use. The page preview, menuing, instantly accessible help, and the reveal-codes screen all contribute to ease of use. It is also customizable, so advanced users will be able to tweak and streamline the program to their liking.

WordStar 5.5: *GOOD*

With experience, WordStar gets much easier to use, and those with an enthusiasm for touch typing will appreciate the control-key approach to managing the various functions. For secretaries who spend a majority of their time typing massive documents and correspondence, WordStar is really worth considering from an ease-of-use standpoint.

ERROR HANDLING

Ami Professional 1.1: *VERY GOOD*
Most errors are captured, and with an automatic timed save and back-up, it takes a real effort to lose data. A four-level undo reverses most activities.

DisplayWrite 4, Version 2: *SATISFACTORY*
There is a backup file, but a power failure can leave portions of text unrecoverable; a special recovery utility may get data back. The Undo command recovers the most recent block delete only.

Microsoft Word 5.0: *VERY GOOD*
Word provides a timed backup, automatic backup on save, an audible "beep" before exiting unsaved files, and special files that accumulate editing changes. The one-level Undo command can even reverse a sort or hyphenation change.

Microsoft Word for Windows 1.0: *VERY GOOD*
There is no timed backup, but rather a timed reminder to save. A one-level undo reverses actions such as formatting and sorting immediately after the action. There is also a Redo feature.

MultiMate 4.0: *GOOD*
MultiMate handles errors easily with a one-level undo for all deletions. There is a built-in undelete for files, but no timed backup. Error messages are sufficiently informative.

OfficeWriter 6.1: *GOOD*
OfficeWriter has a one-level undo that must be implemented right after the error occurs. There is a timed backup and there are multiple warnings when destructive changes or editing changes might be lost.

WordPerfect 5.1: *EXCELLENT*
WordPerfect features plenty of document protection, including a timed backup, promp before exits, and a very effective three-level undo.

WordStar 5.5: *GOOD*
WordStar has a single-level undo, backup files that are created automatically when you save, and a timed backup. We found that the page preview function could be unstable sometimes: When you hit Escape while in page preview, the program can lock instead of displaying an error message; the technical support department led us through a debugging routine that worked, however. This bug detracts from the overall error handling score.

SUPPORT POLICIES

Ami Professional 1.1: *VERY GOOD*
Samna provides a 90-day, unconditional money-back guarantee. Free technical support on a regular phone line is augmented by support available by fax and on CompuServe.

DisplayWrite 4, Version 2: *GOOD*
Only after the current product shipped did IBM add one year of free support on a toll-free line to its support package. As a result, you won't find a tech support number in your documentation.

Microsoft Word 5.0: *VERY GOOD*
Microsoft provides a 30-day money-back guarantee through its dealers; there is also a product usability warranty. There is unlimited technical support on a regular phone line, as well as fax and BBS support.

Microsoft Word for Windows 1.0: *VERY GOOD*
Winword support includes a 30-day money-back guarantee; you must return the product to your dealer for the refund. There is also a 90-day product usability warranty, which guarantees that the product will meet the specifications in the documentation. Microsoft operates a regular phone technical assistance line and offers fax support.

MultiMate 4.0: *VERY GOOD*
A free, regular technical support line is available, and special support is available at various levels and special prices. In addition, there is support on CompuServe and a recorded set of answers to common questions on a toll-free line. There is a 90-day product usability warranty.

OfficeWriter 6.1: *GOOD*
Telephone support is free but on a toll line; and fax support is also offered. There is a 90-day product usability warranty. and fax support is offered.

WordPerfect 5.1: *EXCELLENT*
WordPerfect's support policies are without a doubt the best in the industry. Literally half of this 1,000-plus employee firm works in technical support. The product includes a money-back guarantee, a product usability warranty, extended support, toll-free support (except at night), fax support, weekend support, phone lines open 24 hours, and BBS support. An excellent score understates the generosity of WordPerfect's support policies.

WordStar 5.5: *VERY GOOD*
Support includes toll-free technical support open more than 10 hours

daily, seven days a week, in addition to BBS support on CompuServe and extended support plans available.

TECHNICAL SUPPORT

Ami Professional 1.1: *VERY GOOD*
We called technical support for help and found the technicians informed, accessible, and correct. They often provided extra information about Windows.

DisplayWrite 4, Version 2: *VERY GOOD*
IBM technical support personnel knew the product very well, were helpful and friendly, and answered our questions correctly and quickly.

Microsoft Word 5.0: *VERY GOOD*
Telephone technical support is very good. Our calls produced a short wait on hold and then a well-informed, competent technician who provided good answers.

Microsoft Word for Windows 1.0: *VERY GOOD*
Support from the technicians on the Microsoft support line was good. They answered quickly, were informed about the product, and could respond to a range of issues.

MultiMate 4.0: *SATISFACTORY*
While on occasion the MultiMate phone lines were interminably busy, the several times we did reach them the technical support team, the help was plentiful and knowledgeable.

OfficeWriter 6.1: *VERY GOOD*
The friendly and knowledgeable technicians who manned the OfficeWriter support line answered our questions quickly and correctly.

WordPerfect 5.1: *EXCELLENT*
Highly accessible, toll-free telephone lines specialized by product and function are manned by technicians who know all about the product and its peculiarities. They go out of their way to help with your problem.

WordStar 5.5: *POOR*
WordStar technical support has been notoriously difficult to reach, with a nearly constant busy signal being the standard fare. We did get through one time after four tries, and the support we received was helpful and friendly, and successfully solved our bug problem. However, the inaccessibility overall lowers the score.

VALUE

Ami Professional 1.1: *EXCELLENT*

At $495, Ami Professional is on par in price with the competition, and offers a great deal more than most – especially in its graphics capabilities, which border on the capabilities of lower-end desktop publishing packages. It is a superior graphical office/professional word processor.

DisplayWrite 4, Version 2: *SATISFACTORY*

For $495, DisplayWrite falls considerably short of the office/professional word processing competition, though it sells for the same price. It does not begin to match WordPerfect or Microsoft Word, and doesn't come close to Word for Windows. If IBM standardization is required, DisplayWrite is worth considering.

Microsoft Word 5.0: *EXCELLENT*

At $450, Word 5.0's wide range of features and outstanding performance make it an excellent value. Word 5.0 is less hardware-hungry than the more graphically intensive word processors, so Word is a good choice for an office with slower computers. Its high-quality performance is exceeded in the character-based products category only by WordPerfect. Its compatibility with other products such as Word for Windows is an asset.

Microsoft Word for Windows 1.0: *EXCELLENT*

Word for Windows is less sophisticated as a layout tool or graphics editor than Ami Pro, but a much better word processing program overall, with nevertheless fine layout and good graphic capabilities. At $495, it meets most and exceeds some standards set by WordPerfect 5.1 and will serve any office very well, as long as you have the hardware to handle it.

MultiMate 4.0: *GOOD*

At $565, MultiMate 4.0 costs more than programs with far superior capabilities. If your office is set up on MultiMate, or if you do extensive mail merges but little else, this upgrade is certainly worth consideration. The addition of the grammar checker and support for electronic mail are benefits that will enhance word processing and, consequently, its otherwise satisfactory value.

OfficeWriter 6.1: *GOOD*

At $495, OfficeWriter represents a reasonable value, about on a par with MultiMate but better than DisplayWrite. We prefer OfficeWriter to MultiMate because of its better preview and font management, graceful forms management, and consistent interference.

WordPerfect 5.1: *EXCELLENT*

At $495, WordPerfect represents a fine value. Its extensive features are exceeded by none, and only Microsoft Word and Word for Windows come close to equalling them. Ami Professional and Microsoft Word for Windows outdo WordPerfect with a graphical interface, but for true powerhouse word processing, WordPerfect retains its world championship title.

WordStar 5.5: *GOOD*

At $495, WordStar 5.5 competes at the price level of other heavy-duty products. In this league, WordStar falls somewhere ahead of OfficeWriter 6.0, just barely, but well behind the likes of WordPerfect and Microsoft Word. For the touch typist, it is worth a look.

SIDEBAR

Word Processing, Desktop Publishing Use Different Tackle to Catch the Big Fish

You're out to nab that trophy-size fish. Should you use the deep-sea tackle and power cruiser, or take the Lloyd Bridges stealth approach with your four-band spear gun?

The answer, of course, depends on which system is the best for you. While both methods can catch fish, the hunting styles of each and the types of fish that can be caught realistically differ greatly. The same is true of layout-capable word processors and desktop publishing programs.

There is a temptation – one promoted by product marketing – to pick a "total solution" for a range of tasks. There is, of course, rarely such a solution. Depending on your needs, a sophisticated word processing package may be sufficient for your "publishing" needs, but perhaps you need a word processor for some tasks and a desktop publisher for others. Or maybe you need everything to be fully desktop published. To know how and when to apply which tools, consider the task you've set out to do.

Publishing has three basic editorial components: content editing, copy editing, and copy fitting. In content editing, you don't pay attention to point size, typeface, leading, and other formatting, since these are irrelevant to the task at hand. You do, of course, pay attention to basic character formatting – like boldface and italics – where it's used to enhance the content (by stressing meaning). In copy editing, you check grammar, spelling, and style, and you add coding (or style-sheet tags) to indicate headlines, bylines, and other visually distinct text elements. In copy fitting, you make the text fit the space available while preserving its meaning.

Whether you have a staff of one or 100, you'll want to perform these tasks separately: If you're editing for meaning, simultaneously proofreading for spelling errors will likely result in one or both tasks being compromised.

Desktop publishing programs assume that you use a word processor for the content and copy editing. They make no pretense of being editing programs. It's after these steps are completed that you must decide whether to involve desktop publishing in your layout and production or to stay with your word processor.

What differentiates a desktop publisher from a word processor is that publishing is the merger of verbal and visual presentation. To be effective, you must merge the two forms of presentation interactively and synergistically. The crucial factors are layout type, number of elements, the need to do copy fitting, and fine typographic control. You must decide how crucial each area is – whether you are truly publishing, rather than merely producing, a document.

In a memo, basic formatting is all that's needed for layout: paragraphs, underlining, spacing _ in short, what typewriters have done effectively for more than a century. In an internal newsletter, a word processor's rudimentary layout features are probably sufficient, since you just want a prettier version of what you used to do on mimeograph or copy machines. In a manual, the layout is usually sequential and straightforward, and fine typography is not a major consideration. Again, a word processor is probably fine, although large manuals would benefit from a document processor that can handle cross-references and multiple chapters. In an advertisement, annual report, subscription newsletter, or magazine, you'll want high-quality design and production.

For this last category, you must use a desktop publishing program. Layout-capable word processors, even WYSIWYG engines such as Ami Professional or Microsoft Word for Windows, simply don't have the layout and typographic controls fundamental to both the verbal and visual presentation. Some processors do a reasonable job of straddling the two categories, but integrated packages must sacrifice certain higher-end features or else they become so top-heavy that they are extremely complex to learn and use (see, for example, IBM Interleaf Publisher).

A desktop publishing package offers much more sophisticated multielement control. A newsletter or magazine is composed of several text and graphics elements; the capability to manage multiple threads of text and the graphics associated with each thread is crucial. Something you publish (not merely produce) is not a sequence of stories where one ends before the next begins. Instead, text begins on a page and in a position determined by both its size and relative importance to the other elements, and text jumps to a different page and position, also determined by its size and relative importance. This issue of *InfoWorld* is an example of such multiple threads and files. When you start having a half-dozen or more elements that weave throughout the publication, a desktop publisher is the only way to go.

The third area distinct to desktop publishing is copy fitting, into which come arcane features like tracking and widow control. Most magazines and newsletters must fit onto a certain number of pages, based on press, design, and budget requirements. You can't have a   33-page magazine – it must be in multiples of at least four pages, and typically in multiples of eight. And you probably have ads to fit your text around (you can't shorten or lengthen an ad to make your layout work); and you can't leave parts of pages blank because your copy is too short or just drop text because it's too long.

One of the first things you do is scroll through your layout and start killing widows and tails. A widow is the last line of a paragraph that appears at the top of a column. It is considered unsightly because it is shorter than the other lines in the column and creates unwanted white space in an area that should have none. Some people accept widows if they are at least half the width of the column. A tail is the last line of any paragraph whose length is only a few characters – "few" is a subjective decision. It is both unsightly and wastes a precious line.

You eliminate widows and tails by rewording text more concisely and by tightening the spacing selectively (tracking) in preceding lines in the hope of getting the tail text to move up to the previous line. Tails and widows can easily occupy 5 percent of an article's length, which can be enough to get your text to fit. You can also add widows and tails by loosely tracking text (or using tricks like spelling out common short forms) if your article is a tad short for the space, although this is less common. If the copy is much too long to fit with these techniques, you must go back to the word processor and re-edit it to make it smaller.

This copy fitting requires typographic controls available only in high-end desktop publishing packages such as Xerox Ventura Publisher (for the PC) or Quark XPress (for the Macintosh). It also requires editable WYSIWYG capabilities (not just a full page view that can be seen but not changed), since it's crucial to see the effects of your copy fitting as you do it. The only word processing packages with editable WYSIWYG modes in this comparison are Ami Professional and Word for Windows.

Copy fitting is both an editorial and a design task. An editor must be involved in rewording text, and a designer (or typographer) must be involved in ensuring that the text's appearance is not marred by excessive tracking.

The last area is the art of typography, which only desktop publishing programs truly provide. Unfortunately, this important publishing component is usually the first to be ignored by newcomers to desktop publishing. If you look closely at a magazine, whether Scientific American, Vanity Fair, Time, or InfoWorld, you won't notice how well the spacing between letters and words help carry you along from paragraph to paragraph. You also won't observe how the typography reinforces both the overall feel of the publication and the feel of the content. The fact that you don't notice these things during normal reading is a tribute to the typography, just as not getting confused or bored while reading an article is a tribute to the writer and editor, and not finding grammatical or typographic errors is a tribute to the copy editor.

The crux of this discussion is that a word processor is not a desktop publisher, and a desktop publisher is not a word processor – and there is virtually no need for either of them to be the other. Perhaps some day someone will offer a program that lets you tackle content editing, copy editing, layout, typography, and copy fitting adroitly. But even then, the tasks will be done separately, whether by different people or by one person performing each task in turn. Layout is a component of publishing, but it by itself is not publishing. Whether you choose to solo on a word processor or to bring in desktop publishing power depends on which publishing components you need for the job at hand.

Product Summaries
Word Processing

Ami Professional Version 1.1
Company: Samna Corp., 5600 Glenridge Drive, Atlanta, GA
30342; (800) 831-9679.
List Price: $495.
Requires: IBM PC AT or compatible; hard drive; MS-/PC-DOS 3.0;
640K of RAM (2 Megabytes recommended); mouse recommended; Microsoft Windows 2.X (run-time version included); version
1.2 supports Windows 3.

DisplayWrite 4 Version 2
Company: IBM Corp., Displaywrite Product Support Center, 5 W.
Kirkwood Blvd., Roanoke, TX 76299; (800) IBM-2468, Ext. 126
for dealer information.
List Price: $495.
Requires: IBM PC; PC-DOS 2.1 or later (3.3 recommended); 350K
of RAM; hard drive; versions available for OS/2 Standard or
Extended Edition (compatibility mode) 1.0, 1.1; works with Novell
and 3Com networks; also supports IBM PC Network and Token
Ring Network.

Microsoft Word Version 5.0
Company: Microsoft Corp., 1 Microsoft Way, Redmond, WA
98052; (206) 882-8080.
List Price: $450.
Requires: IBM PC or compatible; PC/MS-DOS 2.0 or later; two
floppy drives; mouse supported; 384K of RAM.

Microsoft Word for Windows Version 1.0
Company: Microsoft Corp., 1 Microsoft Way, Redmond, WA
98052; (206) 882-8080.
List Price: $495.
Requires: IBM PC AT or compatible; 640K of RAM; hard disk; 1 to
2 megabytes of EMS memory recommended; Microsoft Win-
dows/286 or /386 2.x or later (run-time version included); mouse
recommended.

MultiMate Version 4.0
Company: Ashton-Tate, 20101 Hamilton Ave., Torrance, CA
90502; (213) 329-9989.
List Price: $565.
Requires: IBM PC or compatible; PC/MS-DOS 3.1 or later; hard
drive; 384K of RAM, 464K recommended for use of all functions.

OfficeWriter Version 6.1
Company: Software Publishing Corp., 1901 Landings Drive, Mountain View, CA; 94039; (415) 962-8910.
List Price: $495.
Requires: IBM PC or compatible; PC/MS-DOS 2.0 or later; two floppy drives, hard drive recommended; 384K of RAM.

WordPerfect Version 5.1
Company: Word Perfect Corp., 1555 N. Technology Way, Orem UT 84057; (801) 225-5000.
List Price: $495.
Requires: IBM PC or compatible; PC/MS-DOS 2.0 or later; two 720K floppy drives; 384K of RAM.

WordStar Version 5.5
Company: Wordstar International Inc., 33 San Pablo Ave., San Rafael, CA 94903; (800) 227-5609.
List Price: $495.
Requires: IBM PC or compatible; PC/MS-DOS 2.0 or later; two floppy drives; 384K of RAM (for preview and graphics, 512K).

Tackling the Giants: How We Tested Office/Professional Word Processors

Word processors have become so complex that we could no possibly discuss all their capabilities and remain readable. So in this product comparison, we only dwell in te writeup on outstanding or exceptional traits. Our expanded features chart, on the other hand, lists numerous features in great detail.

We evaluated these word processors by comparing performance features and capabilities, employing an extensive laundry list checklist of word processing tools. This provides a baseline for grading the majority of our performance subcategories (except speed, which is based on benchmark results). This method stresses the completeness and effectiveness of tools For this product comparison we supplemented this approach by adding real-life elements. We drew up models representing the kind of documents and results one might wish to obtain from an office/professional word processor, and attempted to duplicate these in each product. Some of these tasks would be very difficult for novice users but relatively trivial for experienced users. The models also place very heavy emphasis on the appearance of the final document.

In the course of evaluating these products, our technicians took extensive notes on how easy or hard it was to execute the various jobs at hand. The data and results we came up with contributed not only to individual performance scores, such as mail merging or outlining, but also to other areas such as ease of use and documentation. The information produced by the Test Center was passed on to our Review Board contributing editor, who is a specialist in word processing. The resulting evaluations were critiqued and edited by InfoWorld editors for accuracy, consistency, and style. The results, consequently, have been scrutinized by several word processing experts.

With the new breed of graphical word processors becoming more common, character-based products face a difficult challenge in such areas as WYSIWYG font handling. Yet character-based products can still receive high scores for most features if they are implemented fully given their interface.

We scored products satisfactory in various tests if they were capable of completing the requisite models, though requiring unnecessary machinations. Products that completed the model with little fanfare or few obstacles receive a score of good. If special features were offered that substantially added to the process of completing the model, very good scores or, in truly exceptional cases, excellent scores were in order.

The testing models we used incorporated mail merging (including labels), graphics, spelling checking, basic editing, formatting, outlining, and table-of-contents generation. The remaining categories were evaluated according to our traditional method of assessing the completeness and effectiveness of features.

All tests were performed on an 8-MHz IBM AT Model 339 80286 with a 30-megabyte hard disk, EGA, and 640K of RAM. Several higher-end packages – Ami Professional, Word for Windows, Microsoft Word, and WordPerfect – were also benchmarked on a Compaq Deskpro 386/20e with 2 megabytes of RAM, a 110-megabyte hard disk, and on-board VGA running under Compaq DOS 3.31 for comparison between our standard configuration and a more optimal setup for these powerhouse word processors.

PERFORMANCE. Basic editing was checked against an existing document with a multiple column table and three differently justified paragraphs. We started with an unformatted document and went to work with each package, attempting to define and move columns with tab functions.

To qualify for a satisfactory score, a package should have left, right, decimal, and center tabs as well as some means of providing left, right, and full paragraph justification. We also looked for case-sensitive search and replace, status-line information (page number, etc.), windowing different documents or the same document, hyphenation options, and date/time stamping.

Our spelling checking model comprised a two-page document with numerous misspellings, some phonetic and some with transposed letters. We also examined the thesaurus. Two grammatical errors were inserted in the model, in the event a product was equipped to catch them.

For a satisfactory score, each office/professional word processor should include at least a 100,000-word spelling checker and a 75,000-word thesaurus, as well as a user dictionary, word replacement suggestions, and a replacement feature that maintains capitalization and punctuation. Bonus items include synonym definitions, multiple dictionaries, and the capability to globally replace words; a grammar checker is worth a bonus. We lower the score for the absence of a thesaurus or case sensitivity.

The mail merge model consisted of a form-letter template with variables representing names, addresses, salutations, and fictional products ordered. We also inserted a date-stamp code. The model was a professional-looking business letter, properly punctuated and formatted on the page. Since it is common practice to print labels for mass mailing, we included this task in our mail merge as well. Our label output consisted of one sheet of 30 labels (in a three-by-10 configuration). We basically require each package to perform error checking (skipping incorrectly entered records) and automatic paragraph reformatting. Bonus features can include mail-merge templates, flat-file managers, programming features (such as conditionals), and database links (DBF or WK1, for example).

Our layout model was one of the most extensive of the group, and the most time consuming. It consisted of a multipage document with numerous font and margin changes, including an 18-point underlined heading, two subheadings, and two 12-point paragraph styles. Products that passed this test were capable of effectively using style sheets or some other method to obtain the same results. We looked at hanging indents, and font- and style-changing capabilities. Basic scored features include multiple columns, right/left-page orientation, column balancing, multiple views/zoom in and out, and other factors affecting page composition.

The graphics model was a single page of two-column text with a straddling headline at the top of the page. Between the columns of text was a vertical dividing line, upon which was centered a TIFF-format graphical image. To pass this test, each word processor needed to snake text in the columns, flow it around the image, and draw the line so that the picture overlaps it. To be able to see this process while it was performed was preferable. We require each package to import at least PCX and PIC graphic file formats and to preview graphics in the document to some degree. We also require the capability to draw at least two styles of lines on the page. Bonuses are given for free-form drawing capabilities, box or circle drawing, fill patterns, and the capability to rotate, scale, crop, or capture screen shot images.

The outlining model was the single most difficult for most of the word processors to pass. This was because few of the products could perform "true" electronic outlining well enough to meet our criteria. While we still considered it satisfactory if basic outlines could easily be constructed, we have updated the criteria to require, for a higher score, the capability to collapse and expand sections automatically as well as easily and automatically to shuffle sections. Our 17-page test document with numerous headings and subheadings was used as the backbone of our outlining sessions. We looked at a product's capability to move a heading from one level to another and retain the text belonging to it. For packages that could not retrofit outline features on an existing document, we generated from scratch an automatically numbered outline to match our model; this capability earned a satisfactory score.

The table of contents and indexing model was reasonably elementary, with styles applied to certain sublevels. Our method of achieving this, however, was not so simple. We used our 17-page document and marked each heading for inclusion in a generated table. If this was possible, we also looked to see if leader characters (typically a period) were available. The inclusion of the first entry as a table-of-contents title was also a desirable goal. Style sheets or their equivalent, where present, came in handy. For indexing, the word processor should be capable of creating an index automatically by "marking" words in some manner. Bonuses were given for the capability to create multiple indexes in the same document, or to create "concordance" indexes (by which you list key words and the program lists every location for those words in the document). For both automatic indexing and table-of-contents generation, we required that each word processor support at least one subtopic level and perform basic formatting. Bonuses were given for cross-referencing capabilities.

To score satisfactory in style sheets, each word processor should be capable of storing a set of styles that include paragraph and character information (line widths, fonts, etc.). Bonuses are given for the capability to store named styles, to record styles by example, or to view styles before they are selected. The formatting/layout category contributed to the style sheet rating, as well.

For most users, font support is a must. Each package should be capable of changing fonts within the text, producing underlined, boldfaced, or italicized fonts, and supporting soft fonts. You should also be able to edit the font as it will appear on the screen (WYSIWYG editing). Bonuses are given for WYSIWYG fonts on the screen. Each product performed at least satisfactorily in fonts overall.

Each office/professional word processor should support footnotes and endnotes. For a satisfactory score, there should be automatic numbering with notes embedded in the text and formatting and automatic superscripting. Bonuses are given for cross-referencing capabilities and on-screen numbering.

Macros are actually short programs that provide automation for manual tasks. Macros provide the capability to customize and perform basic programming functions in a word processor. Many users customize automatic commands, embed functions, and reassign keys to suit their individual tastes and needs. Each word processor should be capable of recording macros and entering commands, as well as saving macros by storing them in the program (not a separate file). Bonuses are given for conditionals or variables support and the capability to reassign function keys.

Printer support: Each word processor should be capable of printing on an HP Laserjet, a dot-matrix printer, and a Diablo-type daisy-wheel printer. Bonuses are given for HP Deskjet or color printer support as well as support for Postscript or for soft fonts such as Bitstream.

Compatibility: Each word processor should import and export ASCII and DCA/RFT files. Bonuses are given for additional file format support, with an emphasis on reading and writing current versions of WordPerfect and Microsoft Word.

We scored speed by comparing the results of all the packages' performance in 11 tests: file loading, file saving, importing an ASCII file, exporting an ASCII file, importing a DCA/RFT file, cursor speed moving from the top to the bottom of a document, manually scrolling to the bottom of a document, reformatting text, searching for the last word in a document, searching and replacing a string of characters throughout a document, and appending a file to the test document. For a satisfactory score, the word processor had to perform quickly and efficiently in a majority of the tests. Higher scores meant the word processor did better overall

Features
Office/Professional Word Processing

■=Feature present □=Feature not present	Ami Professional Ver. 1.1	DisplayWrite Ver. 2	Microsoft Word Ver. 5.0	MultiMate Ver. 4.0
Bullets, automatic	■	□	□	□
Columns				
Parallel	■	■	■	■
Newspaper	■	■	■	■
Auto column balancing	■	■	■	■
Cross referencing	□	□	■	■
Document tracking				
History	■	□	■	□
Summaries	■	□	■	■
Comments	■	■	■	■
Redlining	□	■	■	■
Strikeout	■	■	■	■
Equation generator				
Print equation	□	□	□	□
WYSIWYG equation view	□	□	□	□
Export, file (all support ASCII)				
DCA/RFT	■	■	■	■

OfficeWriter Ver. 6.1	Word for Windows Ver. 1.0	Word-Perfect Ver. 5.1	WordStar Ver. 5.5
□	■	■	□
■	■	■	□
■	■	■	■
□	■	□	□
□	■	■	□
■	■	■	□
■	■	■	■
■	■	■	■
□	■	■	□
■	■	■	■
□	■	■	□
□	■	■	□
■	■	■	■

Features *(continued)*

■=Feature present
□=Feature not present

	Ami Professional Ver. 1.1	DisplayWrite Ver. 2	Microsoft Word Ver. 5.0	MultiMate Ver. 4.0
Word Perfect 5.0	■	□	□	■
Microsoft Word 5.0	■	□	■	■
Other	■	■	■	■
Footnotes and endnotes (same doc.)	□	□	■	■
Footnotes or endnotes (same doc.)	■	■	□	□
Forms processing	■	□	■	■
Frames				
Graphics	■	□	■	■
Text	■	□	■	■
Mixed text/graphics	■	□	■	■
Automatic white space	■	□	■	□
Automatic text wrap	■	□	■	□
Graphics editing				
Bit-map editor	□	□	□	■
Rotation	■	□	□	■
Scaling/cropping	■	□	■	■
Contrast manipulation (gray scaling)	■	□	□	■
Drawing tools	■	□	□	■
Graphics integration				
Insert by code	□	□	■	■
Insert with frame/box	■	□	■	■
File formats				
GEM	□	□	□	□
PCX	■	□	■	■

OfficeWriter Ver. 6.1	Word for Windows Ver. 1.0	Word-Perfect Ver. 5.1	WordStar Ver. 5.5
■	■	■	■
4.0	■	☐	4.0
■	■	☐	■
☐	■	■	■
■	■	☐	☐
■	■	■	☐
☐	■	■	■
■	■	■	■
☐	■	■	■
☐	■	■	☐
☐	■	■	☐
■	☐	☐	■
☐	☐	■	■
■	☐	■	■
☐	☐	☐	■
☐	☐	☐	■
■	■	☐	■
☐	■	■	■
■	☐	■	☐
■	☐	■	☐

Features (continued)

■=Feature present
□=Feature not present

	Ami Professional Ver. 1.1	DisplayWrite Ver. 2	Microsoft Word Ver. 5.0	MultiMate Ver. 4.0
PIC	■	□	■	■
TIFF	■	□	■	■
EPS (encapsulated Postscript)	■	□	■	□
Windows Metafile	■	□	■	□
Other	■	□	■	■
Help, on-line				
Indexed	■	■	■	■
In-context	■	■	■	■
Pull-down menus	■	■	□	■
Hyphenation				
Set zone	■	■	□	■
By formula	■	□	■	□
By dictionary	□	■	□	■
Import, file (all support ASCII)				
DCA/RFT	■	■	■	■
WordPerfect 5.0	■	□	□	■
Microsoft Word 5.0	■	□	■	■
WordStar 5.5	■	□	□	■
Other	■	■	□	■
Indexing				
Single index	■	□	■	■
Multiple index	□	□	■	■
Concordance/ exclusion list	□	□	Optional	□
Kerning	■	□	□	■

OfficeWriter Ver. 6.1	Word for Windows Ver. 1.0	Word-Perfect Ver. 5.1	WordStar Ver. 5.5
□	■	■	□
■	■	■	□
■	w/macro	■	□
■	■	□	□
■	■	■	■
■	■	■	□
■	■	■	■
□	■	■	■
□	■	■	■
□	■	■	■
■	□	■	□
■	■	■	■
■	■	■	■
4.0	■	□	4.0
4.0	4.0	□	■
■	■	□	■
■	■	■	■
■	■	■	■
□	Optional	■	Excl.
□	■	■	□

Features
Office/Professional Word Processing

■=Feature present □=Feature not present	Ami Professional Version 1.1	DisplayWrite Version 2	Microsoft Word Version 5.0	MultiMate Version 4.0
Overall	□	□	□	□
By word	□	□	□	□
By paragraph	■	□	□	□
Line Numbering				
Continuous	■	□	■	■
By page	■	□	■	□
Skip lines	■	□	■	□
List generation (illust, tables, etc.)	□	□	■	■
Macros				
Keystroke	■	■	■	■
Programming functions	■	□	■	■
Mail merge				
W/ conditional record select.	■	■	■	■
W/ ext. database file input	■	■	■	■
W/ spreadsheet file input	■	■	■	□
Miscellaneous				
Electronic mail	□	□	□	■
Grammar checking	□	□	□	■
Mouse support	■	■	■	in graphics
Outlining				
Paragraph Numbering/indent.	■	■	■	■

Office-Writer Version 6.1	Word for Windows Version 1.0	Word-Perfect Version 5.1	WordStar Version 5.5
■	■	■	■
■	■	■	☐
■	■	■	■
☐	■	■	■
☐	■	■	■
☐	■	■	■
■	■	■	■
■	■	■	■
☐	■	■	☐
■	■		
■	■	■	■
■	■	■	■
☐	☐	☐	☐
☐	☐	☐	☐
☐	■	■	■
■	■	■	■

Features *(continued)*

■=Feature present □=Feature not present	Ami Professional Ver. 1.1	DisplayWrite Ver. 2	Microsoft Word Ver. 5.0	MultiMate Ver. 4.0
Collapsing/ expand. sections	□	□	■	□
Page size, custom	■	■	■	□
Pagination, automatic	■	■	■	□
Printer support				
HP Laserjet	■	■	■	■
Postscript	■	□	■	■
HP Deskjet	■	■	■	■
Epson, Okidata, NEC, Diablo	■	■	■	■
Reformatting, automatic	■	■	■	■
Spell. check. (in K words)	130	125	130	110
Style sheets	■	□	■	□
Table of contents generation	■	opt.	■	■
Mult. TOC or other lists	□	■	■	■
Tables of authorities	□	■	■	■
Table generation				
By tab stops	■	■	■	■
By cols. & rows	■	■	□	□
Formatting indiv. cells	■	□	□	□
Math by cols. & rows	■	■	□	□
Import from Lotus 1-2-3, Excel	■	□	■	■
Hot links to spreadsheets 1-way	□	□	□	□
Tabs				
With leaders	■	□	■	□

OfficeWriter Ver. 6.1	Word for Windows Ver. 1.0	Word-Perfect Ver. 5.1	WordStar Ver. 5.5
■	■	□	■
■	■	■	■
■	■	■	■
■	■	■	■
■	■	■	■
■	■	■	■
■	■	■	■
■	■	■	■
80	130	120	100
□	■	■	■
■	■	■	■
■	■	■	■
□	■	■	□
■	■	■	□
■	■	■	□
□	■	■	□
■	■	■	□
ASCII	■	■	■
■	■	■	
□	■	■	■

Features *(continued)*

■=Feature present
□=Feature not present

	Ami Professional Ver. 1.1	DisplayWrite Ver. 2	Microsoft Word Ver. 5.0	MultiMate Ver. 4.0
Centered	■	■	■	□
Right justified	■	■	■	■
Left justified	■	■	■	■
Decimal	■	■	■	■
Thesaurus	■	■	■	■
Tutorial, on-line	opt.	□	■	■
Views				
Graphics/WYSIWYG	■	□	■	■
Editing in WYSIWYG				
graphics mode	■	□	□	□
Magnify	■	□	□	■
Greeked	■	□	■	■
Facing pages	■	□	■	■
Multiple pages	□	□	■	■
Draft mode	■	□	■	■
Guidelines	■	□	■	□
Rulers	■	□	■	□
Windows				
Split screen	■	□	■	□
Edit same doc., 2 or more screens	■	□	■	□
Edit diff doc., 2 or more screens	■	□	■	□

OfficeWriter Ver. 6.1	Word for Windows Ver. 1.0	Word-Perfect Ver. 5.1	WordStar Ver. 5.5
□	■	■	□
□	■	■	□
■	■	■	■
■	■	■	■
■	■	■	■
■	■	□	■
■	■	■	■
□	■	□	□
■	□	■	■
□	■	■	□
□	■	■	■
□	■	□	■
□	■	□	□
□	■	□	■
■	■	□	■
□	■	■	■
□	■	□	■
□	■	■	■

CHAPTER FOUR

Top Spreadsheets That Rule the Number-Crunching Hill

BY **JOHN WALKENBACH**, REVIEW BOARD
WITH **TRACEY CAPEN AND JOHN RICHEY**, TEST CENTER

Believe it or not, spreadsheets have entered their second decade of existence. In 1979, the idea of storing formulas and data in a dynamic row-and-column format materialized on the Apple II as Visicalc. The basic concept remains the same, but today's spreadsheets have powers that are light-years beyond the original vision of Dan Bricklin and Bob Frankston.

In 1990 and 1991 we can expect to see the spreadsheets become even more powerful; we have already seen significant advances in their graphics, output, and database capabilities. The database capabilities of high-end spreadsheets are becoming so sophisticated that many use their spreadsheet as a database. There are other less-familiar areas, such as advanced auditing features, that are also developing quickly.

Another important development in the spreadsheet arena is the move toward applications running under Windows and OS/2 Presentation Manager. Microsoft Excel running under OS/2 Presentation Manager is a front-runner; Lotus 1-2-3/G is another recently released OS/2 spreadsheet.

These writeups are organized by rating categories, in the order given in the Report Card. Products are rated by comparison to on another; for details on scoring, see "How We Tested and Scored Spreadsheets" at the end of this chapter.

EXECUTIVE SUMMARY

This product comparison examines six leading spreadsheets for the IBM PC and compatibles. Now, much more so than in the past, your choice of a spreadsheet will be largely determined by the power of the hardware you'll be running it on.

Lotus 1-2-3, Release 2.2, is a minor upgrade to the company's industry-standard product. Although lacking most of the bells and whistles that characterize the newer crop, Release 2.2 continues to provide basic functionality that will meet the day-to-day needs of most spreadsheet users. The Allways add-in makes it very easy to produce high-quality output.

WordPerfect users might want to consider PlanPerfect, a product that has most of the features found in 1-2-3, Release 2.2, plus more. PlanPerfect is particularly notable for including three interfaces, one of which is a function-key-based WordPerfect-like interface.

Both of these products run quite well on standard 286 (AT-style 10- and 12MHz) systems. Those with more advanced hardware who are looking for more power, speed, and enhanced capabilities will be better served by one of the other products we examined.

Unless you're upgrading from a previous release, SuperCalc 5 doesn't really offer many clear advantages over the other high-end products. A couple of selling points for this product are presentation-quality graphics and 8088 (XT) support, but these strengths are offset by somewhat slow speeds. (An update to SuperCalc 5 promises speed increases of up to 15 percent.)

Of the three remaining products, Excel is perhaps the most powerful from an analytical perspective — although it's more limited in file linking and supports only four fonts per spreadsheet. It is the only true WYSIWYG ("what-you-see-is-what-you-get") product and iscertainly the most "futuristic," thanks to its graphical user interface. Excel for Windows is an excellent way to prepare for OS/2 Presentation Manager.

1-2-3, Release 3, is equally impressive, but it is somewhat hindered by its lack of presentation-quality output (to be fixed by the addition of the spreadsheet publishing program Impress in 1-2-3, Release 3.1). Most notably, this spreadsheet offers truly state-of-the-art 3-D consolidation and linking features. Other new additions, such as live text and graphics, combine to make this a very desirable spreadsheet for those with the hardware to run it.

Quattro Pro combines many of the best elements of 1-2-3, Release 3, and Excel into one extremely powerful package, including impressive 3-D consolidation capabilities and state-of-the-art presentation-quality graphics. It's easy to use and nearly perfectly compatible with the 1-2-3 standard. Our only complaints are the lack of a WYSIWYG edit mode and its relatively slow output.

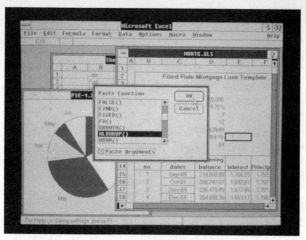

In Excel's elegant Windows-based interface, formulas can be selected from pop-up windows.

INTRODUCTION

Lotus 2.2

Lotus, which dominates the DOS spreadsheet market, offers two versions of its famed spreadsheet: a standard version for most users, and a high-octane version for power users. Lotus 1-2-3 Release 2.2 is the the latest upgrade of its original product. For those new to spreadsheets, this product's name refers to its three main functions: spreadsheet, graphics, and database management. As product upgrades go, Release 2.2 is no great standout. It adds only a few new features: simple file linking, macro libraries, a few new macro commands, and Funk Software's Allways add-in.

With regard to features, Release 2.2 pales in comparison to many other spreadsheets. However, 1-2-3's Add-in Manager keeps the product competitive. Scores of add-in products are available to customize the spreadsheet by adding features that extend its usefulness. In fact, just about every weakness in 1-2-3 can be overcome with an add-in application. Release 2.2 ships with Lotus' Macro Library Manager add-in as well as the Allways add-in for improved printing. Our scoring reflects features tacked on by add-ins that ship with Release 2.2, but not the numerous other add-ins available in the market.

Lotus 1-2-3 Release 3

Lotus 1-2-3 Release 3 is a new high-end version of 1-2-3. This product has the most stringent hardware requirements of any spreadsheet: It needs at least an 80286 system with a minimum of

Report Card
Spreadsheets

	Weight	Excel Ver. 2.1	Lotus 1-2-3 Rel. 2.2	Lotus1-2-3 Rel. 3.0
Price		$495	$495	$595
Performance				
Formulas /analysis	100	Excellent	Good	Good
Compatibility	50	Very Good	Excellent	Excellent
Speed	75	Very Good	Very Good	Very Good
Database	75	Good	Satisfactory	Very Good
Graphics	75	Excellent	Poor	Good
Output	50	Excellent	Very Good	Satisfactory
Macros	50	Very Good	Good	Good
Consolidation and linking	50	Good	Satisfactory	Excellent
Capacity	50	Excellent	Very Good	Very Good
Documentation	75	Very Good	Excellent	Excellent
Ease of learning	50	Excellent	Very Good	Very Good
Ease of Use	100	Very Good	Very Good	Excellent
Error handling	50	Very Good	Poor	Very Good
Support				
Policies	25	Very Good	Very Good	Very Good
Technical support	25	Very Good	Satisfactory	Satisfactory
Value	100	Excellent	Very Good	Excellent
Final Scores:		**8.5**	**6.6**	**7.9**

InfoWorld reviews only finished, production versions of products, never beta test versions.

Products rated within 0.2 points of one another differ little. Weightings represent average relative importance to InfoWorld readers involved in purchasing and using that product category. You can customize the report card to your needs by using your own weightings to calculate the final score.

PlanPerfect Ver. 5.0	Quattro Pro Ver. 1.0	SuperCalc Ver. 5.0
$495	$495	$495
Good	Good	Good
Good	Excellent	Very Good
Satisfactory	Very Good	Satisfactory
Very Good	Excellent	Very Good
Good	Excellent	Very Good
Good	Very Good	Good
Good	Excellent	Very Good
Satisfactory	Excellent	Very Good
Very Good	Very Good	Good
Satisfactory	Excellent	Very Good
Satisfactory	Excellent	Very Good
Good	Very Good	Good
Poor	Very Good	Very Good
Excellent	Very Good	Satisfactory
Very Good	Good	Satisfactory
Good	Excellent	Very Good
6.0	**8.6**	**6.7**

Excellent = Outstanding in all areas.
Very Good = Meets all essential criteria and offers significant advantages.
Good = Meets essential criteria and includes some special features.
Satisfactory = Meets essential criteria.
Poor = Falls short in essential areas.
Unacceptable or N/A = Fails to meet minimum standards or lacks this feature.

1 megabyte of RAM. Release 3 is a significant improvement over Release 2. The most notable enhancement is the addition of a third dimension to your workspace — a feature it shares with SuperCalc 5. Each spreadsheet can have as many as 256 stacked pages.

You can also work with up to 256 files in memory, or as many as will fit. This lets you easily transfer data between worksheets, and also allows you to set up macro libraries by storing all general-purpose macros in a separate file and loading it in when needed. Release 3 also offers state-of-the-art spreadsheet linking, and vastly improved graphics.

Excel

Excel is the only spreadsheet written for Microsoft Windows — and the only completely WYSIWYG ("what-you-see-is-what-you-get")

Benchmarks

High-End PC Spreadsheets 386-Based Tests

	Excel/ Windows	Lotus 1-2-3(2.2)	Lotus 1-2-3(3.0)
CALCULATION			
Arithmetic model			
Recalc partial	<1	1.6	0-1.5
Recalc all	2.3	3.2	4.5
File load	10.3	8.5	9.9
File size	237K	240K	214K
Financial model			
Recalc all	0-19.6	17.5	0-39.5
Scientific model			
Recalc all	0-5.5	6.8	0-10.6
CONSOLIDATION			
Page-oriented model	5.8	N/A[1]	<1
File-oriented model	1.5	N/A[1]	<1

All times in seconds.
[1] Cannot load more than one worksheet into memory at one time.

spreadsheet currently available. You can open multiple spreadsheets in separate windows and easily transfer data between them or specify permanent links between different spreadsheets. Similarly, graphs and macros appear in their own windows, and the product integrates these features well.

The trade-off for all this power and convenience is speed and memory usage. To get the most out of Excel, you'll need a fast AT-class system or a 386 machine. And the more memory you have, the better off you'll be.

Quattro Pro

If it were possible to mate Microsoft Excel and 1-2-3, Release 3, the offspring would probably resemble Quattro Pro. From Excel it borrows the capability to work with multiple files in movable and resizable windows. It also has a slick SAA-style (pull-down) menu system which can be configured as pop-up menus if desired. It lacks Excel's WYSIWYG display but does have a page preview feature. From Release 3 it incorporates such features as direct access to external database files and flexible and powerful spreadsheet linking capabilities. It does not have a three-dimensional mode, but you can work with related groups of files saved as a workspace. Quattro Pro departs significantly from Excel and Release 3 in that it fits easily into 640K and runs well even on an XT. Quattro Pro also has superb graphics capabilities.

PlanPerfect

Version 5 of PlanPerfect was apparently designed in an attempt to broaden the market for this product. In addition to its function-key interface resembling the one found in WordPerfect, Version 5 now includes a 1-2-3-like menu system accessed with the Slash key, plus a pull-down menu system tied to the Escape key.

PlanPerfect is feature-rich, but it had trouble running some of our larger models. It has simple spreadsheet-linking capability, and it lets you work with two worksheets simultaneously. In addition, it has simple database features and presentation-quality graphics.

SuperCalc

SuperCalc was one of the original DOS spreadsheets and is now in its fifth major version. This latest version lets you work with three spreadsheets at a time, supports stacked spreadsheet pages, and has file linking. It also has comprehensive auditing commands and superb graphics. Unlike many of the other advanced spreadsheets, it doesn't require advanced hardware to run; just about any system with a hard disk will do (although operation can be slow).

Performance:
FORMULAS

Excel: *EXCELLENT*

Excel is perhaps the most powerful spreadsheet going in terms of analytic prowess. Besides all the standard built-in functions (and you can develop your own), Excel provides regression analysis, matrix functions, and dynamic what-if tables. In addition, a library of macros extends the usefulness by adding goal seeking, simultaneous equation solving, and several other features. Excel has the broadest range of analytical tools, and we rate it excellent for formulas and analysis.

Excel also has a feature known as arrays that lets you work with

Benchmarks
High-End Spreadsheets — 286-Based Tests

	Excel/Windows Version 2.1	Lotus 1-2-3 Version 2.2	Lotus 1-2-3 Version 3.0
CALCULATION			
Arithmetic model			
Recalc partial	0-2.5	3.9	0-4.7
Recalc all	7.4	9.4	13.0[1]
File load	24.1	30.3	39.3[2]
File size	237K	240K	214K
Financial model			
Recalc all	0-64.6	26.0	0-125.2
Scientific model			
Recalc all	0-17.5	13.6	0-36.2
CONSOLIDATION			
Page-oriented model	16.3	N/A[3]	1.3
File-oriented model	3.8	N/A[3]	1.3

All times in seconds.

[1] 1-2-3 Version 3.0: Does not perform background recalc in manual mode for this test.

blocks of data as a unit. A single formula performs calculations on an entire array and returns a separate value for each array element. Arrays not only simplifies some operations, but also uses less memory.

Lotus 1-2-3 Release 2.2 : *GOOD*

1-2-3 provides a good assortment of built-in functions, including date, time, and string functions. It does not support user-defined functions. It also features a useful Data Table command that can automate what-if scenarios by systematically changing one or two values and building a table showing the effects of these changes on a key dependent variable. It can perform regression analysis and matrix manipulation.

PlanPerfect Version 5.0	Quattro Pro Version 1.0	SuperCalc 5 Version 5.0
5.3	0-5.7	20.4
48.5	11.3	49.6
16.3	39.1	44.2
263K	240K	118K
116.1	0-11.3	104.7
N/A	0-25.7	44.9
N/A[3]	0-7.0	48.0
N/A[3]	<1.0	27.2

[2] Lotus 1-2-3 Version 3.0: Load time includes background recalc.
[3] Lotus 1-2-3 Version 2.2 and Plan Perfect cannot load more than one worksheet into memory at one time.

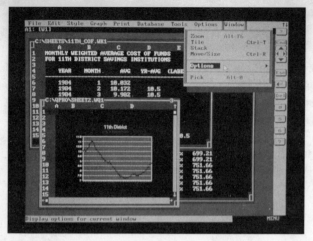

Quattro Pro's pull-down menus and efficient windowing boost its ease of use.

Lotus 1-2-3 Release 3: *GOOD*

Basic analytic capabilities haven't changed all that much relative to Release 2, although the product now calculates and displays values out to 18 significant digits (previously 15). An advantage over other spreadsheets is the expanded 512-character limit per cell. Release 3 also adds some new @functions — primarily in the area of databases. Unfortunately, there is still no facility for developing user-defined functions (unless you're a programmer and purchase the Add-in Toolkit).

Another enhancement is the /Data Table command (used for automating what-if scenarios). It's been expanded to use three variables — perfect for 3-D worksheet orientation.

PlanPerfect: *GOOD*

With the exception of the database functions, PlanPerfect supports all of 1-2-3 Release 2.01's functions, plus several others. It duplicates 1-2-3's regression, matrix, and data table tools, and offers user-defined functions — which can save a significant amount of memory when working with many copies of a complex formula.

On the down side, PlanPerfect's design might not let you develop some highly complex worksheets. For example, we could not load our scientific model benchmark worksheet because PlanPerfect splits the spreadsheet into regions that consist of 128 columns and 256 rows: There is a limit to the number of cell references within a region, and our benchmark file exceeded this limit. Under these conditions, Plan-

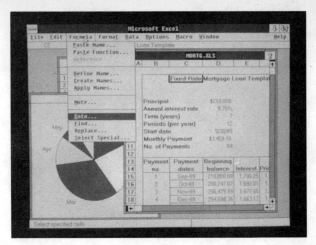

Excel's graphs and data are both live at the same time in separate windows.

Perfect locks up and requires a system reboot. Such deficiencies, though, are balanced by some significant extras — such as user-defined functions — in this category.

Quattro Pro: *GOOD*

Quattro Pro has the usual selection of built-in functions, including several new financial functions. It also supports matrix manipulation, regression analysis, and one- and two-way what-if table creation. Additionally, there's an extensive set of tools to perform linear programming — a mathematical technique that can solve certain optimization problems.

Quattro Pro lacks goal seeking, support for user-defined functions, and support for add-in applications (unlike the original Quattro).

SuperCalc 5: *GOOD*

Aside from the standard complement of built-in functions, SuperCalc 5 sports both matrix manipulation and multiple regression. Unlike competing products, the Regression command handles linear, quadratic, and cubic models. It also has a "what-if" table generator functionally equivalent to 1-2-3, Release 2. SuperCalc 5 does not support user-defined functions, nor does it have a goal-seeking capability.

75

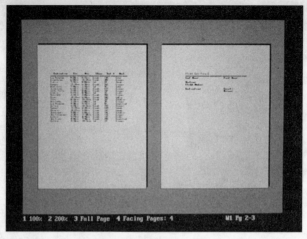

Like WordPerfect, PlanPerfect features dual-page spreadsheet preview.

Performance:
COMPATIBILITY

Excel: *VERY GOOD*
Excel sports a very comprehensive list of compatible file formats. It can read and write 1-2-3 (except Release 3), Symphony, dBASE, DIF, SYLK, and ASCII. Excel will optionally convert 1-2-3 charts when it reads in a WK1 file, and a separate module can translate 1-2-3 macros (but it's a memory-intensive process that requires expanded memory for complex macros).

Lotus 1-2-3 Release 2.2: *EXCELLENT*
1-2-3 can read Release 1A WKS format and Symphony worksheet files directly, and a separate translation program can handle dBASE and DIF files. It can read comma-separated variable files directly, and its Data Parse command lets you read standard text files as strings and break up the strings into component cells. 1-2-3's files have become the industry-standard format for spreadsheet files, and even many non-spreadsheet applications can read and write this format.

Lotus 1-2-3 Release 3: *EXCELLENT*
Release 3 remains extremely compatible with previous versions — in both keystrokes and file support. The enhancements are generally new menu functions rather than modifications of previous commands. There is a new file format, WK3, but Release 3 can read WKS, WK1, and WR1 files directly. You can also read in dBASE files in their entirety or selectively. Release 3 can save files in either WK1 or WK3 format.

76

Release 2 add-ins will not work with Release 3, but some of these are no longer necessary because their features are incorporated into the new product. There are a few minor incompatibilities with Release 2, but they are explained thoroughly.

PlanPerfect: *GOOD*

1-2-3 files can be imported or exported directly, with an option to convert 1-2-3 macros. Macro conversion works only for very simple macros, and imported 1-2-3 macros cannot be executed with the Alt key. Other supported file types include dBASE II and III, PlanPerfect 3.0, WordPerfect files, DIF files, and ASCII files. A standalone conversion program is also included that can translate files in groups.

Quattro Pro: *EXCELLENT*

Quattro's compatibility is the best we've seen in a spreadsheet. It can read and write Lotus WKS, WK1, WR1 file formats, as well as Quattro, Surpass, dBASE, Reflex, and Paradox files. It can also import several types of ASCII files (but not DIF files). SQZ, a file compression program, is built in.

You have your choice of three menu systems: the standard SAA-style pull-down menu system, a system compatible with the original Quattro, or a 1-2-3-compatible command interface. Except for macros that utilize commands unique to 1-2-3, Release 2.2, we found perfect compatibility with all of our 1-2-3, Release 2 macros.

SuperCalc 5: *VERY GOOD*

You can read and write 1-2-3 files directly, and — like Quattro — SuperCalc 5 has an optional 1-2-3 command mode. Pressing "/1" puts you into a menu system that closely resembles 1-2-3. SuperCalc 5 uses this mode to handle 1-2-3 macros. It merely inserts the "/1" characters at the beginning of the macro and executes the subsequent commands in its 1-2-3 command mode. It works fine for simple macros, but you'll usually have to tweak more complex macros.

Besides support for DIF, CSV, and text files, you can also read dBASE III files completely or selectively.

Performance:
SPEED

Excel: *VERY GOOD*

Like most Windows applications, screen updating can be sluggish at times due to the graphics display mode. This is particularly apparent on slower 286 systems. Performance improves significantly with more RAM. In terms of calculation speed, however, Excel posted some of the best times, scoring above average on nearly every benchmark. The product features both minimal recalculation and background recalculation.

Lotus 1-2-3 Release 2.2: *VERY GOOD*

Unlike the new Release 3, 1-2-3, Release 2.2 is written in assembly language. Consequently, it's one of the fastest spreadsheets around. It loads quickly and has the snappiest feel of all these products.

It doesn't support background recalculation, but minimal recalculation is built in and no longer requires an add-in. It performed well in our benchmarks, scoring above average on nearly all of our tests (we were not able to time it on our consolidation benchmarks).

Lotus 1-2-3 Release 3: *VERY GOOD*

Minimal and background recalculation are built in, which means you'll spend less time staring at the flashing "Wait" indicator and — in most cases — you'll regain control of the cursor almost immediately. Release 3 is written in C (rather than assembly language); consequently, it's slower than Release 2.2. Still, it scored above average on four of seven timed tests.

PlanPerfect: *SATISFACTORY*

File loading is fast, but recalc times are somewhat slow. PlanPerfect has minimal recalculation capability that works very well. On our

Lotus 1-2-3, version 2.2 comes with Funk Software's Allways add-in, which enhances graphics and output.

speed benchmarks, PlanPerfect scored above average on only two of the tests (we could not try it on several of the other tests).

On timed benchmark tests, Quattro Pro scored above average in nearly every category. Like 1-2-3, Release 3, it has optional background recalculation. Quattro Pro's memory management system constantly swaps small segments of code to and from disk. This is noticeable only when you approach the limits of available memory.

Also relevant to this category (but not officially scored) are noticeable delays in loading the program and viewing graphs. The product can be agonizingly slow when printing with Bitstream fonts. Nevertheless, Quattro's benchmark performance was impressive.

SuperCalc 5: *SATISFACTORY*

SuperCalc 5 has minimal recalculation, but lacks background recalculation. It's certainly no speed demon — it registered the slowest times on several of our timed benchmark measures, and scored above average on only one of the measures. However, the times are not quite unreasonable.

Performance:
DATABASE

Excel: *VERY GOOD*

Excel has simple flat-file database capabilities; however, like most other spreadsheets, the database must fit into memory. We like its easy-to-use data entry forms and dialog boxes that let you set search criteria and select records. You can sort ranges by rows or columns, using up to three sort keys. A supplied macro lets you cross-tabulate database fields. Lacking only external database capability, Excel offers impressive database performance.

Lotus 1-2-3 Release 2.2: *SATISFACTORY*

1-2-3 defined the manner in which spreadsheets deal with flat-file databases. Spreadsheet rows correspond to records, and columns serve as data fields. Release 2.2 provides a basic assortment of commands and functions to manipulate and extract data that meet your defined criteria. Data must fit into available memory, which puts a damper on manipulating large-scale databases. There is no built-in facility to deal with external databases. (There are several third-party add-ins that give access to external databases, such as dBASE, Informix, and Oracle files.) 1-2-3's sorting capability is limited to row sorts, using one or two sort keys. New to this release is a long-overdue search-and-replace feature that works in both labels and formulas.

Lotus 1-2-3 Release 3: *VERY GOOD*

Release 3 maintains the RAM-dependent database capabilities supplied with previous versions, but now you can set up relations between multiple databases that share a common field. Release 3 also lets you work with external database files via "drivers." A simple dBASE III driver is included, and others will be available through third-parties. You can also modify records extracted from a database and return them to the original table.

This product was designed to interact with database files, and even includes a new function that can send a command to an external database file. However, no drivers are yet available to make use of this facility. Sorting is still limited to row sorts only, but Lotus now lets you use as many as 255 sort keys.

PlanPerfect: *VERY GOOD*

PlanPerfect's database capabilities are similar to those found in 1-2-3, Release 2, though it uses a different method for querying databases. There is no support for directly accessing external database files. You can sort by rows or columns using up to 10 sort keys, and there is also a search feature. You can also develop data entry forms to facilitate data input.

Quattro Pro: *EXCELLENT*

Quattro Pro has the standard spreadsheet database features and also incorporates 1-2-3, Release 3's capability to work with external database files. Quattro Pro can use dBASE II, III, or IV, Paradox, and Reflex database files as if the data were in your spreadsheet. These built-in functions are the best we've seen in any spreadsheet.

Using an external database is a slower alternative to keeping your data in RAM, but it allows much larger tables and eliminates the need to maintain a worksheet version of your database files. A significant advantage over 1-2-3, Release 3 is that Quattro Pro's background recalculation is not disabled while external database functions are being evaluated.

SuperCalc 5: *VERY GOOD*

You'll find a full complement of spreadsheet database features, including the capability to read selected fields and records from a dBASE file. You cannot work with external files larger than RAM without resorting to Silverado, an add-in application that adds relational database features to SuperCalc (and is also available for 1-2-3, Release 2.2). There is a built-in search-and-replace command, and flexible sorting (by rows or columns).

Performance:
GRAPHICS

Excel: *Good*

A significant feature missing from Excel's graphics is the capability to generate three-dimensional charts. If you can live with single-plane graphics, you'll find Excel's graphics among the best available in a spreadsheet. With nearly four dozen different graph types and the capability to add free-floating text and arrows, you can get your graphs to look just right.

Lotus 1-2-3 Release 2.2: *Poor*

This new upgrade provided no major enhancements in the area of graphics, and it's clear that other high-end spreadsheets enjoy a major advantage over Release 2.2 when it comes to graphics. Still lacking are mixed graph types, stock market graphs, dual y-axis graphs, and the capability to customize colors or fonts. Despite a few minor improvements, 1-2-3, Release 2.2's graphics are still not up to our minimum standards.

Lotus 1-2-3 Release 3: *Good*

Release 3's charts are of presentation quality, and you can display a graph alongside your data and watch the chart instantly re-draw as the data changes.

New features include mixed graphs types, stock market graphs, dual y-axes graphs, logarithmic scaling, area charts, and option horizontal orientation. You can customize colors, hatching, and fonts. Still missing is the capability to add free-floating text to graphs, although you can specify two additional lines of text in the form of footnotes. There are also some limitations in terms of changing the fonts and sizes of text in your graph.

The product's three-dimensional worksheet feature doesn't extend to its graphs. You're still limited to charting your data on a single plane only.

PlanPerfect: *Good*

Compared with the previous release, Version 5's graphics have improved significantly. The product now supports mixed graph types and graphs with dual y-axes, but not 3-D graphs. You can, however, display two graphs simultaneously, and the graphs are highly customizable with respect to colors, hatchings, and fonts.

Settings for graphs are stored in separate files, independent of the worksheet for which they were defined. The setting files include cell ranges, but not the actual values. One advantage to this is that you can use the same setting for multiple worksheets with identical layouts. The only graphics file format supported is the WordPerfect graphics file format (.WPG).

Quattro Pro: *EXCELLENT*

If graphics are your prime concern, you can't go wrong with Quattro Pro. It features an "annotation" mode that gives you some of the tools commonly found in paint programs. For example, you can add text, boxes, circles, polygons, and arrows; and you have complete control over size, fonts, colors, and placement. It includes 35 files of clip art to enhance your graphics.

You can generate all the standard graph types, with the exception of true 3-D graphs. It supports mixed graphs, dual y-axes charts, and text-only charts. If you're running in graphics mode, you can insert graphs in your spreadsheet so you can watch them change along with your data.

SuperCalc 5: *VERY GOOD*

Supercalc's graphics are among the best available in a spreadsheet. In addition to the standard graph types, you can get mixed graphs (line/bar and pie/bar), dual-y-axis graphs, area graphs, text-only charts, and even a "radar" graph that uses polar coordinates. It also generates true 3-D graphs — unique among the products reviewed here.

Performance:
OUTPUT

Excel: *EXCELLENT*

Excel's WYSIWYG display is augmented by a fast page preview feature that ensures that your output won't produce any surprises. It supports most printers and plotters, including Postscript. You have excellent control over formatting and fonts, including borders and shading. You can use only four different fonts in a worksheet (most spreadsheets allow eight). It takes advantage of the Windows print spooler, so you can continue working while you print.

Lotus 1-2-3 Release 2.2: *VERY GOOD*

1-2-3 supports most printers and plotters, including Postscript. With the Allways add-in attached, 1-2-3 has a WYSIWYG display and is capable of producing output on par with Microsoft Excel. You can mix fonts, make micro-adjustments to row height and column width, preview page breaks on-screen, and mix graphs with text. Normally, printing or plotting graphs must be done from a separate program. With Allways you can print graphs and text together directly from 1-2-3. Neither option provides background printing. A limitation of

Allways is that you cannot make any changes to your spreadsheet while Allways is active. Consequently, you might find yourself switching between text and graphics mode. Still, Release 2.2's output capabilities exceed those in Release 3.

Lotus 1-2-3 Release 3: *SATISFACTORY*
The separate graph printing program, Pgraph, is no longer included, and graphs are now printed or plotted directly from the spreadsheet. You can mix text and graphs on the same page, and a background print mode lets you continue working while you print. In addition, you can assign print job priorities to control the print queue.

A new feature lets you specify multiple print ranges, separated by semicolons. There is also a new Print Printer Sample option that gives you a hard copy sample printout of all the fonts available on your printer.

Allways, the output-intensive add-in that comes with Release 2.2, does not come with Release 3. Release 3 has enough significant output enhancements to balance the other output features it's missing, such as font display and page preview.

PlanPerfect: *GOOD*
Many of WordPerfect's output capabilities exist in PlanPerfect. The user has full control over the output, including multiple fonts and type sizes. Assigning these attributes to a cell or range is simple; there are no shading or line drawing commands to dress up your output. Although edit mode is not WYSIWYG, you can assign different screen colors for various attributes. There is also a graphics page preview that lets you see one or two pages at a time as they will print.

Compared to Excel or 1-2-3/Allways, complex formatting is more tedious and error-prone because you need to switch between edit mode and preview mode to see how your fonts will look and how the pages will break. The output features are countered by the lack of shading and line-drawing capabilities.

Quattro Pro: *VERY GOOD*
Quattro Pro supports all major output devices, including Postscript. You can enhance your printouts with multiple fonts and type sizes, boxes and lines, and shadings.

Though draft mode is fast, the final print mode uses the graphics mode of your printer and is extremely slow: It's not uncommon to wait 10 minutes or more for a single page in laser 300-dpi resolution.

Though it lacks a WYSIWYG display like Excel and 1-2-3/Allways, Quattro Pro has zoomable page preview. You can print or plot graphs directly from the spreadsheet and insert graphs within your spreadsheet. Unfortunately, there is no background print mode.

SuperCalc 5: *GOOD*

For text, SuperCalc provides direct support for most black-and-white and color printers. Device drivers are provided for plotters, Postscript printers, cameras, and other graphic file formats. You can specify outlining, shading, and multiple fonts in your worksheets, but there is no WYSIWYG page preview feature, and you can't tell where the pages will break until you produce a hard copy. A copy of Sideways is included, but it's the stand-alone version and not a more handy add-in.

Performance:
MACROS

Excel: *EXCELLENT*

Excel stores macros in separate files which can be loaded along with the related worksheet file. Alternatively, you can develop a library of general-purpose macros and load it whenever you run Excel.

Excel has two types of macros: command macros and function macros. Command macros can be recorded as you type, while function macros let you define your own functions. Excel provides everything you need to develop complex and powerful macro-driven applications, complete with dialog boxes and custom help screens. The macro library includes a macro to assist in debugging other macros; there is a macro debugger.

Lotus 1-2-3 Release 2.2: *GOOD*

1-2-3's macro language has always been a strong point: It lets you set up user menus and develop sophisticated models that are easy to use

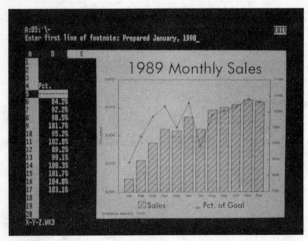

Lotus 1-2-3, Release 3.0 has unique enhancements such as graphs and data that are live concurrently.

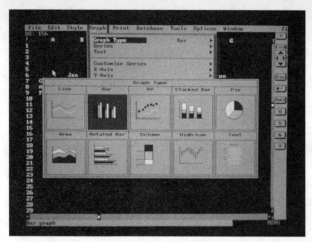

Quattro Pro offers multiple graph types and presents choices using graphical examples.

for end-users. Besides providing new macro commands, 1-2-3 now supports a macro learn mode (without an add-in) and a new add-in provides support for macro libraries. In addition, the former upper limit of 26 keyboard macros per worksheet has been eliminated, and you can now execute macros by name.

Lotus 1-2-3 Release 3: *GOOD*
Release 3 stores your most recent 512 keystrokes in an accessible buffer. This gives you, in effect, a limited macro learn mode; you can

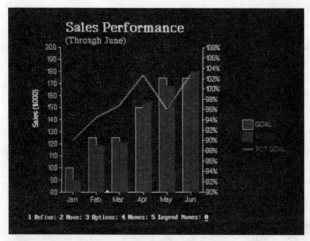

Plan Perfect supports mixed graph types and dual y-axis graphs; the file format is WordPerfect's. WPG.

copy from the buffer to a macro range. An advantage of this is that you can define a macro after the fact. This is a great feature, but we would prefer a larger limit on the number of keystrokes that can be recorded into a macro.

The previous limit of 26 macros has been lifted, and a new macro run command lets you execute a macro by name (up to 15 characters). There is a macro library. The macro language has also been expanded, and now includes keywords for working with the multiple pages and worksheets. You can also turn off the row and column borders under macro control, allowing you to design turn-key applications.

PlanPerfect: *GOOD*

Macros can reside within a spreadsheet or they can be stored individually in files for access from any worksheet. The macro language is the functional equivalent of 1-2-3. While you're recording a macro, you can press Control Page Up to display a point-and-shoot menu of macro commands that can be inserted into your macro. You can also create user menus that mimic PlanPerfect's select-a-number-style horizontal menus. There is no facility for debugging macros.

Quattro Pro: *EXCELLENT*

Quattro Pro has extensive macro debugging capabilities, and macros, in general, are a strong point. You can record macros keystroke by keystroke, or specify that they be interpreted as "command equivalents" so the macros will function without regard to the menu tree that happens to be loaded.

You can designate any worksheet as a macro library. When a macro library file is loaded, the macros are accessible from any other spreadsheet.

SuperCalc 5: *GOOD*

Supercalc's macros can be spreadsheet-specific or file-based macros that work in any worksheet. The macro command language is extensive and lets you develop easy-to-use menu-driven interfaces. Perhaps the only weakness is the lack of any macro debugging capability.

Performance:
CONSOLIDATION AND LINKING

Excel: *VERY GOOD*

For consolidating worksheets, Excel's equivalent to 1-2-3's File Combine command is accomplished via its Edit Paste Special command.

Excel extends the normal method of referencing cells by allowing you to precede the cell reference with a file name. Excel performs two types of external references: simple and complex. A simple external reference is an absolute reference to a cell or range that is not part of a formula. A complex external reference can be a relative reference and can be used in formulas (like 1-2-3, Release 3 and SuperCalc 5).

Clearly, complex external references are more useful, but using them requires that all supporting worksheets be loaded into memory.

For one-time consolidation, Excel earns a very good. The linked file test also resulted in a very good score, and the product received a good score in the linked-page test.

Lotus 1-2-3 Release 2.2: *SATISFACTORY*
Aside from the File Combine command of previous versions, Release 2.2 adds simple file linking. You can precede a cell reference with a file name — but you cannot use these external references in formulas. You can, however, copy the links in a relative manner. Release 2.2 earned satisfactory scores on both our one-time consolidation test and the linked-file test, but received a poor score on the linked-page test since it cannot perform math on linked cells.

Lotus 1-2-3 Release 3: *EXCELLENT*
The original File Consolidation command is still available, but the new multipage feature and the capability of working with multiple worksheets will greatly simplify consolidation of spreadsheets. You can consolidate both active worksheets and those on disk. Performance on our one-time consolidation test is excellent.

You can efficiently reference cells or ranges in other worksheets — either in memory or on disk. You can use these expanded cell references in formulas and copy them in a relative manner. For example, you can set up a link in a single cell and then copy the linking cell to extend the link. This is not possible in Excel, unless the supporting worksheet is also in memory. If you link to worksheets on disk, a separate command will update the links upon request. We award excellent scores for our linked-file and linked-page tests, and we consider this spreadsheet the best at consolidation and linking.

PlanPerfect: *SATISFACTORY*
PlanPerfect lets you link files together by pulling in selected cells or ranges from files on disk. A limitation it shares with 1-2-3, Release 2.2 is that you cannot use these links in formulas. As we noted, you can have two active spreadsheets in memory — but you cannot set links in a point-and-shoot manner.

We put PlanPerfect through our three-part spreadsheet linking and consolidation tests. The capability to work with two spreadsheets at once earns it a satisfactory rating on two of our tests (one-time consolidation and linked-file consolidation), but PlanPerfect earns a poor score on our linked-page test due to its incapability to perform math on values linked from other spreadsheets.

Quattro Pro: *EXCELLENT*

Quattro Pro is a top contender in the consolidation and linking department. It has the standard file consolidation commands, as well as an advanced linking capability.

Linking is accomplished by preceding a cell reference with a file name. The linked file can be in any supported format, including dBASE. If the supporting file is active, you can set up your links in a point-and-shoot manner.

You can save a "workspace" and get, in effect, some of the advantages of a 3-D spreadsheet. The Workspace Save command saves the file names and window settings in an ASCII file (but does not save the actual files).

On our three-part consolidation and linking performance tests, Quattro Pro scored excellent on the one-time and linked-file tests. Lack of true 3-D spreadsheet capability limited its score to very good on the linked-page test. The product is also to be commended for additional linking features: wild-card file references, links to non-spreadsheet files, and automatic link creation when moving a range to another file. Quattro's linking and consolidation is state-of-the-art.

SuperCalc 5: *VERY GOOD*

SuperCalc 5 allows you to work with multiple worksheets simultaneously and — like 1-2-3, Release 3 — it can support three-dimensional spreadsheets in a paged fashion. The program also extends the typical /File Combine process to include multiplication and division (as well as the common copy, add, and subtract options). On our one-time consolidation test, SuperCalc 5 earns an excellent.

Another excellent score was registered for the linked-file consolidation, and it received a very good for the linked-page procedure. A limitation is that SuperCalc lets you work with only the first page from a nonactive supporting worksheet. If you attempt to copy a linked cell, you'll get "N/A" as the result.

CAPACITY

Excel: *GOOD*

Excel was the first of the "new generation" spreadsheets — and also the first that required more advanced hardware. Don't even try to run it on less than a 286 system. Unless your spreadsheets tend to be on the small side, plan on having expanded memory.

Excel is a memory-intensive program, and users who lack expanded memory will frequently encounter out-of-memory errors and be limited in the number of files that can be active. Running it under Windows/386 lets you use all the system's extended memory. You can have as many active spreadsheets as will fit into memory.

Lotus 1-2-3 Release 2.2: *Very Good*

When 1-2-3 was originally written, systems with a full 640K of RAM were relatively rare. Consequently, the program was finely crafted to minimize RAM usage. For users with only conventional memory, 1-2-3, Release 2.2 provides a very large workspace relative to other products. Users with EMS can access up to 2 megabytes of additional memory.

Not unexpectedly, the Undo feature and Allways can take up a lot of memory. In fact, if you have Undo enabled, available conventional RAM will be cut in half because the program allocates an Undo buffer large enough to hold a complete backup worksheet. If you have EMS, however, the Undo buffer will be maintained in expanded memory. If you need more RAM, you can always detach Allways and disable Undo.

Lotus 1-2-3 Release 3: *Very Good*

Not too surprisingly, Release 3 uses much more memory than the previous version. You'll need a minimum of 1 megabyte to run it under DOS. The product can use up to 8 megabytes of LIM EMS (32 megabytes with LIM 4.0) and can address up to 16 megabytes of extended memory (unique among spreadsheets).

As we've mentioned, you can load multiple worksheets into RAM — as many as memory will allow. In addition, each worksheet can consist of multiple pages. We drop our otherwise-excellen capacity rating down one notch since Release 3 cannot run on a 640K system.

PlanPerfect: *Very Good*

PlanPerfect lets you work with one or two spreadsheets at a time, and is the only high-end DOS spreadsheet currently available that can use a hard disk for virtual memory if you run out of RAM. You'll experience slower performance, but it's preferable to getting a memory-full error. However, this doesn't mean you'll never get a memory-full error, as there are some limits in the virtual memory system.

The product also supports expanded memory. The virtual memory capability boosts its capacity rating.

Quattro Pro: *Very Good*

Quattro Pro uses a technology called VROOMM — Virtual Real-Time Object-Oriented Memory Manager. This is a memory management technique that makes use of relatively small (2K to 4K) program over-lays called "objects" that are swapped to and from disk as needed. Preference is given to maximizing data space and minimizing program code in memory. With many copies of a formula, Quattro stores the actual formula only once. You can work with as many multiple spread-sheets as will fit into RAM. You can use up to 8 megabytes of EMS, which can be used to store formulas, labels, and data. There is no disk-based virtual memory, so you will get memory-full errors.

SuperCalc 5: *GOOD*

Without EMS, SuperCalc 5 leaves you with a relatively small workspace. In fact, users without EMS will not get much use out of the multiple spreadsheet feature. It supports up to 32 megabytes of LIM 4 EMS. Relatively limited workspace is offset to some extent by the capability of linking to other worksheets on disk.

DOCUMENTATION

Excel: *EXCELLENT*

Excel's manuals are comprehensive and well-organized. The on-line help system is usually very good, although we have been frustrated by the lack of information it contains on some topics. A feature of the on-line help system is particularly appealing to 1-2-3 users — they can enter a 1-2-3 command, and the program will provide help pertaining to how the same action is accomplished in Excel.

Excel's manuals rival Lotus' for the best in the industry.

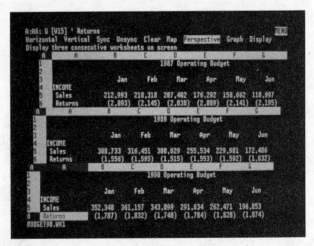

Lotus 1-2-3, Release 3.0 offers state-of-the-art multi-page capabilities.

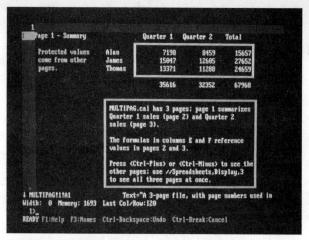

SuperCalc 5 links cells and formats from multiple spreadsheets with ease.

Lotus 1-2-3 Release 2.2: *EXCELLENT*

1-2-3's documentation is superb — from the well-organized and thorough manuals to the easy-to-maneuver context-sensitive on-line help system. The written documentation consists of a reference manual and a quick-start/tutorial book. A separate upgrader's manual offers a concise summary of the enhancements.

Lotus 1-2-3 Release 3: *EXCELLENT*

Release 3.0's documentation consists of a reference manual, an installation guide, and a tutorial book. A separate upgraders manual provides a concise summary of the enhancements, and lets current users get up to speed with minimal delay. The on-line help system has been improved dramatically, and is the best we've seen in a spreadsheet. The help is even more context-sensitive than before, and provides more assistance with error messages.

PlanPerfect: *SATISFACTORY*

A thick three-ring binder and a paperback workbook make up the main documentation. The hands-on workbook covers several specific applications.

There is an on-line help system, but it's not what we would call context-sensitive and is somewhat backwards. Pressing F3 brings up a help screen that asks you to enter the key combination for which you need help. The problem is when that's exactly what you're trying to find out. You can enter a letter, and PlanPerfect will display a screen full of topics that begin with that letter. We found that the help system isn't even operable in many of the menus. The less-than-satisfactory help system downgrades an otherwise good documentation rating.

Quattro Pro: *EXCELLENT*

Quattro Pro is shipped with three paperback manuals and a quick-reference booklet. The manuals are thorough, well-indexed, and easy to read. In addition, a superb on-line help system is always available.

SuperCalc 5: *VERY GOOD*

SuperCalc comes with extensive documentation in the form of a three-ring binder. The manual is well-organized and complete, and there's an additional user's guide, a getting-started booklet, and a quick-reference booklet. Our only complaint with the manual is its sparse coverage of multipage spreadsheets and their limitations. There's a good context-sensitive on-line system.

EASE OF LEARNING

Excel – Score: *VERY GOOD*

Those experienced with Windows or who have used a Macintosh will be able to learn the fundamentals of Excel quickly. It features SAA-style pull-down menus and is accessible with a keyboard or mouse. The command interface is very logical, and an extensive on-line tutorial is included. When you're learning the program, you can work with shortened menus that are less intimidating.

Lotus 1-2-3 Release 2.2: *VERY GOOD*

1-2-3 comes on both $3^1/2$-inch and $5^1/4$-inch disks. Installation consists of copying the disks to a separate directory (or working floppies) and running the Install program to specify your hardware. Lotus provides a good written tutorial — about 150 pages worth in the manual. Users of Release 2.01 will have absolutely no problems adapting to this upgrade.

Lotus 1-2-3 Release 3: *VERY GOOD*

1-2-3, Release 3 is distributed on either 1.2-megabyte $5^1/4$-inch disks or 720K $3^1/2$-inch disks. An improved installation program is included with this version, but we'd still like to be able to change the hardware configuration within the spreadsheet environment rather than via a separate program.

The written tutorial uses sample files to cover most aspects of the product. There is no on-line demo program. Those who are familiar with Release 2 will find this to be a relatively easy upgrade and will experience few, if any, problems in making the transition. Practically all of the Release 2 command sequences still work exactly the same, and you can learn the new features as required. Novices will find this version no more difficult to learn than previous versions.

PlanPerfect: *SATISFACTORY*

PlanPerfect is distributed on a dozen 5¼-inch disks, and includes an installation program to copy the appropriate files to your hard disk or working floppies. 1-2-3 users will feel at home immediately if they use the Slash key menus, but must pay attention because there are some subtle variations in the menu system. Furthermore, the Slash key menus often deviate from the moving-bar menu style to a more cumbersome "enter a letter or number" style. Unfortunately, the documentation almost completely ignores the Slash key menus and the drop-down menus. WordPerfect users will be comfortable with it, but others may be put off by the relatively convoluted user interface.

Quattro Pro: *EXCELLENT*

Quattro Pro is distributed on both 5¼-inch and 3½-inch disks, and an install program guides you through the 10-minute installation process. A getting-started guide provides all the details you'll need to get up and running quickly. A section for 1-2-3 users explains the differences between these products. There's also a written tutorial that walks you through the basics using sample files.

Anyone experienced with either Excel or 1-2-3 will feel right at home very quickly. Once you learn a few basics, it's easy to experiment your way through most of the features. Novices will find this product no more difficult to learn than other spreadsheets.

SuperCalc 5: *VERY GOOD*

SuperCalc doesn't have an installation program; you simply copy the disks to a subdirectory. Both 5¼-inch and 3½-inch formats are supplied. It includes an on-line tutorial to assist in the learning process. Several aspects of this product make it easy for 1-2-3 users to make the transition. Aside from the optional 1-2-3 command interface, the on-line help system can describe the SuperCalc equivalent of a 1-2-3 command.

EASE OF USE

Excel: *EXCELLENT*

You can use Excel without a mouse, but we don't recommend it. Not only does it take away the fun, it's also quite tedious and difficult to remember the key combinations. Excel is packed with minor features that make it a joy to use. The capability to move and resize the spreadsheet, graph, and macro windows is quite efficient. Its consistent use of windows, menus, and dialog boxes — not to mention the overall intuitive design — are bonuses. This product has a smooth and pleasing interface, and its features are well-implemented.

Lotus 1-2-3 Release 2.2: *VERY GOOD*

Once learned, 1-2-3 becomes second nature if you work with it enough. It borrowed the efficient point-and-shoot method of building formulas from Visicalc, which has now become standard spreadsheet fare. The moving-bar menu system is efficient, but doesn't show the full command string like some competing products.

This latest release now features setting sheets. When you issue the Print or Graph command, for example, a full-screen display shows all the current settings appropriate for that command. You can't make changes in this display, but it saves time and can reduce errors. Also new is the capability to change the width of adjacent columns with one command. We especially like the capability to load a worksheet file from the DOS command line.

Despite some nice improvements, some users will miss features such as multiple active spreadsheets, mouse support, and pop-up function building.

Lotus 1-2-3 Release 3: *EXCELLENT*

You can insert new pages as simply as inserting new rows or columns. Ctrl-PgUp and Ctrl-PgDn move between pages, and you can point to cells or ranges exactly as you might expect. The End key can also be used in conjunction with the page movement keys, letting you move quickly to the first or last page in a multipage model. In fact, everything that's possible in two dimensions can be done in the three dimensions.

The Worksheet Window command is enhanced and you can now display three pages and/or worksheets simultaneously in horizontal windows. Surprisingly, there is no option to display multiple pages or worksheets in vertical windows. Another windowing option lets you split the screen vertically and show a dynamic graph in the right window.

Overall, Lotus has done a superb job designing the user interface, and has managed to keep the commands consistent with previous versions. Release 3 is no more difficult to use than the previous versions — and is actually easier in many respects.

PlanPerfect: *GOOD*

PlanPerfect lets you open a text window to edit text for insertion in your worksheet (up to 4K). This mode features easy editing and word wrap. We've already mentioned that you can work with two spreadsheets, and easily copy cells or ranges between them.

An auto-advance feature moves the cursor to the next cell (in any direction) during data entry. You can also use the Tab key to quickly copy a cell in any direction. A unique feature lets you attach a full-screen message to any cell —useful for documenting your work or for providing custom help screens for others.

You can name not only cells and ranges, but also rows and columns. This lets you refer to cells as the intersection of a row and column. If you have a row named "Sales" and a column named "April," the cell at the intersection can be referenced as "April.Sales."

Compared to other spreadsheets, this product's interface is needlessly confusing at times. However, there are other ease-of-use features that compensate for it.

Quattro Pro: *Very Good*

A "mouse palette" lets you specify a series of commands (in macro format) to be issued when a particular button is clicked. You can switch menu systems at any time — particularly useful if you read in a 1-2-3 file that contains macros.

Other ease-of-use features include automatic column width adjustment, an "instant" graph feature, and preformatted date entry. The file manager lets you perform normal file maintenance chores from within the spreadsheet environment, and even tag multiple files to be opened with a single command. Quattro lets you select a range either before or after you issue a command to work on the range. Another option tells Quattro to remember the last option selected on each menu. When you reissue a command, the commands are preselected and you need only press the Enter key. One aspect of Quattro that may affect ease of use is its lack of WYSIWYG display in editing mode. Due to this, you can't really tell how your spreadsheet will look until you print or preview your work.

SuperCalc 5: *Good*

On the surface, this product's multipage spreadsheet mode is quite appealing. But compared to other products, it's somewhat limited. Computer Associates simply didn't extend the product to the third dimension as well as they could. Several commands that work in regular two-dimensional mode do not work across pages. For example, you cannot move a range from one page to another. Also, the Copy command cannot copy a single cell to more than one page at a time.

The lack of consistency in dealing with multipage spreadsheets is our main complaint in the ease-of-use area. Otherwise, this product is very easy to use (although quite different from 1-2-3 in many respects).

ERROR HANDLING

Excel: *VERY GOOD*

You can reverse the effects of most commands by selecting the Undo command. The product also features some handy auditing commands available via a macro, but no automatic file-save feature. The nature of Windows, however, lets you put aside an application and forget about it. If you turn off your system without a graceful exit from Windows (or experience a power failure), your work will be gone. As this potential problem is not specific to Excel, we cannot score it down.

Lotus 1-2-3, Release 2.2: *POOR*

Release 2.2 now prompts you to save your file if you attempt to exit from an unsaved worksheet. However, 1-2-3 still puts your data at risk since you can completely erase an unsaved worksheet and receive no warning.

There is also a new undo feature, but it's quite memory-intensive since it stores an additional copy of the worksheet in memory. 1-2-3 has no auditing capabilities beyond an option to display or print formulas rather than values. Because of the ease with which you can accidentally erase an entire worksheet (with no warning), we must downgrade its error-handling rating.

Lotus 1-2-3, Release 3: *VERY GOOD*

Release 3 is capable of recognizing modified data and provides a warning if you attempt to exit without saving your work or attempt to erase a complete worksheet that has not been saved. There's also a single-level undo that lets you cancel the effects of the most recent action. The File Save menu now includes an option to make a backup copy of your file. What's missing, though, is an auto-save command found in many other spreadsheets.

Also lacking are any significant auditing functions — although a few simple features are included. You can annotate a cell by typing a semicolon followed by descriptive text. Everything following the semicolon is ignored. In addition, there's a "map" view that gives you a bird's-eye look at your worksheet by displaying different characters for labels, formulas, and values. An auto-save and more significant auditing features are the most serious omissions.

PlanPerfect: *POOR*

PlanPerfect always asks if you want to save your file when you issue the exit command. It displays an additional message only if the file was not modified. On the other hand, it lets you erase an unsaved worksheet with no warning.

The product has a timed automatic-backup option, as well as an option to automatically create a backup when you perform a file save. In addition, there is an undo command that can be disabled if desired. Completely lacking are any auditing features. We had no error-handling problems, but must downgrade PlanPerfect's error-handling rating since it's so easy to erase an unsaved worksheet.

Quattro Pro: *VERY GOOD*

You're always warned if you attempt to exit with unsaved data and — unlike 1-2-3, Release 2.2 and PlanPerfect — you also get a warning if you attempt to erase a worksheet that has not been saved. You can always press the Help key for additional information on any error condition. Quattro Pro has a transcript recording technique that records each keystroke to disk. In the event of a power failure, you can recreate your steps and recover your lost work — or create macros after the fact. An undo command will reverse your most recent action.

A map view allows you to identify formulas, values, linked cells, and even circular references. You can annotate formulas by preceding your comments with a semicolon. These are the only auditing features in the product. We'd like to see features such as being able to identify all cells that are dependent upon a particular cell.

SuperCalc 5: *VERY GOOD*

SuperCalc is good about warning you of unsaved data. Pressing Control-Backspace will undo the last action. There is also a good set of spreadsheet auditing features, including the capability to identify dependent cells, and a bird's-eye-view map of your entire spreadsheet.

A complaint with error handling concerns formulas. If you make an error while typing a formula, SuperCalc transforms it into a text string and doesn't indicate the source of the problem.

SUPPORT POLICIES

Excel: *VERY GOOD*

Microsoft's technical support hours are 6:00 a.m. to 6:00 p.m., Pacific Standard Time. You pay for the calls, but you can receive unlimited telephone support. Registered users also receive Microsoft's newsletter, and there is a 30-day money-back guarantee if you're not satisfied with Excel.

Lotus 1-2-3, Release 2.2: *VERY GOOD*

Lotus provides 24-hour-a-day, seven-day-a-week toll-free phone support for Release 2.2 for six months after you buy; thereafter you must pay to receive support. Purchasers can also receive a free six-month subscription to Lotus magazine.

Lotus 1-2-3, Release 3: *VERY GOOD*
Lotus provides six months of free premium support (toll free, 24 hours a day, seven days a week). After this time, you can purchase additional premium support or use the company's standard non-toll-free support. Registered users are also eligible for a free six-month subscription to Lotus magazine.

PlanPerfect: *EXCELLENT*
WordPerfect Corp. provides unlimited toll-free support weekdays between 7 a.m. and 6 p.m. Mountain time, and there is a 90-day money-back guarantee. There is an active Compuserve bulletin board and a newsletter for registered users. Extended corporate support is also available.

Quattro Pro: *VERY GOOD*
Borland provides technical support via CompuServe and has free, not toll-free, telephone support from 8 a.m. to 5 p.m. Companies that purchase at least 100 units are eligible for Preferred Customer Support. This includes toll-free priority technical support, free on-site training, courseware, and reference materials.

SuperCalc 5: *SATISFACTORY*
Computer Associates provides unlimited, but not toll-free, telephone support during regular business hours.

TECHNICAL SUPPORT

Excel: *VERY GOOD*
We made two support calls. In both cases, we were talking to a technician within one minute of dialing the number. We found support to be both friendly and professional.

Lotus 1-2-3, Release 2.2: *SATISFACTORY*
We had mixed luck getting through to technical support. During business hours, the lines were busy. We eventually got through, but hold times were often unreasonable. We had better luck calling after business hours, and got through without time on hold. Support was great; getting there was a pain.

Lotus 1-2-3, Release 3: *SATISFACTORY*
As with our Release 2.2 calls, we found the Lotus technical support lines very busy during business hours and gave up after 10 minutes on hold. We got through immediately during evening hours and spoke with friendly technicians who answered our questions admirably well.

PlanPerfect: *VERY GOOD*
We were connected immediately on both of our support calls, and met with no busy signals (a rarity for a toll-free line). The technicians knew the product well.

Quattro Pro: *GOOD*
Many of our calls to Borland resulted in busy signals. But once we got through, we were connected with a support technician quickly, with minimal time on hold. The support staff was friendly and knew the product well.

SuperCalc 5: *SATISFACTORY*
If you need to call Computer Associates, be prepared for busy signals and lengthy hold times. Once connected, we found the support to be of high quality. The difficulty in making a connection lowers our support rating.

(We tested technical support during December, 1989 and January, 1990; support quality may have changed since then.)

VALUE

Excel: *EXCELLENT*
Excel is powerful, but requires a heavyweight system. If you've got a speedy machine, VGA graphics, and loads of RAM, you'll love Excel; if not, you're likely to be frustrated. Though it's been some time since we've seen an update, Excel was so far ahead of its time when first released that it is still a good prototype for future software. Its $495 price is in line with competitors.

Lotus 1-2-3, Release 2.2: *VERY GOOD*
1-2-3 lists for $495. Unless you require state-of-the-art sophistication in a spreadsheet, it's quite likely that 1-2-3, Release 2.2 will meet the majority of your needs — especially if you explore the world of add-in applications.

Lotus 1-2-3, Release 3: *EXCELLENT*
Release 3 currently lists for $595 (up from its introductory price of $495), making it the most expensive spreadsheet around. If you're a serious spreadsheet user, the price is well worth it. Aside from our problems getting hold of technical support, our only other concerns are the lack of WYSIWYG display and the current dearth of add-ins.

PlanPerfect: *GOOD*
PlanPerfect lists for $495 — the going price for a full-featured spread-sheet. Despite the vendor's apparent attempts to broaden the appeal for

this product, we feel that the audience for PlanPerfect will be Word-Perfect users who are familiar with that interface — which is no small group in itself.

Quattro Pro: *EXCELLENT*

A major consideration is the slow printing and potential frustration inherent in switching between edit mode and page preview. If fancy output is your aim, 1-2-3 with Allways or Impress is a better choice. However, Quattro Pro ($495) is an outstanding product that mixes some of the best elements of Excel and 1-2-3, Release 3 and fits smoothly into 640K of RAM.

SuperCalc 5: *VERY GOOD*

SuperCalc 5 is a worthy spreadsheet that continues to get better with each release. Veteran SuperCalc users will have a lot to like about this upgrade. Although it claims to have most of the multipage features of 1-2-3, Release 3, we found some limitations that are not present with 1-2-3. Regardless, it's a power-packed spreadsheet.

Product Summaries
Spreadsheets

Microsoft Excel Version 2.1
Company: Microsoft Corp., 16011 N.E. 36th Way, P.O. Box 97017, Redmond, WA 98073-9717; (800) 426-9400, (206) 882-8080 in WA.
List Price: $495.
Requires: IBM PC, PS/2, or compatible; hard disk; Windows/286 or 386; graphics display.

LOTUS 1-2-3 Release 2.2
Company: Lotus Development Corp., 55 Cambridge Parkway, Cambridge, MA 02142; (617) 577-8500.
List Price: $495.
Requires: IBM PC, AT, PS/2, or compatible.

LOTUS 1-2-3 Release 3.0
Company: Lotus Development Corp., 55 Cambridge Parkway, Cambridge, MA 02142; (617) 577-8500.
List Price: $595.
Requires: IBM AT, PS/2, or compatible; DOS 3.0 or later; 1 megabyte of RAM; hard disk; graphics display to preview graphs.

PlanPerfect Version 5.0
Company: Word Perfect Corp., 1555 N. Technology Way, Orem, UT 84057; (801) 225-5000.
List Price: $495.
Requires: IBM PC, AT, PS/2, or compatible; DOS 2.0 or later.

Quattro Pro Version 1.0
Company: Borland International, 1800 Green Hill Road, Scotts Valley, CA 95066; (408) 438-8400.
List Price: $495.
Requires: IBM PC, AT, PS/2, or compatible.

SuperCalc 5 Version 5.0
Company: Computer Associates International Inc., 1240 McKay Drive, San Jose, CA 95131; (800) 531-5236, (408) 432-1727.
List Price: $495.
Requires: IBM PC, AT, PS/2, or compatible; hard disk; DOS 3.0 or later.

SIDEBAR
Basic Spreadsheets Can Fill the Needs of Less-Demanding Users

How many users really need or want all the features found in these advanced spreadsheets? Many users don't even begin to utilize all the features in low-end spreadsheets. Is there really a demand for multipage spreadsheets, advanced linking capabilities, and external database capability? If you answer "No" to such questions, read on. Many other spreadsheets are available, most of which can be classified as ``basic'' products. In most cases, these products are priced considerably lower.

LOTUS SPREADSHEET FOR DESKMATE. 1-2-3 it's not, but it can read and write WK1 format files. This spreadsheet ($219) features pull-down menus and includes a run-time version of Tandy's Deskmate graphical interface. On the down side, it lacks a macro programming language, and it cannot use expanded memory or 1-2-3 add-ins.

Lotus Development Corp., 55 Cambridge Parkway, Cambridge, MA 02142; (617) 577-8500.

LUCID-3D. The major strength of this product ($99.95) is that it's RAM-resident. You can pop up a spreadsheet while working in another application, and easily cut and paste data to your underlying program. You can work with multiple files and link them together. It works great with a mouse, and you can read files produced by Dac's accounting packages.

Dac Easy Inc., 17950 Preston Road, Suite 800, Dallas, TX 75252; (800) 877-8088.

MULTIPLAN. Despite its current emphasis on Excel, Microsoft continues to sell its original spreadsheet, called Multiplan ($195). This is a capable spreadsheet, but it lacks graphics and is on the slow side. An interesting footnote is that Multiplan was the first spreadsheet available that featured support for OS/2.

Microsoft Corp., 16011 N.E. 36th Way, P.O. Box 97017, Redmond, WA 98073-9717; (800) 426-9400, (206) 882-8080 in WA.

PRO QUBE. The most distinguishing characteristic of this spreadsheet from Formalsoft ($247.50) is suggested by its name. This product's dataspace is actually a cube of 512 cells on a side, which can be oriented in any of six different directions. Its macro language is among the best we've seen in any spreadsheet.

Formalsoft, P.O. Box 1913, Sandy, UT 84091; (801) 565-0971.

QUATTRO. With the introduction of Quattro Pro, Borland has relegated its original Quattro to a "retail" role — and also reduced the price ($129.95). It's nearly perfectly compatible with 1-2-3, Release 2.01, thanks to a command interface that can be modified. Particular strengths of Quattro include a macro debugger and superb graphics.

Borland International, 1800 Green Hill Road, Scotts Valley, CA 95066; (408) 438-8400.

SMART SPREADSHEET. Part of an integrated package called Smartware II, the Smart Spreadsheet from Informix ($349) is a competitive product capable of standing on its own. It features spreadsheet linking and high-quality graphics.

Informix Software Inc., 16011 College Blvd., Lenexa, KS 66219; (800) 331-1763, Ext. 1000; (913) 599-7100.

TWIN. Mosaic Software currently markets three spreadsheets: Twin Classic (a 1-2-3 Release 1A clone), Twin Advanced (a Release 2.01 workalike), and Twin Level III (a more advanced product with some high-end features, $249). Clearly positioned as a low-cost alternative to 1-2-3, the Twin series fits the bill nicely if you're on a budget.

Mosaic Software, 1972 Massachussetts Ave., Cambridge, MA 02140; (617) 491-2434.

VP-PLANNER PLUS. This spreadsheet from Paperback Software ($249) is compatible with 1-2-3 in terms of keystrokes, macros, and files. It has a unique multidimensional database feature that works with massive amounts of data on disk. An upgrade (VP-Planner 3D) that came out early this year adds "3-D" spreadsheet features like those in 1-2-3 Release 3 or SuperCalc 5.

Paperback Software International, 2830 Ninth St., Berkeley, CA 94710; (415) 644-2116.

Features
High-End PC Spreadsheets

■=Feature present □=Feature not present	Excel/ Windows Version 2.1	Lotus 1-2-3 Version 2.2
Price	$495	$495
Hard disk required	■	□
Maximum rowsq	16,384	8,192
Maximum columns	256	256
Maximum characters in cell	255	240
Disk-based virtual memory	□	□
Supports add-ins	□	■
Number of windows in single sheet	4	2
Multiple active worksheets in RAM	■	□
Pull-down menus	■	□
File compression	□	□
Integrated file manager	□	□
Mouse support	■	□
Formulas and Analysis:		
User-defined functions	■	□
Goal seeking	■	□
Linear programming functions	□	□

Each spreadsheet compared features matrix manipulation, regression analysis and linear programming functions.

Compatibility:		
Read/Write WKS format	■	■
Read/write XLS format	■	□
Read/Write DIF format	■	■
Read/Write CSV format	■	Read

Lotus 1-2-3 Version 3.0	PlanPerfect Version 5.0	Quattro Pro Version 1.0	SuperCalc 5 Version 5.0
$595	$495	$495	$495
■	□	■	■
8,192	8,192	8,192	9,999
256	256	256	255
512	255	255	240
□	■	□	□
■	□	□	■
2	2	2	2
■	■	■	■
□	■	■	□
□	□	■	□
□	■	■	□
□	□	■	□
□	■	□	□
□	□	□	□
□	□	■	□
Read	■	■	■
□	□	□	□
■	■	□	■
Read	■	Read	Read

Features *(continued)*

■=Feature present
□=Feature not present

	Excel/ Windows Version 2.1	Lotus 1-2-3 Version 2.2
Each spreadsheet compared can read and write WK1 and DBF files; they can all also parse text files and execute 1-2-3 macros to some extent.		
Database:		
Search/Replace	■	■
Basic flat-file database	■	■
Selective import from database file	□	□
Access external databsaes on disk	□	□
Sorts by rows/columns	■	Rows
Number of sort keys	3	2
Speed Related:		
Background recalculation	■	□
Each spreadsheet compared performs minimal recalculation and supports a math chip.		
Macros:		
Macro debugger	■	□
Each spreadsheet compared has a Macro Learn mode, supports macros separate from worksheet, has a macro language, and is capable of creating user macro menus.		
Graphics:		
Vertical/horizontal bar charts	■/■	■/□
Vertical/horizontal line charts	■/□	■/□
Pie charts	■	■
X-Y charts	■	■
Area charts	■	□
Combination bar & line charts	■	□
Stock market charts	■	□
Text charts	□	□
Graph annotation with text/drawings	■	□

Lotus 1-2-3 Version 3.0	PlanPerfect Version 5.0	Quattro Pro Version 1.0	SuperCalc 5 Version 5.0
■	■	■	■
■	■	■	■
■	□	■	■
■	□	■	□
Rows	■	Rows	■
255	10	5	3
■	□	■	□
□	□	■	□
■/■	■/■	■/■	■/■
■/■	■/■	■/□	■/■
■	■	■	■
■	■	■	■
■	■	■	■
■	■	■	■
■	■	■	■
□	□	■	■
□	□	■	□

Features *(continued)*

■=Feature present
□=Feature not present

	Excel/ Windows Version 2.1	Lotus 1-2-3 Version 2.2
3-D-look perspective bars/pies	□	□
True 3-D graphs (x,y & z axes)	□	□
Dual Y-axes graphs	■	□
View graphs with worksheet	■	■
Customize fonts/colors/hatching	■	□
Output PIC files	□	■
Output MCG files	□	□
Output:		
Postscript support for text/graphcis	■	■
Multiple fonts	■	■
Number of fonts per worksheet	4	8
Custom cell formats	■	□
Plotter support	■	■
Background printing	■	□
Print graphs with spreadsheet	□	■
WYSIWYG display	■	■
WYSIWYG display (edit mode)	■	□
True page preview	■	□
Adjust screen colors	■	□
Display selected values in different colors	□	□
Expanded display for EGA/VGA users	N/A	□
Cell shading	■	■
Boxes/line draw features	■	■
Consolidation/Linking:		
Multipage (3-D) worksheets	□	□
Multidimensional databsae feature	□	□

Lotus 1-2-3 Version 3.0	PlanPerfect Version 5.0	Quattro Pro Version 1.0	SuperCalc 5 Version 5.0
□	■	■	■
□	■	■	■
■	■	■	■
■	□	■	□
■	■	■	■
■	□	■	■
■	□	□	□
■	■	■	■
■	■	■	■
8	8	8	8
□	□	□	■
■	■	■	■
■	□	□	□
■	□	■	□
□	■	□	□
□	□	□	□
□	■	■	□
□	■	■	□
□	□	■	□
■	□	■	■
□	□	■	■
□	□	■	■
■	□	□	■
□	□	□	□

Features *(continued)*

■=Feature present
□=Feature not present

	Excel/Windows Version 2.1	Lotus 1-2-3 Version 2.2
One-time file combine (copy)	■	■
One-time file combine (add/subtract)	■	■
One-time file combine (multiply/divide)	■	□
Permanent link to cell in active sheet	■	N/A
Permanent link to cell in non-active sheet	■	■
Use active sheet link in formula	■	N/A
Use non-active sheet link in formula	□	□
Can copy (relative) active sheet link	■	N/A
Can copy (relative) non-active sheet link	□	■
Auto-link when cells moved to other sheet	□	N/A
Auditing/security features:		
Identify dependent cells	■	□
Identify circular reference cell	■	■
Annotate formulas	■	□
Map view	□	□
Selective cell protection	■	■
Password protection	■	■
"Seal" worksheet	□	□

Lotus 1-2-3 Version 3.0	PlanPerfect Version 5.0	Quattro Pro Version 1.0	SuperCalc 5 Version 5.0
■	■	■	■
■	■	■	■
□	■	□	■
■	■	■	■
■	■	■	■
■	□	■	■
■	□	■	■
■	□	■	■
■	□	■	■
□	□	■	□
□	□	□	■
■	□	■	■
■	■	■	□
■	□	■	■
■	■	■	■
■	■	■	■
■	□	□	□

How We Test and Score Spreadsheets

Our hardware setup for benchmark testing consisted of an 8-MHz Compaq Deskpro 286 with a 40-megabyte hard drive, a 1-megabyte Intel Above Board, EGA, and DOS 3.31. For graphics-intensive products and products that run under graphical environments (such as Windows) we perform a second set of benchmarks using a Compaq Deskpro 386/20e with a 100-megabyte hard drive, 4 megabytes of RAM, VGA, and DOS 3.31 (when not running OS/2). Our reviewer also used these products with a variety of other systems, including a PS/2 Model 70 (16 MHz), a 386/25 from EPS Technologies, and various 286 systems, all with EGA or VGA graphics.

Many of these spreadsheets are capable of background recalculation, which recalculates the current screen first and returns cursor control so you can continue working while the rest of the worksheet finishes recalculating. Where background calculation is an issue, benchmarks are given as ranges: The first value is how soon cursor control was returned; the second is the actual full recalculation time

Benchmark Tests: We perform a series of calculation tests designed to demonstrate speed of operation in various situations:

Arithmetic model: This test follows a personal net-worth model that calculates the value of assets and liabilities over 253 months. It shows performance in a straightforward recalculation with simple formulas. We report the time required to recalculate the spreadsheet after altering the percent change on all assets (to force a recalculation of the entire spreadsheet). We also record the time required after altering a single asset. This determines whether a spreadsheet can do minimal recalc, also known as intelligent or sparse recalc, in which only the cells affected by a change are recalculated rather than the entire worksheet.

Financial model: Analyzes a variable-rate loan over 360 months. We change the loan amount and time recalculation of the entire spreadsheet.

Scientific model: Constructs a 37-by-37-bivariate distribution matrix. The maximum and minimum values for both variables are defined, as well as sigma and mu. The correlation coefficient is also given. We score the spreadsheet recalculation time after changing the correlation coefficient.

File-oriented consolidation model: Consolidates 24 ranges for seven spreadsheets. Each range was linked into a unique location in the master parent worksheet, and those ranges became part of simple sum formulas used to consolidate the information. The score reported in the chart is the time required to update the parent worksheet after loading all child worksheets into RAM and altering two values in them.

Page-oriented consolidation model: Consolidates a 38-by-12-cell range from 10 identical worksheets. The parent worksheet rolls up the data from each of these worksheets. The score in the chart is the time needed to update the parent worksheet after loading all child worksheets into RAM and altering two values in them.

In addition to performing tests, our technicians reported on features, functionality, quality of documentation, ease of learning and use, and error handling. The reviewer, with much experience in spreadsheet use in a business setting, combined these impressions with his own experience to evaluate the products. Finally, the results were critiqued and edited by InfoWorld editors.

This comparison uses a Report Card that evaluates the most important areas of concern when selecting a powerful spreadsheet. Your requirements may vary; you may wish to adjust Report Card weightings accordingly.

Scoring: *Performance: Formulas/analysis:* This refers to the spreadsheet's basic analytical capability, and takes into account built-in functions and advanced features.

112

An unacceptable score means the product has bugs that can produce erroneous results. We assign a poor rating if: the product lacks common built-in functions (such as string functions); one or more of the functions do not work properly; or it cannot handle reasonably complex formulas or worksheets. A satisfactory rating requires that the built-in functions be generally equivalent to those found in 1-2-3, Release 2.2. A good score requires at least three of the following: matrix manipulation, regression, what-if tables, goal seeking. A very good score requires user-definable functions. An excellent rating is given if all of the above are present, and the product has one or more additional significant analytical features.

Compatibility: This evaluates the spreadsheet's capability to work with other files. Particular attention is given to compatibility with "industry-standard" 1-2-3 files. A satisfactory rating requires that the product read WKS or WK1 files (including formulas) and can import and export ASCII files. The score is boosted to good if it can translate or import dBASE files. A very good rating requires all of the above, plus the capability to read or write two additional file formats (e.g., CSV, DIF, SYLK), translate 1-2-3 macros, and parse text files into component parts. An excellent rating requires all of the above, plus the capability to read two additional file formats and the capability to translate 1-2-3 graph and range names.

Speed: To score speed, we considered relative times on all of our benchmark tests, paying particular attention to recalculation times for the arithmetic, financial, scientific, and consolidation models. Setup and load times play a similar role, and bonus points were awarded for minimal and background recalculation.

Database: This category refers to the product's capability to work with data in field-and-record format. Additional consideration is given for unique or unusual features. A poor score is given if the product has database features but lacks some essential elements compared to 1-2-3, Release 2.2. For a satisfactory rating, the spreadsheet must have the functional equivalent of the flatfile internal database query commands in 1-2-3, Release 2.2. For a good score, it must have all of the above, plus additional sort keys or the capability to sort by rows and columns. A higher score requires user-created data entry templates and/or query-by-example templates, the capability to selectively import database fields and records, or additional database management commands and features.

Graphics: This category deals with a product's capability to generate and customize graphs produced by spreadsheet data. A product is scored poor if it supports only basic graph types, and has no customization of fonts and colors or hatchings. A satisfactory score is awarded if it supports all the basic graph types (line, bar, stacked bar, pie, X-Y) and allows customization of fonts and colors/hatchings. A good score requires support for at least two additional graph types (stock market, text-only, combination bar/pie, true three-dimensional). A very good additionally requires at least four of the following: capability to view graphs and text simultaneously; true 3-D graphs; dual y-axis; mixed graph types; stock market graphs; combination bar/pie. For excellent, the product must meet all of the above criteria, and offer full "paintbrush-style" graph annotation (or some other characteristic that makes it stand out).

Output: Scoring on this category has been revised significantly based on responses to our recent user survey, which shows a strong interest among our readers in high-quality output from their spreadsheets. If print enhancements are possible only via "setup strings" or embedded control strings, we give the product a poor. A product receives a satisfactory score if it allows basic print enhancements (e.g., bold or underline) without embedding printer control strings. If the product allows you to easily mix fonts and sizes and has line drawing and shading features, we give it a good score. A very good requires all of the above, plus page preview or some method to identify page breaks prior to printing. To earn an excellent output score, the product must also offer support for: background printing; WYSIWYG edit mode; printing graphs and text together; dynamic page break display; page preview; and Postscript.

Macros: This category measures the product's "programming" features via macros — keystrokes or commands that can be played back upon request. Products with no macro capability receive an unsatisfactory score. Macros, but no macro language, result in a poor score. To earn a satisfactory score, the product must have auto-record macros and a macro language equivalent to 1-2-3, Release 2.2. To receive a good macro score, the product must have all of the above, plus support for macro libraries (or store macros externally for general use). A very good score needs to have all of the above, plus macro debugging capabilities beyond "step mode." An excellent macro score requires something out of the ordinary.

Consolidation/Linking: We award three separate consolidation and linking scores, which are then averaged into one overall score. The first score is for a one-time consolidation, in which scores are reduced for products that won't let you add values from one worksheet to a cell in another worksheet. Higher scores are awarded to products that let you have multiple spreadsheets in memory, and let you point and shoot in order to create a link.

The second score is for a linked-file model that updates a master spreadsheet with the results from subsidiary spreadsheets. We assigned a satisfactory score to those products that could produce a permanent interactive link among worksheets and that allow you to copy this link to other cells in the spreadsheet. Higher scores are awarded to products that let you have multiple spreadsheets in memory and that consolidate from spreadsheets on disk.

The third and final score tests the product's capability to work with a linked-page situation, in which totals are rolled up from multiple spreadsheets. A satisfactory score goes to a product that will perform math on values linked from other spreadsheets. Higher scores go to products that can view multiple spreadsheets in memory, work with spreadsheets on disk, and allow for multipage models. The final linking/consolidation score is an average of the three subscores.

Capacity: This category reflects a product's capability to work with large files and with multiple files. A satisfactory score requires support for expanded memory. A very good score is awarded if the user can access multiple files simultaneously. An excellent score requires all of the above, plus the use of disk-based virtual memory. Bonus points are awarded for improved memory management techniques or other features. Points are deducted for an unusually small workspace on systems with only 640K of conventional RAM. Incapability to run on a 640K system also detracts from the score.

Other Report Card categories are judged according to the standard criteria described in Chapter 1, with these exceptions:

Ease of Learning: To earn a satisfactory score, the spreadsheets reviewed here must be learnable by novices.

Error Handling: An unacceptable score is given if it is very easy to lose data or crash the system. To earn a satisfactory score, the product must warn the user if exit or worksheet erase is attempted with unsaved data; and it must offer basic protection against data loss and system crashes and have basic error messages. A good score adds the requirement of detailed help for error messages. A very good requires a timed file save/backup feature and an undo feature. An excellent requires all of the above, plus keystroke transcript recording to disk (keystroke logging) or something extra.

Bonus points are awarded for auditing and security features such as cell annotation, map view, identification of dependent cells, "sealing," and network file or cell locking.

CHAPTER FIVE

The Process of Desktop Publishing

Putting the Best to the Test: Aldus PageMaker, Ventura Publisher, and Quark XPress

BY BARBARA ASSADI AND GALEN GRUMAN, INFOWORLD REVIEW BOARD

Desktop publishing is not an activity confined to one program. It is the integration of disparate elements created in a range of applications by people with different skills and needs. As a result, in this comparison we evaluate from a process-oriented view four industrial-strength desktop publishing programs along with the programs that provide their source text and graphics.

In fact, what are commonly called desktop publishing programs are actually layout programs — the linchpins making integration possible and published results better than you could achieve by relying only on your word processor, graphics program, spreadsheet, or other tools. Layout programs should build on — rather than duplicate — the capabilities of the programs that provide the raw material.

For example, a layout package should have basic line-drawing capabilities to add annotations between layout elements, but it doesn't need the capability to draw splines and make graduated fills. Neither does it need sophisticated word processing features like search and replace, since that level of editing should not be done — and is not typically done — during layout and production. A spelling checker, conversely, is an appropriate option to catch typos made during edits.

This is not a typical *InfoWorld* comparison. Instead of detailing performance benchmarks and analyzing features in each desktop publishing/layout program, here we are actually reviewing the process of desktop publishing. As such, we will not dwell or concentrate on the features, support policies, or benchmark scores, although they certainly play a role. Instead, we will focus on the capability of each layout program and its compatible supporting products (such as graphics packages) to produce the same document.

Our report card consists of different, process-related items including categories such as level of integration, text handling, layout, output, and graphics. We also include some of our more common categories that lend themselves well to a process-oriented review, such as ease of learning and use, documentation, error handling, technical support, and value.

For our evaluation of this process, we created an article from a fictional science magazine, *Science Today.* We attempted to produce a three-page layout of the article with the same design specifications using each of the programs.

The main article is in two parts. In "Step-by-Step Analysis" we describe what we did — and what we went through — to create the three-page layout in each of the desktop publishing packages. In "Rating the Process" we score each product on the categories contained in the Report Card. In another departure from our conventions, the scoring criteria for each category is detailed in that category's discussion, rather than in a separate How We Test article.

Though each of these products is feature-filled and powerful, each lacks one or more basic capabilities required to finish our test document easily. These we summarize in a sidebar. In another sidebar we lament the numerous problems introduced by the fact that desktop publishing is an activity that integrates material from many sources: word processors, graphics programs, spreadsheets, and databases, for example, and sometimes across hardware platforms. That means working with different programs from different vendors — a surefire headache. This sidebar also lists our recommendations for the best bets in software to minimize problems.

Important note: As we were going to press, Aldus released Page-Maker 4, a major upgrade. A full separate review of that product appears later in this chapter.

How we tested the products and the process.

Testing a process involves more than testing a program. Thus, this review has two main sections: an examination of the process of creating the same document in all four programs and then a section describing critically (with scores) the products' capabilities to meet our criteria in report card categories. In this latter section, the descriptions of our scoring criteria precede the actual product descriptions and scores. (In most *InfoWorld* product comparisons our testing criteria are described in a separate "How We Test" sidebar.)

Our comparison platforms consisted of a 386-based 20-MHz PC and the Mac II. We included the Macintosh platform especially because it is heralded as the premier system and environment for desktop publishing. The layout programs we used were Aldus PageMaker 3.0 for the IBM PC, Quark XPress 2.1 for the Mac, and Xerox Ventura Publisher 2.0 with Professional Extension (for the IBM PC). PageMaker also comes in a Macintosh version which works nearly identically to its MS-DOS counterpart. PageMaker is also available in an OS/2 version, and Ventura has announced it plans to support OS/2 and the Macintosh in 1990.

We chose the programs in each layout set based on two criteria: The programs should be widely used for their layout features and should save or export data easily in a format used by the layout proram. If the two criteria were in conflict, data exchange superseded popularity.

We chose the following programs to provide the raw material. For PageMaker, which runs under Windows, we created text in Microsoft Word 4.0, graphics in Corel Draw 1.1, and a spreadsheet in Lotus 1-2-3, Release 2 (including a chart based on the spreadsheet data). For Quark XPress, we used Microsoft Word 3.02 for text, Aldus Freehand 2.01 for graphics, and Microsoft Excel for spreadsheet data and charts. For Ventura, we used Word Perfect 5.0 for text, Corel Draw 1.1 for graphics, and Lotus 1-2-3, Release 2 for spreadsheet data and charts.

In addition to the tools described here, when preparing to produce documents you should consider which computers, scanners, printers, monitors, mice, PC-to-Mac transfer products (if appropriate), bit-mapped graphics editors, business-graphics programs, screen capture programs, and text and graphics format translators you'll need. First you'll have to define the range of tasks, then choose the products that meet those needs. The "Desktop Publishers Beware: Perils of Setup Side Effects" sidebar describes some of these setup considerations.

How the process works: A real-world view.

Work flow varies depending on the size of the organization involved, the scope of the project, and the available talent pool. In small organizations and one-person shops, one person may perform most of the tasks. In larger shops, tasks may be assigned to specialists. Either way, the process is similar. Typically, in this process:

- The design director or layout artist starts with a thumbnail sketch of the publication, and implements it as a template in the layout program.

- The design director or graphic artist establishes a graphics style, defining consistent approaches like standard line weights, screen weights, uses of fonts, and placement of keys and text in graphics and charts.

- The design director designs the typographic look, defining attributes such as fonts, spacing, margins, and numbers of columns. This is then implemented as a style sheet in the layout program by the director or a graphic artist. If you use a word processor that generates style sheets that your layout program imports, you implement the style sheet in your word processor. But ultimately you must work with the style sheets in both programs, since the layout programs' style sheets contain typographic controls not available in the word processors' style sheets.

- Coding or type specification may be handled in several ways. In large organizations, an editor may specify only attributes — such as boldface and italics — that affect meaning, usually using the word processor's built-in features. A copy editor may do the fine coding to indicate where to put headlines, bylines, special symbols, and the like. Some layout programs let you determine these in your word processor through style sheets, codes, or a combination of the two. Others force you to implement this during layout, in which case you should devise a set of markup codes for the layout artist.

- The copy editors and graphic artists prepare the text and graphics for layout, coding and exporting them as needed.

- The layout artist lays out the document using the text and graphics files provided, flowing them into a copy of your layout template and overriding template settings when necessary.

- The design director (or perhaps managing editor) approves the layouts.

- The production artist implements final changes and handles fine-tuning such as ensuring that columns align, widows and orphans are removed, and page numbers are correct. The production artist then prepares the final file for output at a typesetter or prep house.

How we duplicated the process.

The descriptions in the sidebar, "A Step-By-Step Analysis of the Desktop Publishing Process," describe and illustrate the desktop publishing process as we performed it using the four layout programs and any accompanying software. It is important to note that these are the main tasks, not the only tasks.

Our *Science Today* project let us cover the full process while revealing differences in features among the four sets of programs. Our design purposely used features we knew were not supported by all programs (like circular wrap and rotated text) to highlight these differences. No set of programs could implement all of our design decisions in a straightforward manner — we had to use workarounds for some. However, the layout chosen is by no means difficult or exceptional; it is a straightforward, typical design, and all three programs could complete the job in our maximum time allotment of 30 hours.

Our test layout posed problems for all the packages we tested. These are the features each program could not handle in our layout:

Aldus PageMaker: A 1½-point rule above the decks (PageMaker has limited rule sizes); rotated text for art credit (PageMaker does not support rotated text).

Quark: Rotated text for the art credit (Quark Version 2.0 does not support rotated text; recently-released Quark 3 does) and spreadsheet import (Quark imports only spreadsheet ASCII files).

Ventura: Spreadsheet import (Ventura imports only spreadsheet print files, which it tries to convert into tables); curved text wrap (Ventura supports only rectangular wrap, and its work-around to simulate curved and polygonal wrap is awkward); and proper hyphenation (it was the only program to mishyphenate words).

Before beginning actual production, we produced a specification sheet defining our typographic design, and a similar sheet to define our layout parameters (margins, numbers of columns, illustrations, etc.). We then began the process of desktop publishing.

You will see two main sections that follow: The first describes the desktop publishing process, and the second scores the various components on our Report Card.

EXECUTIVE SUMMARY

Of the four desktop publishing programs we reviewed, we found **Xerox Ventura Publisher** with the **Professional Extension** for the IBM PC and **Quark XPress** for the Mac to be the most versatile, capable, and well-designed layout programs. Both Ventura and Quark are meant for large-scale publishing projects that involve several professionals per project and support multiple non-layout applications such as spreadsheets and graphics programs. Both use a structured approach that lets you save effort by applying predefined templates to some jobs while still being able to create new designs relatively easily. This structure also lets you learn incrementally, starting out with the core features and moving on to the more powerful — and difficult — features as your confidence and needs grow.

The differences between the two programs come down to high-end features, like anchoring (one of Ventura Publisher's strengths) and text wrap (one of Quark's). Ventura does better in layout and typographic control, while Quark does better in graphics and output control. For most applications, you'll probably find your decision on which to use depends primarily on whether you use MS-DOS or Macintosh computers. Both programs are appropriate for most users, from small-business to corporate settings, since Quark and Ventura ably handle a range of documents and permit growth into their powerful features.

Aldus PageMaker 3 for the IBM PC most closely follows the traditional publishing process — this is both its strength and its weakness. It is an asset because the program is a natural to use for layout artists and designers, allowing them to work much as they've always done by hand. But this is also a detriment because it means the program is more manual than necessary, lacking automation features that are some of the reasons to convert to electronic layout.

The manual orientation makes PageMaker most appropriate for work where almost every document is unique, since the effort to create such documents is about the same in all layout programs. Because of its limited capabilities to let you format typography in your word processor (to keep the jobs of specifying type and layout separate), PageMaker 3 is best suited for one- and two-person shops where the traditional divisions of labor are blurred or don't exist.

Although PageMaker 3 offers some structured features, they are no match for Ventura or Quark's, and PageMaker is hard pressed to match their performance in production of magazines, newspapers, or documentation. PageMaker does offer the advantage of having file compatibility between its Mac and MS-DOS versions. (See also the full review of Page Maker 4, later in this chapter.)

Report Card
The Process of Desktop Publishing

	Weight	Aldus PageMaker Version 3.0	Quark XPress Version 2.12	Xerox Ventura Publisher Version 2.0
Performance				
Text				
Text handling	100	Satisfactory	Excellent	Excellent
Text wrapping	75	Very Good	Excellent	Good
Typography Layout	100	Satisfactory	Very Good	Excellent
Multi-element	25	Good	Very Good	Excellent
Tabular text	25	Satisfactory	Good	Very Good
Graphics				
Graphics editing/ drawing	50	Very Good	Excellent	Very Good
Charting/business graphics	50	Good	Good	Good
Output				
Color	50	Satisfactory	Excellent	Satisfactory
Printing	50	Very Good	Excellent	Very Good
Level of integration	100	Good	Very Good	Excellent
Documentation	75	Good	Very Good	Very Good
Ease of learning	75	Good	Good	Good
Ease of use	100	Very Good	Very Good	Very Good
Error handling	25	Very Good	Good	Satisfactory
Technical support	25	Very Good	Poor	Satisfactory
Value	75	Good	Excellent	Very Good
Final scores		**6.3**	**8.1**	**7.8**

Guide to Report Card Scores
Excellent = 1.0 — Outstanding in all areas.
Very Good = 0.75 — Meets all essential criteria and offers significant advantages.
Good = 0.625 — Meets essential criteria and includes some special features.
Satisfactory = 0..5 — Meets essential criteria.
Poor = 0.25 — Falls short in essential areas.
Unacceptable or N/A = 0.0 — Fails to meet minimum standards or lacks this feature.

A Step-By-Step Analysis of the Desktop Publishing Process

In this section, we describe what it took for us to produce our proto-type Science Today *document. Accompanying this section are step-by-step screen shots illustrating (in parallel, when appropriate, for all four packages) the process.*

SETTING UP THE PROGRAMS:

Fonts: Each layout program has limitations on how it uses fonts. For example, some require that you have both the screen and printer fonts before they will let you use them. Others can use fonts in only selected sizes. If you have special font-size specifications, be sure ahead of time that your package will support it.

Aldus PageMaker: Pagemaker can use the four built-in Windows screen fonts (Helvetica, Times, Courier, and Symbol). It also uses downloadable soft fonts, such as from Bitstream (the installation kit comes with PageMaker and includes 12 fonts).

Quark XPress: As is typical for a Mac program, Quark XPress doesn't come with native typefaces but instead uses the scalable Postscript fonts available on your system. You can specify font sizes between 1 and 500 points in quarter-point increments. A Font Usage box in the Utilities menu lets you see the number of fonts you have specified in any Quark document. Thirteen text attributes (such as all caps, small caps, word-only underline, and superscript) are available on pull-down menus. Quark includes automatic kerning based on the font manufacturer's kerning tables and lets you kern letter pairs in increments of one-two-hundreth of an em space. You can interactively track a passage of text (for example, to make a headline fit on a single line) by keyboard commands that increase or decrease space between characters. Or you can enter specific tracking values in a dialog box.

Ventura: Although Ventura comes with only four built-in typefaces (Helvetica, Times, Courier, and Symbol) for on-screen display, it lets you access any typeface entered into the font-width table. For Postscript, Ventura includes information on 41 typefaces. This capability to use fonts that you don't have means that you can access typefaces that your typesetter or printer has built in without having to buy them yourself. You can download font-width information for other typefaces and their corresponding screen-display fonts from several bulletin boards. (If your printer doesn't have these typefaces, text printing will default to Courier.)

Ventura also allows you to change the kerning tables for any font by editing an ASCII version of the font table created by a utility program. You can also delete width-table fonts, such as unused fonts, or you can create separate tables for different jobs to enforce a consistent look.

Hyphenation Dictionaries: Issues include the capability to insert discretionary hyphens (for preferred breaks or for words like "progress" and "project" that hyphenate differently as nouns than as verbs); add hyphenation exceptions to a user dictionary (to override errors in hyphenation or to add words the built-in hyphenation algorithm does not know); specify the maximum number of consecutive hyphens; and set how many characters after and before which a hyphen may appear.

Aldus PageMaker: PageMaker supports basic hyphenation control, including a 3,000-word ASCII hyphenation-exception dictionary to which you can add unusually hyphenated words and their hyphenation points from your word processor. PageMaker also lets you define a hyphenation hot zone for ragged text, which lets you specify how close to the text's right margin a word may be hyphenated. But you cannot specify how many characters must precede or follow a hyphen in a hyphenated word. (Many typesetters prefer to disallow hyphens unless there are at least three characters before and after the hyphen; the defaults for most layout programs allow hyphens after and before two characters.)

Quark XPress: Quark has a built-in hyphenation feature, which you can modify by entering your own hyphenation choices. A wide range of choices allows you to specify the maximum number of consecutive lines that end in hyphenated words, the minimum number of letters a word must contain to be hyphenated, and the fewest number of characters that must appear before or after a hyphen. You can, if you choose, override the convention of not breaking capitalized words and the first word of a sentence. A Hyphenation Exceptions command lets you select custom hyphenation, overriding the standard hyphenation of that word.

Ventura: Ventura supports full hyphenation control through the Professional Extension's Edco dictionary. (Without this dictionary, you cannot specify the minimum number of characters that must appear before or after a hyphenation.) Adding words to this package's exception dictionary consists of adding them and their hyphenation points to an ASCII file from your word processor.

Program preferences: Some common decisions you must make in setting up each program include: Can you set up preferences such as measurement units, rulers, guidelines, and paragraph and tab marker displays? Are these preferences retained for future sessions? Can you specify preferences within dialogue boxes?

Aldus PageMaker: PageMaker has basic options to set preferences, such as measurement units, greeked text (greeking is the size at which the program stops trying to draw characters; this saves display time), and so on. You cannot tailor individual dialogue boxes.

Quark XPress: Quark's Preferences menu lets you determine preferences for a specific document or change default preferences that apply each time you open a new document. You can set preferences for measurement units, automatic page insertion (to handle text overflow), automatic kerning, character widths, leading mode and automatic leading percentages, where frames should be placed (inside or outside text or picture boxes), guidelines, baseline grid, and the font size below which text is greeked on the screen. A Points/Inch field lets you change the default point-to-inch value of 72, although Quark sizes fonts on the basis of 72 points per inch, regardless of the value you enter in Points/Inch.

Ventura: Ventura lets you customize much of its interface; it saves these preferences when you quit, so they are in place the next time you load the program. Such preferences include measurement units in most dialogue boxes, pull-down or drop-down menus, on-screen kerning size (a large number speeds screen display), greeking, rulers, and paragraph and tab markers.

SETTING UP THE DOCUMENTS:

Creating Templates: *Templates are the basic layout you will use throughout your document. You create templates only once, reusing them for each article by copying the template with a new name before flowing any text or graphics into it. You should be able to alter the basic template on the fly as needed. Issues include ease of creation; ease of local modification; position control (by eye, snap-to ruler, or coordinate placement); number of features that may be included in the template; and the degree of control over widows; orphans; page size; page orientation; and other global layout attributes.*

Aldus PageMaker: PageMaker supports templates through its master pages, which define margins and columns for left and right pages. To include "window shades" (the PageMaker version of a frame) for other text and graphics, you must create dummy text; otherwise, the window shades will not be retained. This incapability to create empty frames for later use, as well as the incapability to predefine their size, makes creating and using templates more time-consuming than it would otherwise be. Once created, you can easily add text and graphics on the fly to your template. Snap-to rulers and grids help make placement accurate, but PageMaker doesn't let you position elements precisely by specifying window-shade coordinates.

PageMaker offers solid control over global attributes like widow and orphan control, page size (including custom sizes), and page orientation (portrait/landscape).

PageMaker illustration 1, the screen shows one master page for our test document. Window shades contain no information about cropping, margins, text wrap, or sizing — you can implement these decisions only when you place text and graphics.

Quark XPress: Quark does not require that you use templates, but it does support them. For publications that have a fixed format from issue to issue, you'll want to prepare a page format so you won't have to design the page from scratch each time. Once you've established the default page, you choose Save As Template. But if you decide to make changes to the default page after working on a few pages of your document, Quark does not retroactively apply those template changes to existing pages, only to pages inserted after the modification of the default page. Quark does not include automatic widow and orphan control, but it does let you control text baselines tightly.

Quark XPress supports portrait and landscape pages, and custom page sizes between one and 48 inches square.

Quark XPress illustration 1, the screen here shows one page of the Quark XPress template developed for our test document. Elements in this template appear on subsequent pages.

Ventura: Ventura is designed specifically with a template orientation. In each layout (called a chapter), you draw frames that can contain text or graphics; size and position them with a mouse or by entering their exact size and coordinates; associate rules and background screens; and specify the margins (both inside the frame and outside it for wraps) and number of columns. You can designate up to six frames as repeating frames, handy for elements like page numbers or logos that appear regularly. Repeating frames can appear on every page, all left pages, or all right pages. You can turn off a repeating frame on a specific page without affecting it elsewhere. Other controls include vertical justification (in Professional Extension only); column balancing (which makes columns within the frame have the same number of lines and appear even with each other); and whether text in other frames should wrap around the selected frame.

Ventura also offers widow and orphan control, portrait and landscape page orientation, and seven page-sizes (5^1/$_2$-by-8^1/$_2$-inch, letter, legal, and tabloid, plus three large-paper formats). You cannot define

Continued on page 134

125

Template Creation: An Important Beginning

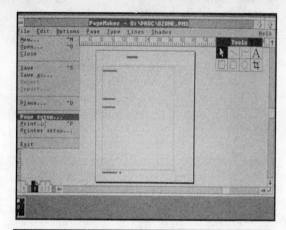

Aldus PageMaker 1

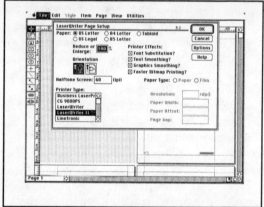

Quark XPress 1

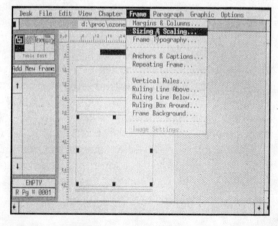

Xerox Ventura 1

Typography

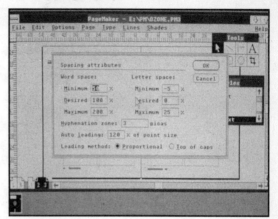

Aldus PageMaker 2

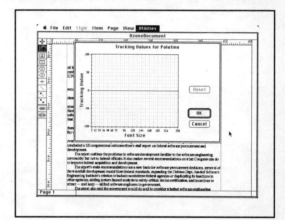

Quark XPress 2

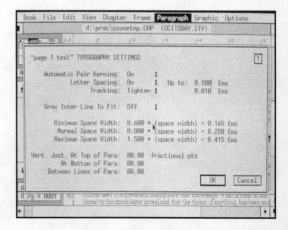

Xerox Ventura 2

Preparing Text Files for Layout

Aldus PageMaker 3

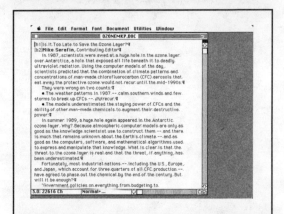

Quark XPress 3

Xerox Ventura 3

Flowing Text into your Document

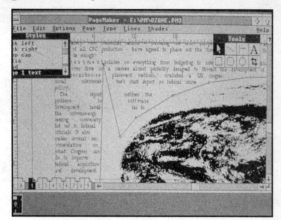

Aldus PageMaker 4

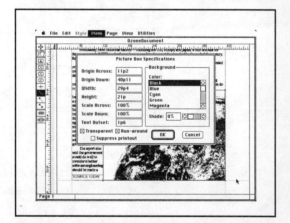

Quark XPress 4

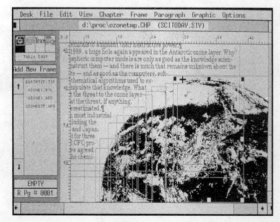

Xerox Ventura 4

Placing Graphics in your Document

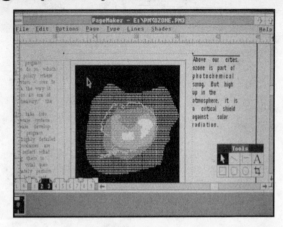

Aldus PageMaker 5

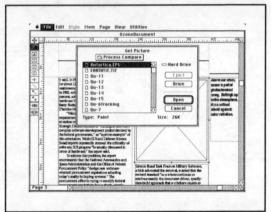

Quark XPress 5

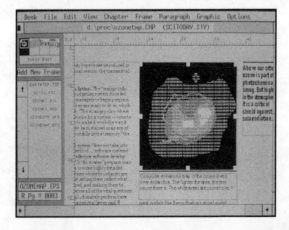

Xerox Ventura 5

Editing Table-Based Data

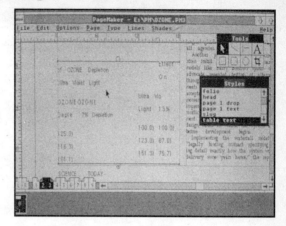

Aldus PageMaker 6

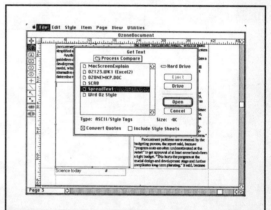

Quark XPress 6

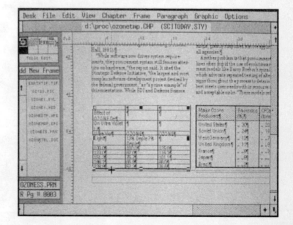

Xerox Ventura 6

The Last Layout Elements

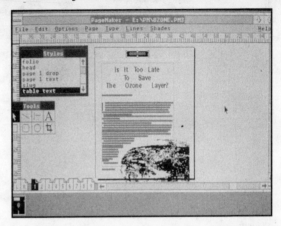

Aldus PageMaker 7

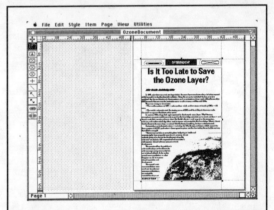

Quark XPress 7

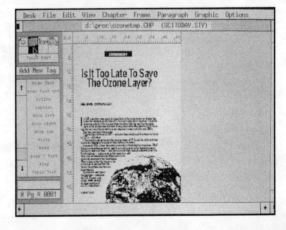

Xerox Ventura 7

The Final Layout

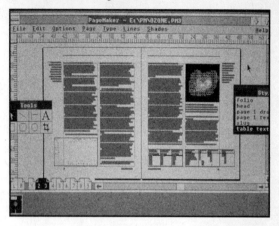

Aldus PageMaker 8

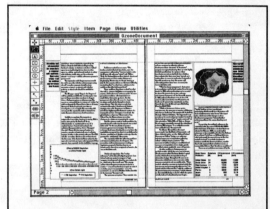

Quark XPress 8

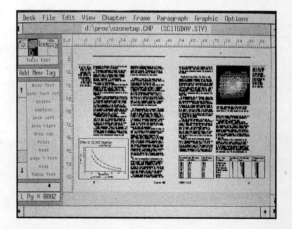

Xerox Ventura 8

custom page sizes, although you can simulate custom sizes smaller than tabloid by creating frames at the custom size. Ventura's layout aids include column and line space and a customizable ruler.

Ventura illustration 1, the screen shows a template for the first three pages of our document. The first page is unique; the second and third are copied on subsequent pages. The frames were placed to hold graphics and sidebars at the back pages of the template so they are available for use as needed. The menu displayed with the first-page template shows frame options; sizing and scaling let you size and position frames precisely, and control whether a wrap is on or off and how graphics are sized and cropped.

Creating style sheets: Style sheets let you apply a set of attributes to all text tagged with a particular style; if you change the attributes of one style tag, all text tagged with it is automatically updated. Issues include ease of creation, ease of local modification, number of features that may be included (degree of control) in the style sheet, and the capability to create a "normal" style sheet containing defaults you want picked up in all later style sheets.

Aldus PageMaker: PageMaker supports style sheets that contain basic typographic settings for typeface and size, leading, paragraph spacing and indents, tab stops, and text color. It does not support sophisticated features like local tracking, kerning, number of permissible consecutive hyphens, overrides for small-cap and superscript size and position, and ruling lines. Aldus PageMaker has the capability of importing Microsoft Word style sheets.

PageMaker builds style tags by recording changes to the tag from which the new one was copied (showing these changes in the dialogue box). Although the font point-size list is limited (although you can set up various font sizes in Bitstream), you can specify point sizes in half-point increments if using a Postscript printer. In our document, the editor manually entered $9^1/_2$ points as the body text's size.

Quark XPress: Quark's style sheets allow you to set paragraph formats, character styles, and tab settings that you use often, saving the effort of defining them for each use. You can either create the style sheets within Quark, or you can import them from Microsoft Word. You can specify more typographic features in Quark than in Word style sheets. The best way to use Word style sheets is to import them for a test document and then enhance them in Quark. For all subsequent documents using the style sheet, Quark substitutes its style sheet for Word's when you import Word files. This lets you use Word style sheets while editing without losing access to Quark's typographic control.

Quark's style sheets maintain their independence from text files, so you can attach one style sheet to several documents.

Ventura: As with templates, Ventura is designed to use style sheets extensively. You can set more than 100 typographic attributes per paragraph style. Any number of documents may use the same style sheet, which is handy if you place separate articles in separate chapters or have a group of publications using the same typographic look. Ventura's unique style-sheet capabilities include defining rules and boxes to be associated with text (handy for change bars and footnotes); tight control over size and position of elements like subscripts and small caps; tight control over spacing and kerning; and automated implementation of drop caps with custom settings and bulleted lists (with a choice of 15 bullet types).

Global typographic control: Layout programs distinguish themselves from word processors by offering typesetter-quality control over kerning, tracking, word spacing, hyphenation, subscript size and position, underline size and position, and the like. Each of the layout programs, however, features various levels of typographical control.

Aldus PageMaker: PageMaker illustration 2, PageMaker offers spacing control globally, letting you set minimum, preferred, and maximum word spacing, kerning, and tracking information.

However, you cannot set these for different style tags, although settings for text like headlines usually are not appropriate for text like body copy.

Quark XPress: Quark XPress illustration 2, you can modify Quark's default settings, such as automatic leading and kerning, and have them apply to all new documents. You can also control typography locally and, since Quark offers such fine typographic control, you may find that you prefer the local option. A utility in Quark lets you precisely control tracking. Tracking controls the amount of space between characters in a selected passage of text; tracking values that are less than zero bring characters closer together than normal, making it possible to fit copy into a space that might not otherwise hold the text.

Ventura: Ventura illustration 2, Ventura implements its typographic control through local style tags, rather than relying on global settings that might not be appropriate for all text. Its few global typographic features include kerning and widow/orphan control, although you can override the global kerning with specific frame   settings or style tags.

In addition to the many settings available in style tags, you can interactively track lines to make them looser or tighter, depending on layout needs. You can also interactively change the point size of high-lighted text.

FILE CREATION:

Editing text files: After importing text from a word processor, this involves specifying basic attributes using native formatting plus tags for major copy elements like headlines.

Aldus PageMaker: PageMaker is strongly tied to Microsoft Word, although it will import text from several word processors. The strong tie-in is due to its support for Microsoft Word style sheets and the fact that Word is the only word processing format to which PageMaker will export. (It also exports in ASCII and DCA formats.)

In this step, the editor used native character formatting for boldface and italics and markup codes for elements like style tags and bullets. A copy editor will replace the markup codes for style tags with Page-Maker's codes; you cannot implement symbols like bullets outside PageMaker.

Quark XPress: Quark imports text files prepared in Mac Write, Microsoft Word, Microsoft Works, WordPerfect, and Write Now. It ignores layout-oriented formatting like the number of columns and margins.

In our document, the editor applied some character attributes in the word processor such as boldface, italics, font, and font size. Many users find Quark's integrated word processor sufficient for writing and editing text; this feature includes a built-in spelling checker and a search-and-replace function that is attribute-sensitive.

Ventura: Ventura reads in nine word processor formats, so editors can usually use their local formatting for boldface, italics, subscripts, superscripts, underline, double underline, and small caps. It ignores word processor formatting for layout (like number of columns), font changes, and tab stops.

We used WordPerfect's native formatting for boldface and italics, and left markup codes for the headline, byline, and bullets for a copy editor to handle.

Preparing text files. This step is performed in a word processor and involves adding all coding and attributes possible, like discretionary hyphens, font changes, and symbol codes. This saves time, because word processors are faster than desktop publishers and because you can often search and replace such codes in your word processor. (Desktop publishers rarely have search and replace.) For small or nonstandard documents, this may not be a worthwhile step.

Aldus PageMaker: You can specify few typographic features in

PageMaker. Using Microsoft Word's style sheets and character-formatting features (not shown here; see the example for Quark, since the programs work similarly) extends this a little to include control over font changes and symbol access.

PageMaker illustration 3: For our document, the copy editor replaced the markup codes for style tags with the PageMaker counterparts (like <HEAD>, which will invoke the headline style tag in Page-Maker). The editor could have also applied Word style sheets (or mixed the two options). Any untagged paragraph acquires the attributes of the last tag used, meaning you don't have to code every paragraph — a nice time saver.

Quark XPress: Quark illustration 3: The editor also used Word style tags to indicate paragraph formatting (someone else created the tags). Instead of using Word tags, you can embed codes for tags, such as "@HEAD = " to invoke the HEAD style tag in Quark (see the Page-Maker screen for an example). A copy editor would traditionally implement these codes.

Ventura: You can specify many typographic features in your word processing file, as well as paragraph tags, with Ventura. Coding in your word processor program is faster than in a layout program.

Ventura illustration 3: For our document, a copy editor replaced the markup codes with the Ventura equivalents. Also added were the paragraph tags (like @HEAD = , which tells Ventura to apply the HEAD style tag to the following paragraph). Any untagged paragraph will have the Body Text style tag applied to it. Unfortunately, however, Ventura will not apply the last tag used to all subsequent paragraphs, meaning extra work if you have paragraphs to which you want to apply the same tag. Ventura has the same limitation with its typographic codes: You must reapply them at the beginning of each paragraph, since a hard return automatically turns them off.

Preparing other files: Graphics programs and spreadsheets both create art and/or data that occasionally must be exported to a desktop publishing program. This can be tricky, especially if the file cannot be saved in a standard format. Nevertheless, it is helpful if files can be used in the layout program.

Aldus PageMaker: We used Corel Draw for Windows to prepare a graphic for export as an EPS (encapsulated Postscript) file. Like most high-end layout programs, PageMaker accepts the popular graphics formats as is, including Macintosh MacPaint and EPS (both Mac and MS-DOS). For some formats, notably HPGL (plotter) and large Lotus .PIC files, PageMaker cannot translate all features.

To prepare a Lotus 1-2-3 (or compatible) spreadsheet for import into PageMaker, you need only save it. If you use Lotus 1-2-3, Release 3, you must first translate the file into Release 2 format.

Quark XPress: We used Aldus Freehand to create a graphic and saved it as an EPS file. In addition to EPS, Quark imports MacPaint, PICT, TIFF, and RIFF files, which you place into predefined picture boxes on the page. There is no real graphics-editing feature other than the capability to manipulate screens and contrast.

For our spreadsheet data, we used Microsoft Excel. Quark does not directly import spreadsheet files. You can, however, save spreadsheet data as text and place it in a text box where you can adjust column alignment by using tabs. You can also save spreadsheet charts to the clipboard and place them into picture boxes.

Ventura: As with PageMaker, we used Corel Draw for Windows to create and prepare a graphic for export as an EPS file. Like most high-end layout programs, Ventura accepts many popular graphics formats as is, including Macintosh MacPaint and EPS (both Mac and MS-DOS) as well as a number of others such as Windows Metafile. For some formats, notably PICT and HPGL, Ventura translates fonts to either Helvetica or Times Roman rather than create a bit map of the original fonts. For Postscript-based graphics, Ventura retains any Postscript fonts.

Ventura does not read in spreadsheet files directly; to use them, you must create a .PRN print file first from your spreadsheet program. Ventura tries to translate these files into tables, but the results usually require much editing. It is easier to create the table in Ventura rather than import it.

DOCUMENT CREATION:

Importing and placing files. File import involves two steps: importing the text or graphics and then placing the text or graphics in the layout. For the first step, the more directly importable the format, the better. For the second step, the layout program should let you place the material precisely, either with snap-to grids or rulers, or by letting you specify the coordinates for the frame that holds the material.

Aldus PageMaker: PageMaker requires that you import each file only when you are about to use it; you cannot import files and leave them in a list for use at any time. The process of importing is simple: Select the disk and directory, and PageMaker displays all the files whose extensions match those of supported formats. Select the file (and any options that go with it, like style-tag data for text files), and PageMaker interprets the file format. If it can't identify the format, it displays a list of formats from which you can choose.

Before we imported our text file, we turned on the option to read-in style tags and left other options at their default settings.

Quark XPress: Quark lets you import text and graphics files, one at a time, into a text or graphics box that you first create on the page. Boxes can contain other, nested boxes. Then, to place the text or graphic, you use Get Text or Get Picture menu selections.

Ventura: Unlike other programs, Ventura lets you import any number of text and graphics files at once. You first tell Ventura the type of file (text, line art, and image) and file format, and then choose the disk and directory on which the files reside. Ventura displays files' default extensions; you can use DOS wild cards to display any pattern of files (Ventura remembers this for the next import session). Once imported, file names appear in a list at the left of the screen. To flow them in, you select the frame you want to place them in and then select the file name from the list. Thus, you are able to create all your frames first and then import your files, import your files and create their frames, or do both on an as-needed basis.

Flowing text. This step involves importing text and placing it in the layout file. The manner in which the layout programs flow text from frame-to-frame and page-to-page, and how easily they wrap around other frames/objects, affects the effort involved.

Aldus PageMaker: PageMaker has three modes of text flow: manual, semi-automatic, and automatic. You must choose the mode before placing your file. In auto-mode, PageMaker will flow all the text, creating as many pages as needed. In semi-automatic mode, PageMaker fills only the current column but creates a new icon for you to place at another column (perhaps on a different page). In manual flow, it places the first column and requires you to activate the placement of any remaining text by double-clicking the bottom of the window shade.

Text wraps in PageMaker are not automatic, but they are versatile. Text will overprint graphics by default. To get a wrap, you select the graphic's window shade and the text-wrap option, which wraps the text rectangularly around the window shade. To create contoured wraps, you can add points to the graphic's window shade and reposition them.

PageMaker illustration 4: In the screen shown here, we simulated a curve by creating a series of short lines. In the screen, the curve is incomplete so you can see the original position of part of the graphic's window shade (at left).

Quark XPress: Flowing text into a Quark document is a snap. If you're placing a text document that's larger than the text box into which you are placing it, Quark lets you place the excess text exactly where you want it using a linking tool to point the way to the spot in the document where you want the text to continue.

Quark XPress illustration 4, Quark is exceptional in how it wraps text around graphics. You can specify exactly the offset distance from the graphic to the text, and text can wrap around virtually any shape. You can have text run around the outside of the picture box or around the shape of the object in the picture box, or even behind a picture box. Because Quark places text only on one side of an opaque line, you can draw an invisible opaque line to control even more closely the text wrap around an object. This is useful for keeping text from entering unwanted areas of a run-around graphic.

Ventura: Flowing text is just a matter of selecting the frame it goes in and the name of the text file. The text will flow in the frame using the margins and columns set up for the frame. If the frame has not been set up, you can do so after flowing in the text. If you select another frame and click the same text file name, the remainder of the text will flow into that frame and the two frames will be linked. You are able to do this with any number of frames.

Ventura illustration 4, With the text flowed in, you can place other frames containing text or graphics over it to create wraps. However, Ventura wraps only rectangularly, along frame borders,   and not around irregularly shaped objects. To achieve polygonal or curved wraps as in this screen, you must turn off wrap for the frame containing the image, which means the text will overprint it. You must then create a series of frames on top of the image to simulate its general contour. For close fits, you must create many frames, a time-consuming task.

Placing graphics. Issues in placing graphics include sizing, scaling, display quality, and minor graphics editing (like adding arrows and rules for annotation).

Aldus PageMaker: Graphics placement works just like text placement: You select and place the file. Once placed, you can crop and resize the image dynamically on the screen.

PageMaker illustration 5: Because our EPS file shown here was created in Corel Draw, which provides a bitmap for screen display, we were able to see our drawing on-screen. Many applications, as well as Macintosh EPS files transferred to PCs, do not provide this bitmap; in these cases, PageMaker draws a gray box to represent the image size and proportions. PageMaker's built-in graphics are rudimentary — basic lines, gray shades, fill patterns, and boxes. The program's bonus features include the capability to specify rounded corners. These features are sufficient for minor graphical additions and touch-ups, but the program does not go beyond that.

Quark XPress: To place a graphic in Quark, you first create a graphics box and then place the graphic. You can modify the size and proportions of an active picture box in increments between 10 and 1,000 percent of the original size. For special effects, you can vary the selection of Scale Across and Scale Down to distort the picture. If you use equal Scale Across and Scale Down values, scaling is much more accurate than resizing with keyboard commands or with the mouse. Quark's simple built-in graphics include lines and arrows in a variety of widths and patterns. Arrowheads and tails are included, as are fill patterns that can be shaded between zero and 100 percent. Quark also includes a frame feature for outlining a text box or a page with a number of predesigned patterns, or you can create your own patterns.

Quark XPress illustration 5: The screen shot shows a selected picture box and the Get Picture selector box.

Ventura: Graphics placement works the same as text placement: you click the destination frame and then the graphic file name. Ventura sizes the graphics so they fit completely within the frame without distorting the proportions. To distort the proportions or to crop the image for a better fit, you must use Ventura's non-WYSIWYG sizing dialogue box. Ventura's built-in graphics are rudimentary — basic lines, boxes, and ellipses — coupled with user-defined line weights, gray fills, and optional arrowheads for lines. They are sufficient for minor graphical additions and touch-ups, but they do not go beyond that.

Ventura illustration 5: Because our EPS file was created in Corel Draw for Windows, which provides a bitmap for screen display, you can see what the image looks like. As we mentioned with PageMaker, many applications do not provide this bit map; in these cases, Ventura draws an "X" to represent the image size and proportions.

Placing tabular data. *If a table editor is available, how easy is it to use? If none is available, can you build tables easily with a combination of tabs and style sheets? For spreadsheet import, it is important to determine if you easily apply style sheets to the text and add elements like rules.*

Aldus PageMaker: PageMaker has no table editor, so you must use tab stops and drawing features to create a table with rules. We first typed in the data, defined the tab stops, drew the box around the table, drew the lines between columns, and then added a gray box with a rule around it to place behind the table title.

PageMaker illustration 6, during spreadsheet import, PageMaker requires that you specify which cell range you want imported (something you may not have written down). With PageMaker, imported text requires a great deal of editing and formatting — it is easier to rekey the data in it and define the tab stops as you do so.

Quark XPress: Quark does not include a table editor, but we found it fairly easy to create a table using its tab-setting feature. Right, left, centered, and decimal tabs are supported, and you can precisely place them by entering coordinates in a Position field in the Tab dialogue box.

Quark XPress illustration 6, we also saved an Excel spreadsheet as text, imported it to a Quark text frame, and then adjusted the alignment of the cell entries by use of tabs.

Ventura: Ventura offers a sophisticated WYSIWYG table editor (available only in the Professional Extension). You specify the number of rows and columns, margins, where lines should be drawn, and relative column sizes; Ventura creates an empty table in which you enter your text. Cells automatically grow to the size of the largest size in each row. You can also merge cells within rows and columns and apply screens over table cells.

You can use Ventura style tags to augment the table editor's capabilities. For example, we used the table editor's feature to draw the box around the table and the vertical lines between columns, but we used the Ruling Line Below feature in the table title's style tag to draw the horizontal line below the title. (Our design called for a ruling line below just the title row, not every row.)

Ventura illustration 6: When Ventura imports a .PRN spreadsheet file, it tries to create a table automatically to put it in. As the screen above shows, the result often needs much editing and fine-tuning.

Final layout elements: These elements include how easy it is to add layout elements like decks, folios, and cross-references that are created within the layout program. Also, how easily can any of these be automated? What other steps must be taken that could not be handled elsewhere (like drop caps)?

Aldus PageMaker: To finalize the PageMaker layout, we had to place the drop cap manually on the first page. We also had to add window shades manually for the decks (we couldn't put these in the master pages, like we did the rules above them, because the holding text would also duplicate from page to page). There are no cross-referencing features. See PageMaker illustrations 7 and 8.

Quark XPress: Once you've placed the major elements on a page, you can add additional frames to handle items like slugs and decks. You can also fine-tune baseline placement, and you can make last-minute tracking adjustments to fit headlines. See Quark XPress illustrations 7 and 8.

Ventura: Ventura's frame orientation makes it easy to add frames for decks (pull quotes), sidebars, and other elements. Its anchoring feature lets you associate such frames with points in text so that as text moves, the frames associated with it moves, too. Automatic page numbering, headers, footers, index generation, and cross-references round out Ventura's layout-finalization features. See Ventura illustrations 7 and 8.

Layout production. Tasks include ensuring columns align and elements are positioned correctly. This can be a time-consuming task, since it involves manual fine-tuning and repetitive printing of drafts to ensure correctness.

Aldus PageMaker: PageMaker offers no vertical-justification or frame-balancing features. To ensure alignment, you can use snap-to rulers and grids, although this is a painstaking process.

Quark XPress: Quark supports vertical justification in the form of an invisible baseline grid against which you can lock paragraphs, aligning text from column to column. You can lock text to this grid paragraph by paragraph, and you can specify the grid's baseline interval values.

Ventura: Ventura's Professional Extension offers a vertical justification feature meant to ensure that text aligns along the bottom of all columns by adding space between paragraphs. However, the results of this feature are often worse than the original, since it tends to over-space text in most cases. We found it easier to manually add spacing (using 1-point paragraphs) between paragraphs to achieve the same result.

Typographic production. Tasks in the typographic phase of production include finalizing page numbers, eliminating bad hyphenations, removing space in loose lines, and fixing improperly imported text (like untranslated quotes and dashes).

Aldus PageMaker: PageMaker automatically translates typewriter quote marks and double hyphens into true typographic quotes and dashes upon import. You can also add discretionary hyphens to fix bad breaks or to override PageMaker's breaks (perhaps to improve spacing). And PageMaker's automatic page-numbering feature saved us the effort of manually entering page numbers on the folios.

Quark XPress: Once you've entered Quark's page-number keyboard command, page numbers are automatic, as are page number references in continued lines. When you use the Get Text function, Quark lets you convert quote marks to their true typographic equivalents. Double hyphens in the text file are automatically replaced with em dashes. If the text you use in text wraparound has been justified, you may want to realign that portion of the text as right- or left-aligned to avoid loose space between words.

Ventura: Ventura's automatic page numbering makes this task simple. Its Show Loose Lines option displays in reverse video all lines spaced wider than the style-sheet maximums (this occurs because some words cannot be hyphenated to achieve the desired settings), letting you manually hyphenate, selectively tighten the spacing on highlighted text (to less than the style tag's minimum settings), or accept the spacing. While Ventura can automatically translate typewriter quotes and dashes into their typographic equivalents, quote conversion is flawed when importing text files (although it is documented). Quotes appearing after non-alphanumeric characters like parentheses and hard spaces are ignored, so you must manually fix these quotes.

DOCUMENT CONTROL:

Change control. Are changes made in your word processing and desktop publishing text files automatically made to both? If not, can you set the desktop publisher to export the changed text or to import the changed text?

Aldus PageMaker: PageMaker's limited export capabilities hinder version control, especially since exported files lose special symbols like bullets. But PageMaker does offer an option to always import the latest version of the word processor file, which can help you manage versions (but changes made to the earlier text will be lost if you use this feature, unless you manually made the changes in your source file as well).

Quark XPress: When you place a text file in a Quark document, Quark uses a copy of that original file; original text files are not affected by any of the edits you do in Quark. This hinders change control, but you can export text from Quark into any of the five supported word processors' formats, as well as into ASCII format.

Ventura: Unlike most layout programs, Ventura uses the source text files instead of copying them into the layout. This means that edits made in Ventura are automatically saved back to the source file and changes made in the source file are automatically seen by Ventura the next time you load a chapter using the text. This makes version control nearly automatic.

File transfer. To move a layout from one disk to another, are all files — graphics, text, and layout — automatically copied? If not, is there some sort of archiving option to transfer files? These are issues critical to file transers.

Aldus PageMaker: PageMaker copies all constituent files into the PageMaker publication (except for TIFF files or other large bit-mapped images over 60K), so copying a document is as easy as copying the publication file. However, when moving files, PageMaker tracks printer options and recomposes a publication on a new PC even if the only change between the original and new location's setup was the printer port. This recomposition is time consuming.

Quark XPress: When you copy a Quark document from one disk to another, the entire document is copied. This includes all formatting, style sheets, templates, text, and graphics information.

Ventura: Ventura's dynamic-link approach has a price: Because Ventura chapters are really a collection of files linked together, it is easy to forget to copy all the constituent files when moving chapters from one PC to another. You must use Ventura's Copy All feature to copy all of a chapter's constituent files to make this transfer easier.

OUTPUT:

Printing. To be effective, desktop publishing programs must support Hewlett-Packard PCL (for PC-based programs) and Postscript printers. For Postscript, the standard for high-resolution output, packages are more valuable and useful if they support image control such as for sharper screen density.

Aldus PageMaker: PageMaker supports Postscript and PCL printers, as well as image control like line-screen resolution and type and contrast control for bit-mapped files.

Quark XPress: Like other high-end layout packages, Quark supports Postscript printers at their maximum resolution. Printing to high-end or color high-resolution output devices is not only possible but common among Quark users. It also supports control over the line screen and angle that make up images and lets you control image contrast. Because it is Macintosh-based, it does not support the IBM PC-based Hewlett-Packard PCL printer standard.

Ventura: Ventura supports major printers. For the high-quality Postscript standard, Ventura supports several special features through a special driver (which you must install manually if you want to use it), including gray and outline text. You can also edit the Postscript driver to change the screen density from the newspaper-level default (90-line screen) to any level (like 120-line for magazines) to increase clarity. Within the program, you can alter the line screen and line type (dots, ellipses, or lines) that make up a gray-scale TIFF image, but not for other bit-mapped images. It also offers no contrast-control features.

Color Support. *Color definition should be simple and WYSIWYG (within the limits of the screen display). The layout package should produce spot-color overlays and let you assign colors to graphics, rules, and boxes produced within the layout package, as well as to text. Support for the Pantone Matching System (PMS) and process-color separation for user-defined colors enhances a layout program's versatility.*

Aldus PageMaker: PageMaker lets you define colors for use in spot-color printing; an add-on package called PageMaker Color Extension provides color support, but this is only available for the Macintosh version of PageMaker. There is a third-party utility available, called Colorsep/PC from Ozette Technologies in Seattle, that will do CYMK color separations.

Quark XPress: With Quark, you can prepare color separations, including four-color separations. Quark accepts images scanned in color and lets you modify or customize colors. We like how Quark lets you select and edit PMS colors, although the screen colors are often more vibrant than what shows on a printer's Pantone chart. Four standard color models are supported — PMS, CMYK, HSB, and RGB — and it's easy to switch between models. Quark is the only program here that provides useful color features for traditional high-quality publishing.

Ventura: Ventura lets you define colors and gray levels for use in graphics, frame borders and backgrounds, and text. It will output spot-color overlays. On a VGA monitor, you can see the grays and colors you define.

How the Packages Perform: Rating the Process

Performance:
TEXT HANDLING

Each layout program should allow the use of native formatting (like boldface and superscripting) in several major word processing formats. Within the layout program, at minimum there should be a basic text editor. Bonus points are issued for supporting a broad variety of formats, word-processor style-sheet compatibility, the ability to code style tags and typographic features for the layout program in the word processor, automated cross-referencing (such as "See reference on page XX"), automated page numbering, spelling checking, and dynamic links with source text files (where changes in the word processor are reflected in the layout program and vice versa).

Aldus PageMaker: *SATISFACTORY*
PageMaker's emphasis on Microsoft Word and its lack of support of word-processor-generated typographic coding add to the editor's and layout artist's workload. Support for Word style sheets helps somewhat, but PageMaker still lacks sufficient support for text preparation. The built-in editor is satisfactory for minor revisions. But the difficulty in version control due to import and export limitations will cause headaches in larger organizations. Microsoft Word is powerful and straightforward to use, combining a menu-based orientation with function-key shortcuts. Overall, because of PageMaker's text handling limitations, we rate text handling no higher than satisfactory.

Quark XPress: *EXCELLENT*
Quark's straightforward approach to handling input from a variety of Macintosh word processors is appealing, and the various formats import well into Quark. The built-in word processor is fully functional and can handle many text tasks. Quark accepts Microsoft Word style sheets, an important consideration for many office environments, and lets you enter manual tags if you use a different word processor. Although Quark is missing the capability to link dynamically to source files, the built-in spelling checker is a great feature, useful for making a quick check after a last-minute editing session. Given its superb text-

handling advantages when compared with the other layout programs, we rate text handling excellent.

Ventura: *EXCELLENT*

Ventura's wide support of word-processing formats, support of embedded coding in word-processing files, and dynamic linking between the layout and source files mean text handling is flexible and powerful. Ventura's built-in editor is capable for minor revisions. Likewise, we found WordPerfect, as a source of text for Ventura, to be versatile and capable, although its function-key orientation took a while to learn.

Performance:
TEXT WRAP

Each layout program should be able to automatically wrap text around other text and/or graphics. It should also have the option to turn off a wrap to achieve special effects like text overprinting graphics or even text overprinting text. Bonuses are in order for features such as the capability to wrap non-rectangular (such as polygonal or curved) images.

Aldus PageMaker: *VERY GOOD*

PageMaker's polygonal text wrapping capabilities are both powerful and elegant. You have the option of wrapping text around an image or having it stop above and resume below it. Our only complaint is that text wrapping is not automatic.

Quark XPress: *EXCELLENT*

Quark's text-wrap capability is the most powerful of any of the products reviewed here. Wrapping can be turned on and off and closely controlled. Text can be wrapped around the outside of an object or inside a shape.

Ventura: *GOOD*

Ventura's text wrap is functional, providing what's needed. However, it is limited to wrapping rectangular shapes, which keeps its score to no better than good.

Performance:
TYPOGRAPHY

The layout program should give you control over word spacing, letter spacing (tracking), line spacing (leading), hyphenation, kerning, indents, and tabs. Bonuses are awarded for automated drop caps;

automated bullets; support of half-point type and leading increments; separate typographic control for each paragraph tag; the capability to override local tracking and point size; and the capability to define settings for attributes like subscript size and position, small-cap size, and underline weight and position.

As part of typography, we tested the programs' hyphenation accuracy by checking a sample document to see how many common words were incorrectly hyphenated or were not hyphenated that should have been. The sample document had narrow (7-pica) columns with unlimited hyphenation to allow as many hyphenations as possible. The number of lines in the document was about 1,200, depending on the layout package's spacing settings.

Aldus PageMaker: *SATISFACTORY*

PageMaker lacks fine typographic controls basic to publishing. The control it does offer is global, meaning you must find the least unacceptable compromise for important presentation issues like word spacing and tracking. In our hyphenation test, PageMaker did better than the other programs: It made no errors and missed only six hyphenation opportunities. Unfortunately, it offers no control over the maximum number of consecutive hyphens and how many characters must appear before and after a hyphenation. Because PageMaker offers the basics, we rate typography satisfactory.

Quark XPress: *VERY GOOD*

With the capability to size fonts in quarter-point increments, Quark gives you a lot of control over typographical effects. The program excels in most of our scoring criteria for typography, with only one exception: While drop caps can be created, they are not automatic. Quark also scored quite well on our hyphenation test, mishyphenating no words and missing only 10 hyphenation opportunities.

Ventura: *EXCELLENT*

No other desktop publishing package offers the richness and fine control over typography found in Ventura. You have control over word, character, and paragraph spacing, as well as the capability to define ruling lines, underscores, and super/subscripts. You also have complete and automated control over drop-cap size and position for each paragraph. However, Ventura's Edco hyphenation dictionary is flawed, despite being better than the base version's dictionary. In our test, it was the only one to make a hyphenation error (mishyphenating "test-ing" as "tes-ting" and "Eng-land" and "En-Gland"). It also missed nine hyphenation opportunities that would have improved spacing. Overall, however, Ventura's superior typography is rated excellent.

Performance:

MULTIELEMENT LAYOUT

Each layout program should let you easily handle multiple elements, such as graphics and sidebars, in a layout. We award bonus points for the capability to anchor elements together or to text so they move with their related elements or text as the layout changes.

Aldus PageMaker: *GOOD*

While you can work with multiple elements, PageMaker lacks features like frame anchoring and the capability to import several files and hold them ready to be placed at any time (this helps when trying to figure out how several pieces best fit together). However, it is easy to place, move, and resize elements.

Quark XPress: *VERY GOOD*

Quark's capability to nest text and graphics frames in a hierarchical structure makes it possible to move grouped boxes around on a page. However, we would like to see more flexibility in being able to copy nested boxes from page to page; Quark's orientation for moving nested boxes is more page-oriented. Still, it is easy to have a wide range of page elements together on a Quark page.

Ventura: *EXCELLENT*

Ventura's frame orientation and very capable anchoring features make it well-suited for multielement layouts.

Performance:

TABULAR TEXT

The layout program should let you define several types of tab stops — decimal, left, right, and centered — with the option of at least dot and line leaders for each paragraph tag. Imported spreadsheet data should be supported at least as a print file. Bonuses are issued for user-defined leaders, other types of tab stops (e.g., justified), built-in table-editing features, and native support of spreadsheet data.

Aldus PageMaker: *SATISFACTORY*

PageMaker offers basic tabular-text capabilities with its tab stops, but nothing sophisticated.

Quark XPress: *GOOD*

Quark supports left, right, centered, and decimal tabs. You can use any character as a fill between the tab character and the tab stop (the default is a blank). Quark's numeric selection of tab locations makes it possible for them to be precisely placed. Native spreadsheet data saved as text comes into Quark nicely, but not without the need for some manual tabbing intervention.

Ventura: *VERY GOOD*

Ventura's table editor in Professional Extension is easy to use and intuitive, and is a very useful enhancement to the program. The program's tab features are comprehensive. However, it does not import spreadsheet data in native format.

Performance:
GRAPHICS EDITING/DRAWING

Graphics programs used to generate illustrations for layout programs should include high-end features like splines, rotation, skew, multiple layers, and a wide range of screen and rule types. Layout programs should let you size and crop imported graphics and provide basic drawing features like lines and rectangles for simple annotations and illustrations. In the layout program, we give bonus points for arrowheads, user-defined line weights, a wide range of drawing shapes, and bit-map editing. We also take into consideration the graphics program's capabilities, such as a wide format support and for including a display bitmap when exporting/saving to Postscript.

Aldus PageMaker: *VERY GOOD*

PageMaker offers basic graphics drawing features, although they are limited in areas like available line weights. It supports a wide range of graphics formats and lets you crop and size them dynamically. Corel Draw, which we used to generate graphics for PageMaker, offers sophisticated features that match in many cases what is available in Macintosh programs like Aldus Freehand (although it is not yet at that level).

Quark XPress: *EXCELLENT*

For manipulating graphic objects, Quark provides a ruler and movable rule guides and displays the coordinates of these tools. A full suite of line styles and fills earns extra points, as does the page and text box-framing capability. Aldus Freehand as a graphics front end provides very sophisticated drawing features, such as the capability to fit text around polygons and curves.

Ventura: VERY GOOD

Ventura's graphics features, coupled with the capability to associate rules and boxes to both text and frames, are sufficient for most layout uses. Its support of a range of major graphics formats is marred only by its incapability to crop and size those images dynamically. As with PageMaker, Corel Draw offers sophisticated drawing features.

Performance:
CHARTING/BUSINESS GRAPHICS

Charting capabilities in programs (such as spreadsheets) generating files for use in layout programs should support a range of chart types (including scatter plots, area graphs, bar charts, and pie charts). The layout program should be able to import common formats. Bonus points are awarded for support of user-defined line weights, node shapes, and fills.

Aldus PageMaker: GOOD

PageMaker treats charts like any other graphics. We found Lotus 1-2-3's graphic options to be sufficient, although we would prefer more control over shapes and fills used in charts.

Quark XPress: GOOD

Quark imports charts, but doesn't let you edit them once they are on the Quark page. We used Excel for the business chart in our comparison and found it more than amply met our needs.

Ventura: GOOD

Ventura treats charts like any other graphics. As with PageMaker, we found Lotus 1-2-3's graphic options adequate (although we'd like more control over shapes and fills in charts).

Performance:
COLOR OUTPUT

Effective color support means being able to specify colors either in the standard Pantone Matching System (PMS) or by building colors through the traditional process-color method and being able to generate the process-color separations a print shop would need for reproduction.

Aldus PageMaker: SATISFACTORY

PageMaker's color-definition features are easy to use, and the capability to apply color to text and basic graphics is handy. However, because PageMaker does not use the standard PMS or create process-color separations for the user-defined colors, its color features are useful only if you are printing to a color printer (unless you are using the third-party utility cited earlier). It cannot produce what a commercial print shop would need to reproduce your colors correctly. We can rate color no higher than satisfactory.

Quark XPress: *EXCELLENT*

With spot-color and four-color support, Quark is strong in color support. It earns additional points for supporting full PMS colors, user-defined colors, and three additional color models.

Ventura: *SATISFACTORY*

Ventura's color-definition features are easy to use, and the capability to apply color to text and basic graphics is handy. However, as with PageMaker, Ventura does not use PMS colors or create process-color separations for user-defined colors, its color features are useful only if you are printing to a color printer.

Performance:

PRINTING

Printing support in a layout program should default to the output device's maximum resolution and, of course, should match the on-screen layout in text line breaks and element size and location. The program should support popular American paper sizes: letter, legal, and tabloid (11-by-17-inch). Postscript and Hewlett-Packard Laserjet PCL support are required. We issue bonus points for image control (such as changing the line-screen resolution and line type for gray-scale elements); thumbnail printing (printing small views of the page); European page sizes; or user-defined page sizes.

Aldus PageMaker: *VERY GOOD*

PageMaker's output uses the output device's maximum resolution, providing clean results. While not offering access to Postscript special effects, it lets you define your own page sizes and supports image control and contrast control.

Quark XPress: *EXCELLENT*

Quark's output uses the output device's maximum resolution, providing clean results. It offers basic page sizes plus user-defined sizes, thumbnail printing, image control, and contrast control.

Ventura: *VERY GOOD*

Ventura's output uses the output device's maximum resolution, providing clean results. While limited to basic page sizes, Ventura offers advantages in font support and Postscript special effects that earn it a very good printing score.

Performance:
LEVEL OF INTEGRATION

If marketed as a stand-alone product, the layout program should support the main formats for each type of element (text and graphics). If marketed as part of an integrated environment, the programs used in that environment should require no format translation to be used.

Aldus PageMaker: *GOOD*

PageMaker works well with files from popular packages, both MS-DOS and Macintosh. However, its exclusive strong tie-in to Microsoft Word and version-control problems limit it needlessly. (Word users, of course, will benefit from PageMaker's devotion to it.) Furthermore, Windows users will find that PageMaker does not support many Windows applications, since most were written after its latest version and use formats it does not support. Furthermore, it does not support DDE, the dynamic data exchange link common to many Windows products (as well as others) for creating "hot links" You can also access database files by filtering dBASE fields and assigning styles to them. Given this mix, PageMaker's support for both Mac and PC formats is an advantage, and we rate its level of integration good.

Quark XPress: *VERY GOOD*

One of the Macintosh's selling points is the high level of integration between software packages. Quark is no exception to this standard, although it is not marketed as part of an integrated environment. It supports all leading Macintosh text and graphics formats, and we rate level of integration very good.

Ventura: *Excellent*

Ventura's capability to work with popular programs from all popular platforms — MS-DOS and Mac — makes its environment irrelevant. It shines on a mixed-platform environment, letting you concentrate on picking the right tool for the job.

DOCUMENTATION

Documentation scores reflect the quantity and quality of both written and on-line information. At a minimum, documentation should describe the product and how to use it. Scores can be raised for a quick-start guide, on-line tutorial and help programs, a quick-reference card, or a written tutorial. Poor organization, missing information, or an incomplete index lowers the score.

Aldus PageMaker: *GOOD*

PageMaker's reasonably organized manuals and several guidebooks cover the basics, especially for new users. However, we found the spotty index and tendency to sprinkle details throughout the documentation made it hard to use them as a reference. We were constantly bouncing between manuals. The on-line documentation is not context-sensitive but is well-written and useful as a reminder for experienced users.

Quark XPress: *VERY GOOD*

The Quark reference manual has carefully organized, thoughtfully presented material made more useful by a detailed index. It is an especially good source on typographic terms and their application. The tutorial is competent, but it suffers from a skimpy index and table of contents. On-line help, which you access from the Apple-icon menu, is not context-sensitive, but it is well-structured and easy to maneuver through.

Ventura: *VERY GOOD*

Ventura's documentation is very well designed and the best of the lot. The one manual and several guidebooks cover a wide range of material but do so in depth. Well-indexed and well-organized, the manual is excellent as both a learning guide and reference book. A series of appendixes provides helpful detail on everything from printer configurations to kerning tables. The on-line help is context-sensitive but spotty in its coverage; some screens are excellent, but others are merely obvious and uninformative.

EASE OF LEARNING

The programs should be designed so new users can do basic tasks while learning the more powerful features.

Aldus PageMaker: *GOOD*

PageMaker is easy to learn, thanks to its strong mimicry of the traditional publishing process and straightforward interface. Additionally, the Windows environment with its standard operation eases the learning curve. The reference/user manuals are only adequate and can actually be a learning impediment, since they are sparsely indexed and cross-reference each other too much.

Quark XPress: *GOOD*

Let's face it: Any program as feature-rich as Quark XPress takes time to learn simply because it includes so many options. The tutorial that accompanies the package is very well done and will definitely shorten your learning curve. Most users should be up and running on Quark XPress by the end of a day's use of the program. The manual is sparsely indexed but otherwise well-written.

Ventura: *GOOD*

Ventura requires an initially steep learning curve because its approach rewards planning over on-the-fly experimentation (which is also true of Quark). Still, its features are designed so that you can start with basic layouts and work up to complex ones. Its well-written, well-organized, and well-indexed manual is full of detailed, clear explanations and useful appendixes that enhance learning.

EASE OF USE

The layout programs should be straightforward to use by moderately experienced users.

Aldus PageMaker: *VERY GOOD*

The capability to save preferences would help experienced users concentrate on their layout work, but this is a minor complaint. Page-Maker's automation features, such as adding multiple pages, enhance the program's ease of use. Depending on the system you use, Page-Maker can be slow (as can most any Windows package), and EMS memory is not a bad thing to have installed. PageMaker is generally very easy to use thanks to a clear, intuitive interface.

Quark XPress: *VERY GOOD*

Once you've reached the downward slope on the learning curve, you'll appreciate how intuitive and logically oriented Quark is to use. Menu options are easy to access and understand.

Ventura: *VERY GOOD*

Ventura is easy to use, thanks to a clear interface, consistent approach and the capability to retain many user preferences. Its vast numbering capabilities are a great convenience, and it is optimized to be capable of modifying existing documents with a minimum of hassle. However, the program lacks some automation features that would improve its ease of use, such as the capability to add and delete more than one page at a time.

ERROR HANDLING

To earn a satisfactory score in error handling, a program must prompt you to save files and shouldn't do anything to corrupt data   or make it easy to lose information. Packages that offer basic error messages get a satisfactory score; we also expect all of the packages to have at least a one-level undo command. Bonuses are awarded for programs whose error messages clearly explain the problem or, ideally, that offer suggestions on how to resolve the problem. All four   programs have an abandon/revert-to-previously-saved-version feature, so we didn't single this feature out for special attention.

Aldus PageMaker: *VERY GOOD*

PageMaker helps prevent lost work by automatically saving documents to a backup version each time you move to a new page. This incremental backup doesn't replace your actual document, so you can still abandon to previous versions without having unwanted changes saved; you can use Revert, which reverts back to the last saved version, and Shift-Revert, which lets you revert to the last page-turn save. PageMaker also offers an Undo feature, and warnings and messages are generally clear and contain technical reference numbers (useful if you call technical support).

Quark XPress: *GOOD*

Quark uses the typical Macintosh dialog boxes to warn you of error conditions such as deleting an element that contains other elements. The program also gives you the chance to save your file if you quit without having saved changes. There is an Undo feature but no automatic incremental backup.

Ventura: *SATISFACTORY*

Ventura gives meaningful error messages; warns you if it starts running low on memory so you can save your work; and always checks to make sure that you've saved before you quit. You can also configure the program to automatically back up the previous version when you save. But there is no undo or automatic backup of incremental changes. Because there is no undo command, we cannot rate error handling higher than satisfactory.

SUPPORT

Support consists of both support policies and technical support, but because we are rating the process of desktop publishing as opposed to the layout programs specifically, we are not including ratings of support policies. Technical support scores are based on the quality of service we received in the course of multiple anonymous calls to the vendor and the availability of knowledgeable technicians. We will call technical support up to 10 times over a period of days to confirm the existence of support problems, if any.

Aldus PageMaker: *VERY GOOD*

Support technicians know not just PageMaker but Windows and — very important — publishing. They offer advice unrelated to the immediate question asked and take the time to discuss related applications like Windows.

Quark XPress: *POOR*

Quark's technical support staff no longer answers the phone directly, which used to save the time of being routed through a switchboard operator. Because of the volume of calls, you must now leave a message with an operator and wait for a call back, which we found can take as long as a day and a half. Once we got through to technical support, they easily answered our questions. Although the quality of the answers we got was fine, we must limit Quark's technical support score to poor because it took so long to have calls returned.

Ventura: *SATISFACTORY*

Technical support has recovered somewhat from its slump last spring and summer, although being put on hold or having to leave a message is still common. Support technicians are consistently knowledgeable, although not up to the standards we experienced with the previous version's support staff.

VALUE

This score reflects the price vs. the effectiveness and capabilities of the layout program and its associated products.

Aldus PageMaker: Good

At $795, PageMaker is a better-than-average value since it is among the least expensive of the desktop publishing programs and offers a solid set of features. It is an especially reasonable value for smaller shops that concentrate on one-of-a-kind designs.

Quark XPress: Excellent

XPress is near the top of its class in typographic controls, offering sophisticated features that you might expect to find in high-end type-setting systems. Furthermore, it has strong layout features, and color support is another nice bonus. At $795, Quark XPress offers a lot for the money.

Ventura: Very Good

At $1,490, Xerox Ventura Publisher combined with the Professional Extension are expensive — and that doesn't include the EMS memory needed to use it effectively. On the other hand, it offers sophisticated features for sophisticated publishing needs while also handling basic publishing tasks, and the basic version of Ventura (without Profession-al Extension) will run even on a IBM PC XT configuration. Overall, Ventura is a workhorse program and, as such, its value is very good.

Desktop Publishers Beware:
Perils of Software Setup Side Effects

While testing these programs, we spent considerable time figuring out strange problems caused by the various programs' interactions with each other and how well they conformed to the publishing process. In fact, handling these oddities consumed more time than using the layout packages to create the test document. The problems came in several major areas, explained below.

Version Control. Having the latest version of your source programs (your text, graphics, and spreadsheet programs) isn't necessarily a good idea. If the programs were released after your layout program, you may find they use new formats your layout package can't read, even if it supported the old formats. Of course, new releases may extend the export options, making a previously inappropriate source program usable in desktop publishing.

For the Windows-based Aldus PageMaker, we originally used the Windows-based Ami Professional 1.1 word processor and Microsoft Excel 2.01 spreadsheet editor, but we found that the applications did not fit well together.

PageMaker is strongly tied to Microsoft Word; PageMaker supports Word style sheets and, although it imports several word-processing formats, it exports only to Word format. We could have exported from Ami to Word to PageMaker, and then imported into Ami the Word-format text exported by PageMaker when we wanted to edit text, but that precluded use of Word's style sheets and added an unnecessary burden.

Microsoft Excel was similarly disqualified. PageMaker can only read in Lotus 1-2-3-format spreadsheets and charts. Excel can export 1-2-3-format (.WK1) data but not 1-2-3-format (.PIC) charts.

For Quark XPress, we started to use Microsoft Word 4.0, but Quark supports only Versions 3.0 and earlier. (Word 4.0 was released after XPress.)

Similarly, we backed down from using Lotus 1-2-3, Release 3, and switched to Release 2 for PageMaker and Ventura Publisher because PageMaker cannot read the new .WK3 format. Ventura can't read spreadsheet files directly (it reads in the .PRN print files you can create in a spreadsheet program), but we used the older version of 1-2-3 for consistency.

Environmental Concerns. There is a great push to use integrated, graphical environments for all tasks. However, this is probably inappropriate for desktop publishing that is based on integrating distinct activities.

For example, an editor needs a good word processor, not something to format copy, because a layout artist will take care of that. Likewise, an editor doesn't need a graphical interface, while a layout artist does. Giving an editor control over formatting wastes both time (and skills) and conflicts with the layout artist's responsibilities. The money spent on a WYSIWYG system with WYSIWYG features are not relevant to the task — editing — and could be better spent elsewhere. And chances are that a non-WYSIWYG word processor is faster than its graphical counterpart.

Also, most publishing is carried out by different people using different systems. The editor's user interface need not be similar to the layout artist's or graphic artist's. Of course, if you have a small, do-it-all-yourself operation, the value of interface consistency is worth exploring.

The same is true for hardware. In our companies' operations (one of us works for a publisher of technical trade magazines, the other for an insurance company's corporate communications department), we both use a range of hardware and software, picking the right tools for each job. While we use different combinations, based on our personal and our companies' needs and preferences, we both found environment is not an issue.

Why is a mixed environment not a problem for us? Because high-end desktop publishing programs are usually well-equipped to handle both the popular MS-DOS and Mac formats. They let us worry about publishing, not technical-environmental concerns.

Factors such as disk formats (a problem within both the PC and Mac worlds) loom much larger for us than whether the source of a graphic was a Mac while the text came from a PC, or whether the screen shots came from a Mac but one image was scanned into a PC.

Imposing an environment can actually hinder productivity. The work-arounds required to do desktop publishing exclusively in Windows, described above, are one example. Even if we had determined the work-arounds to be acceptable in our deadline-oriented work, we found that even with 2 megabytes of RAM (whether configured as extended or expanded), we could not run any two of PageMaker, Corel Draw, and Excel under Windows/286, Version 2.11. We could run Ami Professional with one of these, but it soon returned out-of-memory errors.

Of course, the chances of one user needing to load all these programs simultaneously are very small, since the tasks involved in publishing are not typically done in tandem. Thus one advantage of such an integrated environment — dynamic, simultaneous data exchange — becomes moot.

For small organizations or projects with small staffing, where economies of scale dictate that one person should perform several or all of the publishing roles, the staff still needs a system with the appropriate tools. But in such settings, it may be best to avoid a standardized environment with tools not well suited to desktop publishing. Instead, choose tools that work well together even if they use different interfaces or hardware.

Overpowered Source Programs. There is a danger that buying word processors or document processors with layout and WYSIWYG preview features will be a waste. Much of the formatting in these programs will not translate to the layout program you use, resulting in wasted effort. While layout programs will read in paragraph tags and some will read in embedded codes for character formatting, they won't read in information like the number of columns per page, the location of text and graphics, or margins.

If you use such word processors, make sure your staff knows *not* to worry about layout formatting if their work will be used in desktop publishing. Obviously, they should pay attention to issues such as what text is boldfaced, which text should be tagged as headlines, and the like.

Should You Do It All Yourself? The most important element of setting up a system is the staff. One incentive to use desktop publishing is to reduce staffing: An *InfoWorld* survey found that while only six percent of the respondents were interested in desktop publishing to reduce labor costs, 39 percent of those using desktop publishing saved labor costs. And when asked what jobs desktop publishing could eliminate, 55 percent said typographers, 30 percent said pressmen, 29 percent said layout artists, and 20 percent said production artists. Only 8 percent surveyed thought desktop publishing would eliminate editors (perhaps because they would absorb the other jobs).

There is a temptation to move layout tasks to the editor's desk. And this is encouraged by programs like IBM Interleaf Publisher and FrameMaker that are almost totally self-contained and like PageMaker that don't let you handle some editing tasks in your word processor. That's fine if the editor is skilled in typography, layout, and production — and has enough time to take on these tasks while still editing. But publishing is akin to product manufacturing: Imagine deciding that the team that designed an automobile should therefore also engineer it, manufacture it, and deliver it to dealers, all because of computerization.

Of course, there are areas where job integration is appropriate. If typography and layout control aren't important for the final product — products like memos, simple flyers, and basic reports — formatting might be an appropriate editorial task. For such applications, sophisticated word processors, document processors, and low-end desktop publishers probably suffice. But these are not substitutes for real publishing tools any more than an editor is a substitute for other publishing positions.

Recommended Setups. Based on our experience and tests, we recommend these setups for the four layout packages:

PageMaker. Word processor: Microsoft Word (MS-DOS). *Artwork:* Aldus Freehand (Mac), Adobe Illustrator (Mac), Corel Draw (MS-DOS/Windows), or Micrografx Designer (MS-DOS/Windows). *Business graphics:* Any program that saves in EPS or .PIC format, like Harvard Graphics. *Images:* Any popular program that saves in .PCX, TIFF, or Windows Metafile format, like PC Paintbrush and Hotshot Graphics. *Spreadsheet:* Lotus 1-2-3, Release 2 or compatible (avoid products like Microsoft Excel that can save data in 1-2-3's .WK1 format but not charts in its .PIC format).

Quark. Word processor: Any popular Mac package, including Microsoft Word, WordPerfect, and Mac Write. *Artwork:* Aldus Freehand or Adobe Illustrator. Business graphics: Aldus Persuasion and similar programs that save in EPS or PICT, Version 1 formats. *Images:* Any program that saves in MacPaint or TIFF format. *Spreadsheet:* Microsoft Excel.

Ventura. Word processor: Any popular MS-DOS package, including WordPerfect, Microsoft Word, Xywrite, or WordStar. *Artwork, business graphics, spreadsheet* (although you have to print to a file), and *images:* See PageMaker.

—Barbara Assadi and Galen Gruman

Product Summaries
High End Desktop Publishing

Aldus PageMaker for the IBM PC Version 3.0
Company: Aldus Corp., 411 First Ave. S., Seattle, WA 98104;
(206) 622-5500.
List Price: $795.
Requires: IBM PC or compatible; PC/MS-DOS 3.1 or later; 640K
of RAM; hard disk; Microsoft Windows (run-time version included); CGA, EGA, VGA, or Hercules graphics; mouse.

Quark XPress Version 2.12
Company: Quark Inc., 300 S. Jackson, Suite 100, Denver, CO
80209; (800) 543-7711.
List Price: $795.
Requires: Macintosh Plus, Macintosh SE, or Macintosh II; 1
megabyte of RAM and a hard disk; System 5.2; Macintosh II and
color monitor needed to view color.

Xerox Ventura Publisher Version 2.0
Company: Xerox Desktop Software, 9745 Business Park Drive,
San Diego, CA 92131; (800) 822-8221
List Price: $895 (includes Bitstream font manager); Professional
Extension costs additional $595; currently, a promotion running
through March includes Professional Extension free if you buy
the base package or the network server.
Requires: IBM PC or compatible; PC-/MS-DOS 2.1 or later; 640K
of RAM; hard disk; CGA, EGA, VGA, or Hercules graphics; mouse;
GEM operating environment (run-time version included); EMS
memory highly recommended, and required with Professional
Extension (512K without Professional Extension's hyphenation
dictionary, 1 1/2 megabytes with it).

PageMaker 4 Touts Improved Typography, Text Editing

This version offers well-implemented features, and is up to par with Quark XPress' strengths.

BY GALEN GRUMEN, Reviews Board

After we published the foregoing in-depth analysis of desktop publishing packages, Aldus released their long-awaited upgrade to PageMaker. Our standalone review follows.

The expanded typographic, file management, color, long-document, and layout capabilities of Aldus PageMaker 4.0 for the Macintosh both broaden the program's user base and deepen its functionality. Despite this added breadth, veteran PageMaker users will find that the program retains the feel and approach that has characterized the program since its inception.

These new features put PageMaker on par with Quark XPress (reviewed in the preceding article) in areas such as typography, color, and word processing, where Quark has traditionally led the field. When Version 3.0 of XPress ships (in the summer of 1990), Quark might again lead the field in typographic capabilities, but PageMaker 4.0 should fulfill the needs of all but the most demanding desktop publishers. The only significant area Aldus neglected to update in this version is graphics, although this release can use Pantone Matching System (PMS) colors.

FEATURES:

Most of the new features added to PageMaker 4.0 meet the needs of professional publishers, who need finer control over layout and text elements than the previous version provided.

Perhaps PageMaker's most significant enhancement is its improved typographic capabilities —the program now lets you specify tracking, word spacing, and kerning information independently for each stylesheet tag; control widows and orphans; associate rules above and below paragraphs; and override some default settings (for small caps, subscripts, and superscripts). In addition, the new version offers a broader range of type sizes (from 4 to 650 points in one-tenth-point increments) and leading (also now in one-tenth-point increments), and allows you to compress and expand type from 5 to 250 percent.

PageMaker has also improved its text-handling features. Enhancements include a "story editor," which is a non-WYSIWYG simple text editor that includes search and replace, a spelling checker, standard document editing features such as cut and paste, and indexing and table of contents generation. You can either create your original document in the story editor, or place a word processing file in PageMaker and use the story editor for editing. The story editor can't replace a word processor, but it works much faster than editing text in the layout view. Other text-handling additions include text rotation in 90-degree

Benchmarks
Macintosh Desktop Publishing Software

	Aldus PageMaker Version 4.0	Aldus PageMaker Version 3.02	Quark XPress Version 2.12
ASCII file import	0:15	0:14	0:08[1]
SHORT DOCUMENT[2]			
Open document	0:09	0:07	0:05
Jump to last page	0:04	0:03	0:03
Change view	0:06	0:06	0:07[3]
Save/continue	0:02	0:02	0:03
Print	5:19	3:03	2:07
LONG DOCUMENT[4]			
Open document	0:07	0:06	0:04
Jump to last page	0:02	0:02	0:02
Change view	0:07	0:07	0:04
Save/continue	0:02	0:02	0:04
Print	6:02	4:53	4:24

Times in minutes:seconds, unless otherwise noted. As a test platform, we used a 5-megabyte Mac IIcx with a 40-megabyte hard disk.

[1]Quark: Numerous blank pages and pages of control characters were noted.

[2]Short document is four pages.

[3]Quark: Two menu commands were required; no command-key equivalents were available from the pull-down menu.

[4]Long document is approximately 18 pages.

Report Card
MAC DESKTOP PUBLISHING SOFTWARE
PageMaker Version 4.0

Performance		
Layout	(75)	Very Good
Word processing	(75)	Excellent
Speed	(75)	Good
Typography	(50)	Very Good
Graphic objects	(50)	Good
Graphic images	(50)	Good
Output	(50)	Very Good
Documentation	(100)	Very Good
Ease of learning	(100)	Very Good
Ease of use	(150)	Very Good
Error handling	(75)	Very Good
Support		
Support policies	(50)	Good
Technical support	(50)	Very Good
Value	(50)	Very Good
Final score	**7.4**	

PRODUCT SUMMARY
Company: Aldus Corp., 411 First Ave. S., Seattle, WA 98104-2871; (206) 622-5500.
List Price: $795.
Requires: Macintosh Plus or higher; hard disk; 1 megabyte of RAM; System 6.0.3 (Mac Portable, SE/30, or II series with 2 megabytes of RAM are recommended).
Pros: Sophisticated typographic and color support; long-document features; design-oriented layout approach; word processing capabilities.
Cons: Limited graphics creation capabilities; manual orientation for many layout tasks.
Summary: A well-rounded desktop publisher for a range of publications, from newsletters to magazines, with enough long-document features for the occasional production of manuals and reference books.

increments (Quark XPress 3.0 allows you to rotate text in one-thousandth degree increments), a line-break character (soft return), and a "keep with" command that lets you keep text with its associated paragraph, column, or page.

Version 4.0's new long-document features include index and table of contents generation, automatic page numbering, and links management, a new feature that allows workgroup PageMaker users the option of having their documents updated automatically when changes are made to a source file. For example, if someone altered the text in a linked Microsoft Word file, the placed text in PageMaker would also be altered.

PageMaker now also provides PMS colors and the capability to display and print 24-bit color graphics. In addition, you can create four-color separation files, which require an Aldus Open Prepress Interface (OPI) compatible application such as the just-shipped Aldus Preprint ($495) to process. Printing enhancements include the capability to batch print multiple documents; output individual pages as EPS files for reuse in graphics and publishing programs (as a cover thumbnail in a contents page, for example); and print odd and even pages separately.

PageMaker's new layout features include in-line graphics, which tie a graphic to a block of text so it remains with the associated text when it is moved. However, PageMaker cannot automatically wrap text around an in-line graphic. A separate table editor application included with Version 4.0 makes it easy to create and import row-and-column tables, which you can export as text or PICT files into a PageMaker document.

PERFORMANCE:

PageMaker uses the familiar pasteboard approach to layout. Its layout capabilities, including text wrap, text and graphics placement, and master pages, work basically as they did in Version 3.02. Version 4.0 retains the flexible but manual approach that best suits design-intensive publications. You can now position graphics on master pages and wrap placed text around them in the layout view, which is helpful if you wish to wrap text around a logo on each page.

You can use style tags to specify whether a particular paragraph style ends with a column or page, continues with a following paragraph, or flows normally.

The new links-management feature greatly eases workgroup document production. With the links, you can specify which files PageMaker should automatically update when you open PageMaker files. You can also see the last creation date for each file, as well as the time and the date that the file was placed in PageMaker, which is helpful if an old version of a text file gets inadvertently linked to your publication. However, the link does not work both ways: When you change files in PageMaker, the source files, such as graphic images or text files, are not automatically updated. We rate layout very good.

The story editor significantly enhances PageMaker's word processing capabilities. Although you will probably still use your word processor for major changes (something that you can easily do now, since the new links feature ensures that PageMaker will use the most up-to-date text file), the story editor lets you quickly perform global changes and moderate editing such as adding or deleting paragraphs story by story. You can select the typeface and font size you wish to use, too, for easier viewing.

The story editor's search-and-replace feature lets you replace both text and attributes such as typeface and style tag, either independently or in tandem. The spelling checker is handy for detecting editing errors. Since you see a text-only version of your document in the story editor, it's much faster than editing in layout mode. When you leave the story editor window, the publication automatically reformats with the altered text.

Though capable, the new table editor module can't match the sophistication of Xerox Ventura Publisher's on the PC. PageMaker 4.0's table editor offers expected features such as cell sizing, merging, and shading, plus some bonuses such as the capability to sum data in a range of cells. Unless you want to import just the text from your table, you must import these tables into PageMaker as graphics files. This means that you can't edit the content of the tables in PageMaker.

The new long-document features — contents and index generation — should please documentation writers and book publishers, especially when coupled with the "books" feature, which lets you index or create a contents list across a group of PageMaker files, as well as print out that group as a whole with one command. Curiously, while you can cross-reference topics, you cannot do an automatic cross-reference such as "see page X" within your document.

With its spelling checker and search-and-replace function, the new story editor and the word processor file-linking feature significantly enhance PageMaker's text editing capabilities. We rate word processing excellent.

In our updated benchmark tests introduced with this review, which include both a four-page and an 18-page document, PageMaker 4.0 performed a little slower than Version 3.02. Opening a document and file import were slightly slower, printing more slowly than both Version 3.02 and Version 2.12 of XPress. You can speed up screen redraw by turning off the graphics display or having the program use standard display resolution for high-resolution artwork. We rate speed good.

The new control over character spacing and the capability to specify all typographic attributes separately for every paragraph tag put Page-Maker's typographic features on par with those of XPress 2.12's and almost on par with Ventura Publisher for the PC.

Most significant are the spacing controls, which let you specify tracking, word spacing, and kerning for each paragraph. In earlier versions, you had to find a compromise value that worked decently with both headlines and text — an almost impossible task for most documents. Now you can fine-tune each text element as needed. You cannot, however, specify tracking values (you choose from five options, ranging from "very tight" to "very loose"), and you cannot edit the table that contains kerning information (which means you can't ensure that certain kerning is always done automatically). As a layout aid, you can have PageMaker highlight overly loose or tight lines.

The added capability to associate rules above and below paragraphs comes in handy for elements such as footnotes, which often have a rule above them, and decks (or pull quotes), which often have rules above and below. As in previous versions, PageMaker limits you to a finite set of rule sizes and types (you cannot define them manually), but you can control the placement of the rules both vertically and horizontally.

You can now compress and expand type, which widens the range of type effects you can produce with your existing typefaces, without having to resort to treating the text as a graphic object.

These new features duplicate most of what the typographically strong XPress offers in Version 2.12. We rate typography very good.

PageMaker's handling of graphic objects remains almost unchanged from earlier versions, offering basic drawing features, limited fill patterns, and a limited selection of line weights. Both Timeworks Publish-It and Design Studio surpass PageMaker here. There are no sophisticated graphics manipulation features such as flipping, rotation, or reversal, which are offered in Design Studio; Aldus assumes you perform such actions in a separate graphics program. But PageMaker now allows you to specify Pantone colors, in addition to those created using the CMYK (cyan/magenta/yellow/ black, the offset printing standard), RGB (red/green/blue, the screen-display standard), and HLS (hue/luminance/saturation, a painting standard) models. We rate graphic objects good.

Similarly, PageMaker's graphic image capabilities include a few enhancements but no radical additions. You can now choose from three levels of graphics display: grayed out (for faster performance);

normal resolution; and high resolution (which displays up to 24-bit images). You can also import 24-bit-color EPS and TIFF files, new to this version. As far as printing goes, you can adjust the resolution, gray levels, and contrast of only black-and-white bit-mapped images. Page-Maker continues to offer standard cropping and resizing features. We rate graphic images good.

PageMaker 4.0 provides significantly enhanced output control. A series of print options for PostScript output let you specify such things as suppressing the printing of bit-mapped files, which is handy if you used such files in your layout for positioning but intend to have the printer mechanically strip the photo into your negatives at a higher resolution.

You can output spot color separations from PageMaker, but you need to use an OPI application such as Preprint to output continuous-tone (four-color) separations; however, you can print the four-color separation file to disk, which is convenient for sending the file to a service bureau. Quark lets you directly produce four-color separations for colors specified and created within Quark, but it does not support the separation of color TIFF files, even with a separator program. Because most people using colors in page-layout software use them for fills and simple graphics, the lack of direct separation support in PageMaker is a hindrance.

If you select four-color separations as an output option, PageMaker will also separate any Pantone colors used in the equivalent "build" of cyan, magenta, yellow, and black required to reproduce them with the OPI application. (The Pantone menu also displays these builds after you select the Pantone colors; we found that they closely matched builds suggested by our commercial printers.) Aldus equips Version 4.0 with a powerful range of output controls. All that we missed is a built-in OPI capability. We rate output very good.

DOCUMENTATION:

Aldus reorganized the documentation for this new version. The old user and reference manuals have been merged into a shorter reference manual. The new index is more complete, and the manual now offers handy "See also" lists with each menu description to help you find relevant material quickly. A getting-started manual contains a tutorial for new users, but some of the tutorial examples don't match the results you get with the on-line file, such as extra tabs in the "Brief History of Publishing" table. The manual could stand more coverage of utilities and operating system-level details such as how to modify printer-description files to increase output resolution, but on the whole it is fairly complete.

The on-line documentation has been significantly revised. The program retains the on-line help arranged by topic, and you can now select a help icon and click a menu option to get detailed help on that option. Documentation is very good.

EASE OF LEARNING:

Although richer in functionality, the retention of PageMaker 4.0's original menu and icon structure makes it easy for experienced PageMaker users to learn the new version — most functions will work as expected. Users should be able to easily grasp altered functions and learn new features as needed.

Newcomers to PageMaker will benefit from experience in other Mac-based layout packages, since the basics tend to work similarly. Those with no experience will have the toughest time simply because of the inherent complexity of a desktop publishing package. PageMaker's pasteboard metaphor will help artists with traditional experience but not those used to documentation systems. The program's logical arrangement, use of Macintosh conventions, and documentation all help you learn to use the program rapidly. Despite some inconsistencies, we found the tutorial to be helpful. We rate ease of learning very good.

EASE OF USE:

PageMaker's adherence to its familiar pasteboard metaphor and the generally straightforward implementation of new features make it easy to use. In the story editor, for example, you can select the typeface and size that is most readable for you. The links-management feature's capability to show you the last update and link status for each file is another handy addition, as is the capability to generate a table of contents and an index for use with long documents. One minor complaint is that PageMaker retains a manual orientation for such features as placing graphics in columns; in XPress, you can just type in the coordinates of where you wish to place the graphic. Ease of use is very good.

ERROR HANDLING:

PageMaker offers a single-level undo for most commands; you can also revert to the previously saved version if you've made disastrous changes to your layout. A mini-save feature automatically stores changes when you move from page to page or when you close the story editor, but you can still revert to the previous version. Error messages are clear and self-explanatory.

The only oddity we discovered, which Aldus documents in an appendix, is how Version 4.0 handles super- and subscripted characters imported from Word 4.0: Rather than using your PageMaker styles, as in Version 3.02, the program uses Word's settings. A work-around is to retag paragraphs manually in PageMaker. We rate error handling very good, better than any of the other current Mac desktop publishing contenders.

SUPPORT:

Registered users are entitled to 90 days of free technical support via a toll number, from 7 a.m. to 6 p.m. Pacific time. After that period expires, you may buy one of two annual support policies or pay $15 per call. Support is also available on CompuServe. Support policies are rated good.

Technicians made an effort to understand the context surrounding our question so they could provide the most appropriate answer. We also were able to get through to support technicians with minimal waiting.

We rate Aldus' technical support very good.

VALUE:

At $795, PageMaker's price is the same as that of Quark XPress and Design Studio. For most high-end publishing needs, PageMaker offers well-implemented features at an appropriate price. In particular, the links management, table editor application, and the story editor set the program apart from its contenders.

We rate PageMaker 4.0 a very good value.

CHAPTER SIX

Publish or Perish

InfoWorld looks at six affordable DTP packages for the nondesigner on the IBM PC.

BY GALEN GRUMAN, REVIEW BOARD, AND
ERIC AZINGER AND JEFF ECKERT, INFOWORLD TEST CENTER

Low-end desktop publishing programs are aimed at a different audience than the old standbys, PageMaker and Ventura, reviewed in the previous chapter. If you are in charge of producing your company's monthly newsletter, corporate bulletins, or want occasionally to add some sparkle to memos or price sheets, one of the six packages reviewed here may be for you. These DOS programs – Avagio, Express Publisher, Finesse, GEM Desktop Publisher, PFS:First Publisher, and Publish It – are designed to be easy to use and to have the right balance of features for occasional users who own IBM PC compatibles – not for publishing professionals.

If you want to design a book, however, or if you are a layout artist needing access to the most sophisticated typographic tools, you're probably better off in the PageMaker or Ventura camp (or, on the Macintosh, using Quark XPress or PageMaker). These programs are more difficult to learn and cost more, but offer fuller features sets and capabilities (such as table-of-contents generation) that most of the low-end packages can't touch.

As the desktop publishing (DTP) market evolves, both the high-end and low-end program vendors are seeing the market redefined. "Low-end" now means laser-printed output, not just dot matrix – as it did when this category of software was introduced. Low-end DTP users want some of the same features that once were the sole province of this category's giants, namely extensive layout and typographic controls.

High-end programs offer increasing flexibility for both highly creative documents such as advertisements, and highly complex documents such as consumer magazines and books. Automated layout and formatting, version control, fine typographic control, dynamic manipulation of layout elements, and the capability to make global changes easily are critical in this market. These programs also offer a range of specialized features such as index generation, table editing, spot-color overlays, nonrectangular text wrap, the capability to anchor graphics to specific places in text, and customizable page numbering.

Low-end programs are, of course, much less expensive than the high-end programs – $100 to $300 compared to $700 to $1,000 for those at the high end. Despite all their fancy new features, the low-end programs are limited in what they can do. For example, they typically have limited typographic controls, limited font selection, and reduced file import capabilities.

Low-end desktop publishers also tend to keep layout activity manual, rather than automating tasks such as creating multiple columns, text flow, and text wrap. Because they are designed to create simpler documents, this approach is acceptable.

LOW-END DTP VS. THE WORLD

The competition for low-end desktop publishing dollars is fierce. Word processors now offer basic layout capabilities and even some typographic features. High-end programs beckon many users – especially those in business – who are willing to invest in the extra hardware, more expensive software, and training. More users are attempting to do layouts.

Deciding which path to take – word processing or high- or low-end DTP – is not always easy, especially if you are new to publishing. Clearly, magazines and advertising agencies will want a high-end program. A company or customer newsletter will have to choose between the high-end programs and those more affordable at the low end. For these users, the sophistication of the newsletter's design and the method chosen to print it will be determining factors – if you use many graphics, text elements, and typographic effects, and intend to produce the newsletter through offset printing, the high end is a better bet.

Users looking to create fact sheets, flyers, bulletins, and other such documents have the toughest choice. The low-end programs offer WYSIWYG implementations that give you instant feedback about your layout and design choices, but word processors like WordPerfect and Microsoft Word that have layout features and page preview offer similar capabilities wrapped in a familiar interface. For these users, the critical factor may be the frequency of their publishing needs. Infrequent users can easily stick to a familiar word processor – or perhaps to a layout-capable upgrade of it – but those who have a continuing need to produce "designed" documents are better off using a program made especially for layout.

A GUIDING HAND

Low-end DTP programs must focus on the business user, providing a sound foundation for basic yet quality publishing while not overwhelming the user with the sophisticated features of the high-end products. The programs should be easy to learn and guide publishing novices through the process of creating a graphical document that works.

As this comparison shows, most of the products in the low end of this market still have a way to go to meet their business-publishing goals. We found most implementations uneven, with many features plagued by limitations – the many footnotes our features chart required to mark limited implementations attests to this.

Many programs compromise on basic layout features, while offering surprisingly sophisticated bells and whistles. Of the products we review here, GEM Desktop Publisher and Publish It have the highest aspirations – the most features, and naturally, the highest prices.

Avagio and Express Publisher represent the middle ground in desktop publishing packages, while First Publisher and Finesse represent the low end of the market.

EXECUTIVE SUMMARY

Business-oriented, low-end desktop publishers are all over the map in terms of features and functionality. This is due partly to the recent integration – at varying levels – of professional features such as typography and a new emphasis on multi-element layout. But it's also due to emphasizing a few sophisticated features, often at the expense of basic ones, in an apparent effort to differentiate themselves.

Avagio first appears to be a layout-oriented package as well as a DTP product; unfortunately, its real emphasis is on gee-whiz graphics features, not on the publishing component –which makes its usefulness limited to a handful of tasks that have been the traditional domain of graphics editors.

Express Publisher falls in the middle ground of desktop publishing. The features offered by the program are neither extraordinary nor abysmal. Graphic images are particularly nice in this product.

PFS:First Publisher and **Finesse** address basic publishing, representing the low-end's low end. (But they are not so low end as to be confused with dot-matrix-only mimeograph-style page-formatting programs.) First Publisher, now in its third major version, is the least sophisticated in this comparison. With the advent of preview mode, word processors, document editors, and truly layout-oriented programs, First Publisher looks more and more like an anachronism. Although Finesse is basic, it is not primitive. It offers the appropriate features for its niche and executes them well in that context.

Report Card
Low-End Desktop Publishing Software

	(Weighting)	Avagio Version 1.1	Express Publisher Version 1.1
Price		$299.95	$149.95
Performance			
Layout	(75)	Good	Satisfactory
Word processing	(75)	Satisfactory	Satisfactory
Typography	(50)	Satisfactory	Good
Graphic objects	(50)	Good	Good
Graphic images	(50)	Excellent	Very Good
Speed	(75)	Poor	Poor
Output quality	(50)	Very Good	Good
Documentation	(75)	Poor	Very Good
Ease of learning	(100)	Satisfactory	Satisfactory
Ease of use	(125)	Satisfactory	Poor
Error handling	(75)	Satisfactory	Good
Support			
Support policies	(50)	Good	Satisfactory
Technical support	(50)	Good	Satisfactor
Value	(100)	Good	Satisfactory
Final scores		**5.4**	**5.0**

InfoWorld reviews only finished, production versions of products, never beta test versions.
Products rated within 0.2 points of one another differ little. Weightings represent average relative importance to InfoWorld readers involved in purchasing and using that product category. You can customize the report card to your needs by using your own weightings to calculate the final score.

Finesse Version 3.1	GEM Desktop Publisher Version 2.01	PFS: First Publisher Version 3.0	Publish It Version 1.12
$179	$299	$149	$195.95
Good	Good	Poor	Very Good
Poor	Poor	Satisfactory	Satisfactory
Satisfactory	Satisfactory	Poor	Satisfactory
Poor	Good	Satisfactory	Very Good
Good	Poor	Good	Good
Satisfactory	Good	Satisfactory	Satisfactory
Good	Good	Poor	Good
Satisfactory	Satisfactory	Satisfactory	Satisfactory
Good	Good	Good	Good
Satisfactory	Poor	Good	Good
Satisfactory	Good	Satisfactory	Satisfactory
Good	Poor	Very Good	Poor
Good	Satisfactory	Good	Satisfactory
Satisfactory	Poor	Poor	Very Good
5.1	**4.5**	**4.8**	**5.8**

Excellent = Outstanding in all areas.
Very Good = Meets all essential criteria and offers significant advantages.
Good = Meets essential criteria and includes some special features.
Satisfactory = Meets essential criteria.
Poor = Falls short in essential areas.
Unacceptable or N/A = Fails to meet minimum standards or lacks this feature.

INTRODUCTION

Avagio

Avagio is the latest entry in the low-end desktop publishing market. It has an odd mixture of high-end features and low-end implementation. The product uses its own graphical interface, which lacks the feedback that both GEM and Windows supply, making the program awkward to use.

Avagio's strength lies in its graphics capabilities. Features include gradient fills, type special effects (such as printing letters in mixtures of outlines and grays), and mingling (which lets you overlap text and graphics and have the overlapped portion of text, for example, print in white over the graphic). None of these features is available in high-end layout programs such as PageMaker and Ventura.

For layout and text handling, Avagio offers basic style sheets, drawing tools, a word processor, graphics file support, and wrap capabilities. It supports basic editing and hyphenation (including discretionary hyphens) and a wide variety of dot-matrix and laser printers.

Unfortunately, Avagio is annoyingly slow and somewhat difficult to learn, and the documentation lacks basic detail about the program and its features.

With Avagio's mixed feature set, its appropriateness is based more on the type of publication you are creating. The more important graphics editing and type special effects are to you, the more appropriate Avagio is for your needs.

Express Publisher

Express Publisher is a relative newcomer to the low-end desktop publishing market, and offers many features commonly associated with high-end desktop publishers for layout, typographic control, and graphics manipulation. Although intended for simple needs such as small internal newsletters and flyers, it is a major upgrade to the basic layout program, Pages, which Power-Up Software acquired from Pinpoint Publishing. Express Publisher uses its own graphical interface; unfortunately, the interface can be very awkward at times. Overall, the product is in the middle of the pack.

Express Publisher's advanced layout features include the capability to position and size frames by coordinate, lock frames in place to prevent accidental changes, and wrap text around an image's contour. It uses style sheets for text and can set a wide range of character attributes, including subscripts and monospacing (where each letter takes the same amount of space regardless of width – helpful for certain tables and some documentation conventions).

The program's typographic controls include kerning, tracking, indents, and special symbols. Its text-editing capabilities include search and replace.

In graphics, Express Publisher offers a bit-map editor, rotation, flipping, reversing, and the highly unusual capability to export graphics (to PCX format).

Finesse

Finesse has few bells and whistles. It is intended for simple business documents and short, straightforward newsletters. Although limited to basic tasks, Finesse performs them well, making appropriate trade-offs in functionality and simplicity. If your needs are relatively simple, Finesse may be the right product for you. Finesse uses the GEM/3 operating environment.

Finesse's layout approach is frame-based but manual: You create a frame for each column and then manually link frames to control text flow. Finesse does not use style sheets, although it lets you copy paragraph attributes, such as spacing, from one paragraph to another.

Typographic support is likewise basic: typeface, point size, tabs, indents, kerning, and hyphenation. You cannot control leading (although you can add more space between paragraphs) or tracking.

Finesse also offers basic graphics capabilities: It can import the common bit-map formats, size and crop them, and wrap text around them. It has basic gray levels and line weights. It does not offer drawing tools for circles, rectangles, or other shapes – only lines.

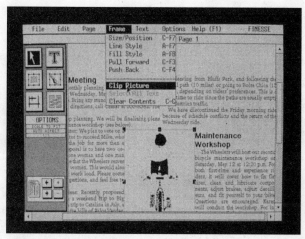

After you import a graphic, Finesse will let you size and crop your image to fit.

GEM Desktop Publisher

An early pioneer in the now-defunct midrange DTP market, GEM Desktop Publisher has not seen a major upgrade in a year and so retains several flaws and limitations that its competitors have fixed or avoided. Its lack of an update has let those competitors redefine the market, and as a result GEM Desktop Publisher has slipped into the upper reaches of the new low-end market. If you are comfortable with the GEM interface, this might be the product for you.

GEM Desktop Publisher is useful for business needs such as simple newsletters, fact sheets, and corporate communications – especially if you use other GEM-based programs (word processors and drawing packages). It offers essential layout, type, graphics, and text handling features in a user interface that strongly resembles Ventura Publisher. Its frame-based style-sheet approach lets you format structured documents and modify them on the fly.

To provide its feature set, the program is a memory hog. It uses about 560K, yet does not support extended or expanded memory.

PFS: First Publisher

PFS:First Publisher retains its basic approach from previous versions, offering few of the features now considered standard in desktop publishing such as multiple page views, style sheets, hyphenation, or typographic controls. Although it now supports downloadable fonts, First Publisher retains its dot-matrix orientation. This program is best applied to memos, flyers, and other such simple documents that don't have multiple text elements on each page.

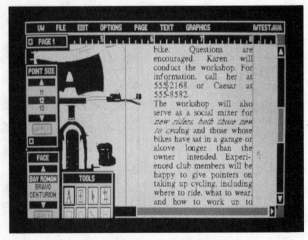

Avagio offers basic drawing tools for rectangles, lines, and ellipses.

First Publisher has a nice interface, similar to the GEM interface. The major changes in Version 3.0 include 300-dpi resolution and the layout gallery, which lets you automate the layout process by providing a set of 21 thumbnail sketches; you find the one you want and the text reformats to that sketch.

The layout features include automatic text wrap around graphics, the capability to determine the order of text flow among columns, and the capability to change the width of specific lines or parts of columns.

First Publisher's typeface options are largely dot-matrix-resolution typefaces available in limited sizes, although it now supports seven of Bitstream's high-resolution, scalable fonts. The program will install Bitstream fonts automatically.

Graphics are the program's strong suit: First Publisher offers sizing, cropping, 90-degree rotation, mirroring, and flipping. The drawing features include ellipses, rectangles, lines, and a freehand tool, but no gray screens or fill patterns.

Publish It

At first glance, Publish It resembles high-end programs such as Ventura Publisher. Like its closest competitor in the low end, GEM Desktop Publisher, Publish It offers a GEM-based interface that uses frames and style tags. And like GEM Desktop Publisher, Publish It is intended for the business communicator seeking a simple but capable program for office-quality documents. To provide this, the program offers frame orientation for layout, style sheets, essential typographic control, and some advanced drawing tools.

The layout features are strong, including standard capabilities such as text wrap, guidelines, and rulers, plus some high-end capabilities such as the capability to place and size frames by coordinate. Style sheets cover professional typographic issues such as word spacing, tracking, discretionary hyphens, indents, and tab settings.

The program does not support many typefaces – eight for Postscript users and seven for others. It also does not support popular downloadable fonts such as Bitstream's or Adobe's. Publish It also has a version for the Macintosh, which is quite different from the PC version.

Performance:
LAYOUT

Avagio: *GOOD*

Like Pagemaker, Avagio uses the manual pasteboard approach to layout, augmented with auto-flow features. When you import text and place it, the program flows the text into a frame it creates; you can then size and position that frame. You can create additional frames for additional columns and then link the frames together so the text flows from one to another. If you select the auto-flow and specify the number of columns per page before importing text, Avagio will flow the text from column to column, creating new pages until all the text is used. Graphics placement is similar: You import the file, position a frame on the page, and then size and crop it.

Avagio lets you use master pages to define a basic template and repeat information like folios and logos. You can also set up automatic page numbering.

Avagio does not automatically wrap text around graphics. You must select all the text frames affected by the graphic and then select the wrap option. Fortunately, you can select multiple text frames at a time for wrapping. There is no option to set margins around the graphic to prevent the text from bumping against it. You must put a larger, empty frame behind your image and wrap around it to simulate a margin.

The program offers several page views, layout rulers, and snap-to guides. You can also have the program show the cursor's position,

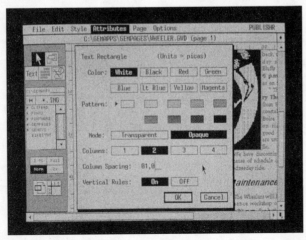

GEM Desktop Publisher's drawing capabilities allow you to choose from gray, color, or other fill patterns.

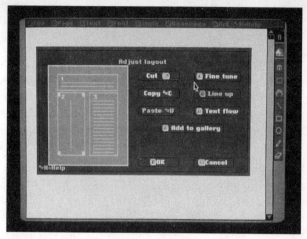

*PFS:First Publisher allows you to adjust your layout with
options like cut, copy, and paste.*

which helps you place frames precisely. Another option lets the frame
grow automatically as you enter text, which is handy when you enter
text during layout. Another plus is the capability to lock frames, which
prevents you from accidentally moving or resizing them. Unfortunately,
Avagio is limited to working in inches.

Express Publisher: *SATISFACTORY*
Express Publisher implements many of its sophisticated layout features
awkwardly, defeating their advantages. For example, the program does
not let you automatically flow text. It does not support multicolumn
frames – you must create a frame for each column or break an existing
frame into smaller ones. And it supports only one view, which makes it
hard to select items that extend outside the screen's border, because the
screen will not scroll if your cursor moves past the screen's edge.

Fortunately, it does let you link and unlink frames to control text
flow, position and size frames by coordinate for exact placement, and
lock frames to prevent accidental changes.

Express Publisher's most sophisticated feature is its capability to follow an image's contour when wrapping text around graphics. Wrapping
is not automatic – you must select each frame affected by a wrap one at
a time.

If you do not want your text to wrap around the contour, you must
create a transparent rectangle (or other shape) behind the image and
have the text wrap around it. When you import a graphic, the program
automatically creates a frame for it; unfortunately, that frame is the size
of the original graphic, which usually makes it much too large for the

layout. You must then resize the frame with the mouse (which is difficult because of the single-page view) or with a resize dialog box (which makes you guess the percentage of reduction or enlargement).

Express Publisher offers a powerful set of Copy Many features that lets you duplicate frames in four ways: all that will fit across the page in a row, all that will fit down in a column, filling the page as a table, or in custom positions. Text in the original frames will not be copied. Express Publisher also has adequate style sheets. .

Finesse: *GOOD*

Finesse's manual approach to layout is time-consuming. However, features like snap-to grids and "position by coordinate" ensure that the layout is accurate. The capability to link and unlink text frames gives you complete control over the placement of text, especially in multidocument layouts. The automatic wrap feature for graphics (which you can turn off if you want text to overprint graphics) does the job well. It does not have the capability to place a margin around the graphic so text does not bump against it. This can be accomplished by placing an empty, slightly larger frame behind the graphic's frame.

A bright-red page corner at the bottom of the frame serves as a simple but strong reminder that a frame's text is longer than the current frame, and lets you know to place that text elsewhere in your layout or adjust your text size to make the full text fit.

Unfortunately, Finesse's manual approach to character formatting is

Publish It allows you to specify a frame around graphics so text will not bump against your graphic.

not as trouble-free. To format text, you must highlight it and then apply text attributes such as typeface and size. Fortunately, you can select all the text in a story (no matter how many frames it is in) and apply that formatting globally.

Finesse does not include style sheets, so you cannot change one paragraph and have all similar paragraphs change automatically. If you do change basic formatting – whether paragraph or text – you must highlight all the text you want changed. Finesse does offer helpful features such as page numbering and master pages, which let you place repeating text, graphics, and margins. You can have separate masters for left and right pages.

GEM Desktop Publisher: *GOOD*

GEM Desktop Publisher uses the popular frame-based approach to layout, where you specify frames to hold text and graphics, and manipulate the frames on the fly to accommodate requirements such as number of columns, position, and size. If frames overlap, the text in the newer frame will wrap around the other frames, whether they contain graphics or text. You cannot set margins around frames; the space between the text in one frame and the graphic or text in another cannot be controlled. As a work-around, you can put a larger, empty frame behind the graphics; the text will wrap around this frame, simulating a margin.

The program offers the standard layout capabilities, including editable text flow, several page views, and snap-to-guide layout rulers. You can also have the program show the cursor's position, which helps you precisely place frames.

Unfortunately, the program hides text frames when in text (editing) mode, so you cannot see the frame margins while entering or editing text (important feedback during layout). While this ``feature'' is documented, it is disconcerting.

The style-sheet tag covers the basics, letting you set typeface, spacing, size, and tab attributes. But you must specify line spacing in inches or picas – you cannot use the traditional measurement of points.

One higher-end feature GEM Desktop Publisher offers is an automatic page numbering capability, including your choice of numbering schemes and the starting page's number.

PFS: First Publisher: *POOR*

First Publisher's rudimentary layout capabilities let you create simple documents: You select the number of columns per page and the order in which text flows among columns, and then import your text; the program will add pages until all the text is used. The new Layout

Gallery feature gives you a choice of 21 layout templates (which you can modify and add to) and fine-tuning controls. Unfortunately, if you want to use more than one text file, First Publisher will insert each subsequent file at the beginning of your document, pushing the other text to the back. You probably won't want the same layout on each page (the first page, for example, would have room for a title that the other pages wouldn't), so you must reformat (manually or with the Layout Gallery) the other pages.

Because First Publisher assumes there is one story per page (no matter what layout is chosen), having multi-element pages is very difficult. You cannot unlink a column in a layout from the other columns or otherwise keep some layout areas for other imported text files. You can partially get around this by manually entering stories (or cutting and pasting imported text) in the columns you choose. Because the text flow among columns is not independent of the stories, First Publisher will treat the various pieces as if they were in one large document, so adding or deleting text will cause pieces from one story to move into the column for another. One option is to manually enter independent text on the graphics layer. Still, it is nearly impossible to produce a newsletter or other document with several independent text files on one page. Because this is a basic need in publishing, First Publisher's deficiency limits its score.

Publish It: *VERY GOOD*
Publish It uses a frame-based approach to combining text and graphics, which makes layout simple. Its use of master pages makes it easy to define basic templates and handle repeating elements with minimal effort. Publish It has a good set of layout aids, including rulers (in picas, centimeters, or inches) and five page views. It also offers header and footer functions.

The program does not include automation features such as automatic text flow and the capability to create multicolumn frames. To be able to place multiple columns of text in a document, you must draw a frame for each column – a tedious task. Fortunately, using the copy feature and snap-to grid (or the position-by-coordinate feature) makes sizing and placement accurate, if not fast. It is one of the few low-end programs to offer the capability to specify a margin around frames, which means that text wrapping around a graphic won't bump into the image.

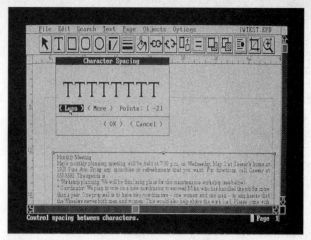

Express Publisher allows you to control spacing between each character.

Performance:
WORD PROCESSING

Avagio: *SATISFACTORY*

Avagio imports four word processing formats, covering several standard formats except RFT/DCA. It retains most character formatting information, including small caps, superscripts, and subscripts – and even some paragraph formatting such as indent and spacing. But there are no sophisticated features such as quote and dash conversion. The text editor is the standard desktop publishing type, providing cut, paste, and insert operations. Avagio also provides search and replace.

The program will export selected text, but only in ASCII (plain text) format, removing all formatting and paragraph-tag information and thus making the exported files nearly useless for version control or reuse in other documents.

Express Publisher: *SATISFACTORY*

Express Publisher imports standard word processing formats (Word-Perfect, DCA, Microsoft Word, and WordStar) plus ASCII, although it cannot read character formatting from DCA files. The text editor offers typical cut, paste, and insert operations. The program also offers search and replace. But you cannot export edits for use elsewhere or for version control.

Finesse: *POOR*

Finesse supports most basic word processor formats except RFT/DCA. However, it ignores character formatting such as boldface and italics, making you reapply those attributes manually during layout. It also cannot export edits or read the latest version of your text file, making text reuse and version control more difficult. Finesse offers basic editing capabilities like cut and paste, as well as the more sophisticated capability to search and replace text. The lack of attribute support during import hurts the score.

GEM Desktop Publisher: *POOR*

GEM Desktop Publisher supports the major word processors. However, the import filters do not work within the program – even though they appear on the menu. The filter packs are available through the company for $15 each. To import word processing files, you must use the appropriate utility at the DOS level.

The program automatically saves editing changes made during layout to an ASCII (plain text) file. You can edit this ASCII file from your word processor when it is more convenient than using the built-in text editor; when you load the file again, the changes made in the ASCII file will be reflected on-screen.

The text editor provides basic insert, cut, and paste functions. Text formatting lacks such features as subscript, superscript, and overstrike.

PFS: First Publisher: *SATISFACTORY*

First Publisher offers the basics in word processing. Although it supports a wide range of word processors (more than any other program in this comparison), its text formatting is limited to bold, italic, and normal – no underline, superscript, or other such attributes. The method of getting bold italic is nonstandard. Most programs let you select bold and then italics (like a word processor) and know to access the bold italic style. But in First Publisher, you must select bold italic as a separate face. This is not readily apparent in the default settings; as bold italic is not automatically installed, you must do so manually. Text editing functions are the typical cut, paste, and insert.

Publish It: *SATISFACTORY*

Publish It supports several major text formats, but not RFT/DCA. Its import function leaves out character formatting such as boldface and italics in some file formats (Microsoft Word, Version 5.0, for example) – an inappropriate omission that will be fixed in Version 1.2. The text editor provides cut, paste, and insert operations. The program also provides search and replace capabilities. However, Publish It has no export features, so you cannot reuse text created during layout.

Performance:
TYPOGRAPHY

Avagio: *SATISFACTORY*
Avagio's typographic features are basic and few. It comes with five typefaces that are clones of popular typefaces. It supports other manufacturers' HP-format fonts with a conversion utility.

In the style sheets, you can set basic type specs like typeface, face, size, indent, leading, and tab stops, as well as turning on hyphenation. But the hyphenation routine ignores most opportunities to hyphenate, resulting in awkward gaps that you must fix by manually inserting discretionary hyphens. You cannot control tracking or word spacing, but you can manually kern letters. On the plus side, Avagio also offers sophisticated type-manipulation features, including mirroring, flipping, reversing, compressing, and expanding.

Although Avagio has some impressive high-end features, some basic typography features are lacking.

Express Publisher: *GOOD*
Express Publisher offers an attractive set of well-implemented typographic features. It offers the capability to create screen and printer fonts on the fly for the HP printers and dot-matrix printers. Express Publisher supports downloadable fonts for dot-matrix and HP printers through a utility program.

The process to create a style-sheet tag and apply it is error-prone and not intuitive. You must first select all options that your tag will override from the default style and then make all the changes. Then you must apply the tag. Updating a tag means creating a new tag with the same name as the old one. Some settings are tied to the text frame, not to the paragraph tag. While the ability to set such defaults at first seems to offer flexibility, it actually hinders it because too many local attributes are included in these global defaults. An example of an inappropriate attribute for such defaults is whether a paragraph's first line is indented. Because of this, getting headlines not to be indented while leaving body text indented is a difficult chore.

Finesse: *SATISFACTORY*
Finesse allows you to set basic type specifications such as typeface, size, indent, and tab stops. It also has a hyphenation capability. The discretionary hyphen capability (undocumented in this release and

accessed via Alt-hyphen) lets you refine the hyphenation to avoid awkward spacing. You cannot control leading, tracking, or word spacing, but you can manually kern letters. Finesse also comes with very limited typeface selections. Your choices include: Dutch and Swiss, plus Symbol for Laserjet users.

GEM Desktop Publisher: *SATISFACTORY*

GEM Desktop Publisher offers a rich set of typographic settings, including the capability to set tracking for each paragraph tag. Its support of hyphenation is strong, including all professional features except the capability to decide how many consecutive hyphens may occur.

For Postscript output, you can select any size from 6 to 720 points in 1-point increments. Hewlett-Packard and dot-matrix output is limited by your soft fonts' size range. However, you may use only eight typefaces in a document, which limits your flexibility. This limitation seems unnecessary, especially as Bitstream's Fontware program – which gives you access to hundreds of typefaces – is bundled with GEM Desktop Publisher.

Worse, you cannot move any of the 11 built-in typefaces from one width table to another without purchasing (for about $200) each typeface to be moved. And you cannot use Adobe's Postscript typefaces because they come in binary files (PFB) that the program cannot read; you must use ASCII font files (PFA) generated by Bitstream's Fontware.

PFS: First Publisher: *POOR*

First Publisher offers less typographic control than most word processors. You cannot set tabs or define indents, let alone control hyphenation or spacing. The only settings are type size, typeface, leading (which can only be set for the entire page or selected columns, not for selected text), and justification. Version 3.0 supports Bitstream scalable typefaces (these are scaled during installation, not on the fly). The program requires Bitstream's 2.0 version of the Fontware Installation Kit, and so does not support older versions of Bitstream fontware; this prevented us from using the Charter typeface we used in other programs.

Publish It: *SATISFACTORY*

The program offers such essential typographic features as control over spacing, which distinguishes publishing programs from mere page formatters. Its implementation of attributes, through style sheets containing paragraph tags, is well done.

A more important limitation is the small number of supported type-faces and its incapability to support standard downloadable fonts from such vendors as Bitstream, Agfa Compugraphic, and Adobe. HP Laserjet users will be unable to use any font cartridges they may have, and Postscript users can access only eight of the standard 11 typefaces.

Performance:

GRAPHICS OBJECTS

Avagio: *Good*

Avagio offers basic drawing tools for rectangles, lines, and ellipses, but there are no advanced features for freehand drawing or curves. When drawing shapes, you can constrain them to create perfect squares and circles. Avagio offers you a choice of line patterns and user-defined sizes. You also have the option of several types of rounded corners for boxes. Avagio lets you specify gray backgrounds in 1-point increments from 0 to 100 percent, an unusually flexible feature.

Express Publisher: *Good*

The program's drawing editor covers the basic lines, ellipses, and rect-angles. It does not have freehand drawing capabilities. The program offers a very wide selection of fill patterns (74) and gray screens (14), as well as a reasonable selection of line weights.

Finesse: *Poor*

Finesse's drawing editor creates only lines, limiting its usefulness. You can get rectangles by creating an empty frame and specifying a border for it. You can also choose from eight levels of gray for a frame's background. Finesse's drawing editor does give you a choice of 14 rule weights and types (including several dashed lines) and the ability to place and size rules by coordinate – an unusual but thoughtful feature. Despite these pluses, the incapability to draw basic shapes such as circles and ellipses limits the score for graphics objects.

GEM Desktop Publisher: *Good*

GEM Desktop Publisher's basic drawing capabilities are simple to use, including ellipses, lines, and rectangles. Advanced capabilities include automatic intercolumn rules, user-defined line size, and a choice of three line endings (square, rounded, and arrowhead). You can also specify frame borders, gray screens, and colors.

PFS: First Publisher: *Satisfactory*

In addition to the basic drawing tools, First Publisher provides free-hand drawing, a feature that few others offer. But it has a very limited selection of line sizes and does not have gray screens or fill patterns.

Publish It: VERY GOOD

Publish It has several advanced graphics drawing features as well as the basic ellipses, lines, and rectangles. The program also has a wide range of fill patterns and gray screens.

Performance:
GRAPHICS IMAGES

Avagio: EXCELLENT

Avagio's import capabilities are limited to TIFF, PCX, PIC, and two Unison-specific formats; you can also convert some Encapsulated Postscript files (such as Adobe Illustrator's but not Corel Draw's or Aldus Freehand's) to Unison's own format. Avagio offers typical WYSIWYG sizing and cropping tools.

It also offers several higher-end capabilities, including the capability to mingle text and graphics so that type printing over a graphic automatically changes to white or black (whichever contrasts with the graphic under it) and the capability to print text at user-defined gray levels and with or without outlines. The mingle feature also works with graphics, letting you define the pattern and gray level that will print where separate elements overlap. It also provides 25 fill patterns.

Express Publisher: VERY GOOD

Express Publisher imports seven bit-map formats but only one vector format (EPS). It also can load only small files (those that take less than 64K) – of four of those bit-maps formats: IMG, PCX, Mac Paint, and Compuserve's GIF. Cropping is not available for Encapsulated Postscript or TIFF files. You can reverse any of the bit-map formats supported and edit them with a bit-map editor. You can also export changed versions of the graphics as PCX files – an unusual but welcome feature. The program also offers flip and rotation functions.

Finesse: GOOD

Finesse's program fares better in image handling. It imports the common bit-map formats – TIFF, IMG, and PCX – but only the GEM vector format. Once imported, you can crop and size your image. Like most packages, you can have the program fit the image (to its best ability) in the frame or distort the aspect ratio to match the frame's. When using Finesse, you can also activate a scanning program for use with Logitech's Scanman scanner and directly import scanned images.

GEM Desktop Publisher: *POOR*

The program's image capabilities are very limited. It supports only two graphics formats, GEM Draw's GEM vector and IMG bit-map formats, which limits you to GEM-based art packages. To use popular formats such as TIFF, PCX, or PIC, you can buy filter packs ($15) for each format. Graphics display is also crude compared to other programs.

Graphics cropping is not WYSIWYG; instead, you must select from a dialog box the vertical and horizontal size that you want your image to be, doing so repeatedly until the image is cropped where you want it. A plus is the capability to distort an image to fit the frame, which lets you compress or expand an image along one dimension for special effects. The default setting maintains the aspect ratio and fits the graphic as closely as possible in the frame. Compared to other programs, GEM Desktop Publisher's image handling is weak.

PFS: First Publisher: *GOOD*

The program fares better with graphics images, since it can import several bit-map graphics formats and has sophisticated features such as rotation and flipping, in addition to cropping and sizing. However, because only certain types of TIFF files are supported, we had difficulty importing several TIFF files. The program supports no vector formats (such as Encapsulated Postscript or Lotus PIC). Furthermore, its cropping tool only truly works on high-resolution images. Fortunately, you can fool First Publisher into thinking your image is high-resolution by typing a resolution value of higher than 72 when importing your graphic.

Publish It: *GOOD*

The program imports only four graphics formats. It could not import several of our PCX files (those exported by Corel Draw). We also had problems using IMG graphics: While Publish It imported them, it only displayed the graphics when we had selected the default rescale-to-fit option, which distorts an image to fit the size of the frame containing it. When we selected the option to maintain the original's aspect ratio (the typical setting for a graphic), the image disappeared from the screen. (This problem did not occur with PCX files.) We were informed that technical support has a patch available for this problem. Other limitations include the incapability to crop GEM and PIC files, but the program does offer a bit-map editor so you can retouch IMG and PCX graphics.

Performance:
SPEED

Avagio: *POOR*

The user interface runs at an annoyingly slow pace, (reflected in the change of view times) even on a 386-based computer. You can speed performance a bit by hiding graphics, but even all-text pages redraw slowly. The program's tendency to redisplay text and graphics when you select a frame adds unnecessary delay to the already slow interface.

Benchmarks
Low-End Desktop Publishing Software

	Avagio Version 1.1	Express Publisher Version 1.1	Finesse Version 3.1
Flyer document (two-page file)			
Open document	0:11	0:05	0:06
Jump to last page	0:03	0:02	0:01
Change view	0:07	0:01	0:01
Save & continue	0:05	0:03	0:01
Print	4:50	2:04	5:50
Newsletter document (four-page file)			
Open document	0:15	0:09	0:10
Jump to last page	0:03	0:03	0:01
Change view	0:12	0:01	0:02
Save & continue	0:05	0:05	0:02
Print	9:59	5:16	10:44
Prnbench ASCII			
Flow text	0:13	0:54	0:45

All times in minutes:seconds.

Express Publisher: *POOR*

Express Publisher is the slowest of these programs at text flow. Even on a 20-MHz 386, it is excruciatingly slow for functions such as text wrap. But even simple operations such as applying a style tag or selecting a text frame for editing cause noticeable pauses. On the AT-class machines that we would expect a low-end desktop publishing user to have, the waits are intolerable.

Finesse: *SATISFACTORY*

Finesse performed adequately, usually causing no frustrating or unexpected waits, except when flowing text into a document.

GEM Desktop Publisher Version 2.0	PFS:First Publisher Version 3	Publish It Version 1.12
0:10	0:04	0:06
0:01	0:03	0:02
0:01	0:01	0:02
0:12	0:06	0:04
3:51	0:14	5:01
0:19	0:06	0:20
0:02	0:03	0:02
0:06	0:01	0:04
0:23	0:15	0:12
7:36	37:43	10:30
0:05	0:07	0:31

GEM Desktop Publisher: *GOOD*

The program performed adequately in terms of speed. It is neither blindingly fast nor excruciatingly slow. Text flow is the fastest, and Save and Continue is the slowest. A feature to hide graphics helps keep screen display reasonable.

PFS: First Publisher: *SATISFACTORY*

First Publisher works at an acceptable speed. It frequently displays the wait icon, but the icon usually disappears very quickly. First Publisher is relatively quick in flowing text and changing views; unfortunately it was agonizingly slow when printing our test documents.

Publish It: *SATISFACTORY*

Publish It generally performs quickly. The only time it gets bogged down is when saving files and importing graphics. It was also the slowest in opening our four-page document. An option to hide graphics speeds screen redisplay during layout.

Performance:

OUTPUT QUALITY

Avagio: *Very GOOD*

Avagio's output was the best in this comparison, although not quite perfect. The program supports Postscript and HP Laserjet printers.

Express Publisher: *GOOD*

Express Publisher supports HP Laserjet and Postscript printers up to 300-dpi resolution. The output quality was very nice overall, however the shaded box did not reproduce accurately.

Finesse: *GOOD*

Because of its support for HP Laserjet and Postscript printers through GEM's print spooler, Finesse's output conforms to those printers' standards. The headline font sizes differed dramatically from our test document. Otherwise, the quality was quite acceptable.

GEM Desktop Publisher: *GOOD*

Because GEM Desktop Publisher supports Postscript and HP Laserjet printers, its output is crisp. The fonts were clean; however, the line weight was quite thin.

PFS: First Publisher: *POOR*

The program supports HP Laserjet and Postscript printers. Entering and printing text is difficult because all text in a document must be in one continuous stream. If you enter a headline it will move as text is entered or deleted above it. You can create static text or headlines by specifying them as "graphic text," which renders them as graphic objects. You will lose any high-resolution output; even a 300-dpi Bitstream font will be limited to at most 150 dpi.

Publish It: *Good*

Publish It supports the HP Laserjet series and Postscript printers. The output looks crisp and clean.

DOCUMENTATION

Avagio: *Poor*

Avagio's documentation lacks basic detail about the program and its features. The text is both cursory and badly organized. There is no index, and more than a quarter of the manual is taken up with incidental material like pictures of the 150 clip-art files included with the program.

Among the details missing are how to wrap text around graphics (a manual feature that does not work intuitively) and how to access special symbols such as bullets and accented characters, which the program does support. When features are covered, treatment is often sparse. For example, the explanation of hyphenation settings only incidentally mentions how to insert a discretionary hyphen.

The on-line help menus help but cannot overcome the manual's many weaknesses.

Express Publisher: *Very Good*

Express Publisher's manual follows the basic recipe approach. The organization and exposition are clear, while the appendixes on troubleshooting and system configuration are useful. The tutorial is also very competent.

But the most welcome facet of the documentation is the explicit detail on the program's limitations. This lets you know exactly what you can and cannot do. Most manuals leave out details on what the product cannot do, making you guess whether an omission is not supported or if it is merely not documented. Express Publisher's manual hides nothing.

Problems are few: While basically sound, the index is missing a few index entries (like "symbols"), and the square-bound manual is hard to lay flat while you are using the computer.

This is supplemented by on-line help screens that provide good recaps.

Finesse: *SATISFACTORY*

Finesse's documentation includes a recipe-style format preceded by a quick tutorial. The writing and organization are clear, but the manual lacks background and context that would be helpful for users applying Finesse to their tasks. It also lacks information on Finesse's hyphenation capabilities and accessing multiple printers, but it includes helpful appendixes on symbol and special character sets and on using Bitstream's Fontware installation program. The index is adequate.

The on-line help covers the basics and is a good reinforcement for the manual's material.

GEM Desktop Publisher: *SATISFACTORY*

GEM Desktop Publisher's documentation has adequate technical information, but lacks context to help you understand how things work. The focus is more on learning steps than on the process of using the program as a layout tool. Still, the exposition is clear and organized.

The index is sparse, making it hard to find some information. Helpful details such as a table of extended characters for symbols, bullets, and accented characters – which the program supports – are missing.

The manuals are all square-bound, which makes it hard to lay them flat while using the program. On-line help is almost nonexistent: There are two screens that display keyboard shortcuts.

PFS: First Publisher: *SATISFACTORY*

First Publisher's manual is complete and well organized, with an adequate index and tutorial. Its rec.ipe format tends to neglect explaining the program's use as a layout tool, but the required information is there and is readable. The only problem we had with the documentation was its square binding, which makes it difficult to lay flat. The on-line help is adequate, although many screens simply refer you to the relevant chapter in the manual.

Publish It: *SATISFACTORY*

Like many of its competitors, Publish It focuses on a laundry list of features and a recipe approach to execute them, rather than explaining the process behind them. However, it contains the required information and is reasonably well organized. It also contains useful appendixes covering definitions, extended character sets for symbols and accented letters, and hardware information.

However, the manual contains a claim that the program supports Bitstream typefaces and that it can size text at 72 points. According to a technical support representative, neither claim is accurate for the current version. There is no simple way to use the Bitstream fonts. Timeworks suggests buying the full GEM desktop interface, as Publish It only comes with a run-time version. The capability to size text up to 72 points is dependent on the printer selection. The on-line help screens are adequate for quick reminders.

EASE OF LEARNING

Avagio: *SATISFACTORY*

Avagio's Pagemaker-like interface will help people familiar with that program. Chances are that people familiar with Pagemaker would not be using a low-level desktop publisher. Nonintuitive icons (for example, the plus for text-frame linking) and multiple-meaning icons (for example, the letter "A" is used for both text editing and text-frame creation, not just for text editing, as is typical in other interfaces) can confuse users, especially those unfamiliar with layout tasks. Some odd menu groupings further hinder your ability to learn the program.

The manual's tutorial jumps from one topic to another, making it hard to see connections between tasks and the typical order of layout tasks. For example, the manual describes how to select typeface and size, then graphics import and positioning, and then text entry. The text tasks should be grouped.

Express Publisher: *SATISFACTORY*

Express Publisher's strong manual orientation and awkward layout implementation make it hard to learn layout tasks at first, especially for functions such as style sheets. These are fundamental tasks that newcomers need to learn clearly and fully before they can effectively use a layout program. The major difficulties lie in the use of many icons for many different tasks rather than the usual approach of limiting the number of icons to basic task types, and having the appropriate functions for each task appear (either as icons or menu items) when the task icon is selected.

But the manual and the logically arranged pull-down menus make the other functions – graphics, file management, and typography – easy to learn. While the many icons can be confusing, the manual's tutorial will help guide you to their meaning, as well as explain the different tasks needed to lay out a document.

Finesse: *GOOD*

Finesse is straightforward to learn, thanks to a consistent interface that for the most part is logically arranged. (An exception is the placement of the Select All option in the Frame menu, not in the usual Edit menu.) Because of the GEM interface, most people will be able to concentrate on learning the program rather than its menu structure and icon meanings.

The manual's tutorial also covers enough of the product to help new users become familiar with most of the program's capabilities. While it could go into more detail, Finesse's manual is sufficient to get you going for typical layout tasks.

GEM Desktop Publisher: *Good*

The GEM interface and familiar icons make GEM Desktop Publisher relatively easy to learn. Anyone used to working in GEM applications will be able to start using the program immediately; those used to other graphical interfaces like Windows and the Macintosh will likewise have a head start. Those not used to such an interface will find that the interface's simplicity and intuitive icons let you concentrate on learning the program rather than the interface.

However, there are unnecessary impediments to learning, such as unintuitive grouping of options under the pull-down menus that make you play hide and seek to find the function you want.

A written tutorial helps overcome these oddities by running you through the basic design and layout steps, teaching both the program and its use.

PFS: First Publisher: *Good*

First Publisher is easy to learn, thanks to a combination of limited functionality and a familiar interface. The interface, although unique to this program, resembles most other graphical interfaces. It also uses readily identifiable icons to represent major tasks, helping you select the appropriate action.

The only impediment is the interface's segregation of art functions into low-resolution and high-resolution "layers." The split of graphics into two layers is not intuitive and forces users to remember what resolution a graphic has when they want to select the layer that contains it.

Otherwise, the division of labor among icons and menus is generally well conceived. The manual's tutorial section does a good job of explaining the basics in several steps so you can apply the knowledge from one lesson to the next, while also learning basic layout skills.

Adding to ease of learning is the availability of context-sensitive help.

Publish It: *Good*

Publish It is easy to learn because of its straightforward, intuitively arranged interface. Its use of the GEM interface aids users new to graphical interfaces and users familiar with other interfaces. The program's use of basic icons to represent task types (modes) helps newcomers narrow down their choices when learning functions, and reinforces their understanding that a layout is composed of separate components (such as text and graphics) that are to be integrated in a desktop publishing program.

A quick-start section in the manual aids new users in learning the program and basic layout skills. It is aided by liberal use of screen shots.

EASE OF USE

Avagio: SATISFACTORY

Once learned, Avagio is straightforward to use, thanks to a consistent interface. The capability to define user preferences for how drop-down menus work, the many zoom levels, and the movable toolboxes all aid ease of use. The capability to add and remove toolboxes, some of which display helpful aids like a clock and current cursor position, is also a plus. Another helpful feature is an undo function.

However, the display is difficult to read because of its CGA-level (low-resolution) graphics. (Avagio uses its own graphical interface, not a standard one like GEM or Windows.) The interface lacks feedback to tell you, for example, which file is in the current frame or which tag is applied to the current paragraph. Its slow speed also hinders ease of use.

Express Publisher: POOR

Express Publisher's interface and awkward implementation of layout features hinder the program's ease of use. Interface flaws include not being able to tell which icon has been selected because the icon does not become highlighted (you must rely on the cursor to tell you the current mode), and screen fonts that differentiate boldface and roman text almost imperceptibly for some serif faces at typical body copy sizes.

However, the interface is consistent, the tasks are well organized and offer sufficient aids such as rulers and measurement-unit choices.

Still, the extreme speed problems, and interface quirks will hinder you even after you've learned the program.

Finesse: SATISFACTORY

Finesse is easy to use. The capability to set preferences such as menu type (pull-down or drop-down) and rulers is helpful. Unfortunately, settings are not saved for future documents and you are limited to inches and millimeters as measurement units. Oddly, you can use the text tool only in normal view, not in the full-page or facing-pages views; this makes it hard to select all text on a page. The screen fonts do not distinguish between types of serif and types of sans serif (for example, between Dutch and Charter or Swiss and Universe – see the Glossary appendix for the terms serif and sans serif), making it hard to tell what your final document will look like or what typefaces are being used.

GEM Desktop Publisher: *Poor*

Although straightforward to use, GEM Desktop Publisher suffers from oddities in its user interface. The most awkward is the disappearance of the text frame when you are in text editing mode. This removes feedback on how close you are to the edge or bottom of your text frame until you actually reach it. The limitation to inches and millimeters for line spacing is a consistent annoyance, as those measurements are both nonstandard and inappropriate. Also, if you alter preferences through the Set Preferences dialog, you must also invoke the Save Preferences dialog to make these changes permanent from each session – an extra, easily overlooked step.

There are some good features in the interface, including the capability to load another GEM application directly from GEM Desktop Publisher. Another nice option is a status dialog box that shows how much disk space and memory you have, as well as how many frames and files have been used and loaded.

The lack of error messages for the nonfunctional text-import filters, and the requirement that you use DOS-level batch files to convert your word processing files, seriously hinders use in this key area.

PFS: First Publisher: *Good*

First Publisher is easy to use. The use of function-key equivalents for major functions will help users new to mouse-based applications. The menu options and tools are straightforward, so you can concentrate on the task you're trying to accomplish rather than the set of steps needed to implement it.

However, the interface does have some quirks. When highlighting text, we had to place the text icon below the text, not on it, as is standard elsewhere. Also, the new capability to set up fonts directly from First Publisher is marred by the fact that the program does not return to the layout you were working on (although it does save it), which is a natural expectation. But these are minor problems.

Publish It: *GOOD*

Publish It is straightforward to use, thanks to its clean interface. Its tools work in a straightforward manner, so they don't get in the way of the task you're trying to complete. Menu options are likewise organized so you don't have to seek out the option you want from a confusing arrangement. Publish It's unassuming interface is one you don't really notice – which means it's doing what it should.

Helpful features include the capability to customize some settings, such as ruler and dialog-box units. Unfortunately, these preferences are not saved for later sessions.

ERROR HANDLING

Avagio: *SATISFACTORY*

Avagio prompts you to save your changes before quitting. The error messages we encountered were simple and to the point.

Express Publisher: *GOOD*

Express Publisher prompts you to save if you try to exit after making changes, and its error messages are clear.

Finesse: *SATISFACTORY*

Finesse's error messages are generally clear. If you try to quit after making changes, the program prompts you to save your work.

GEM Desktop Publisher: *GOOD*

GEM Desktop Publisher consistently checks to see if you have saved before quitting. It also automatically writes any changes to your text made during layout to a coded ASCII copy of your word processor file each time you save. This preserves your original file in case of severe mistakes. The only difficulty we had was the lack of an error message when trying to use the nonfunctional text-import filters.

PFS: First Publisher: *SATISFACTORY*

First Publisher's error messages are clear. The program always prompts you to save your changes. However, each time you save, it asks you if you want to overwrite the file name; this prompt is not necessary in this situation.

Publish It: *SATISFACTORY*

We found Publish It's error messages to be adequate. The program always prompts you to save before you quit your document. Unfortunately, it always prompts you, even when you've made no changes. Also, when saving a current document, it asks if you want to overwrite it. The program's inability to distinguish exiting with unsaved changes from a normal exit, and saving a modified version of a file from overwriting a separate file, are annoying and potentially dangerous. A user may ignore the prompts and thus eventually abandon changes or overwrite a separate file accidentally. These flaws hurt the program's score.

SUPPORT POLICIES

Avagio: *Good*
Unison World offers unlimited support via a toll-free number from 8 a.m. to 5 p.m. Pacific time, Monday through Friday.

Express Publisher: *Satisfactory*
Power-Up Software offers unlimited technical support to registered users through a toll number.

Finesse: *Good*
Logitech offers non-toll-free unlimited technical support seven days a week, as well as BBS support.

GEM Desktop Publisher: *Poor*
Digital Research provides 90 days of free (but not toll-free) support, which includes mail, fax, and Compuserve. After the 90 days, support is available for $95 per year, which includes a toll-free number.

PFS: First Publisher: *Very Good*
Software Publishing offers unlimited technical support, although the number is not toll free. SPC also offers fax and BBS support as well as a 30-day, money-back guarantee.

Publish It: *Poor*
Timeworks offers 60 days of free phone and fax support, by toll number, Monday through Friday, 8 a.m. to 5 p.m. Central time. An extended support plan that includes a toll-free number is available for $100 per year. Timeworks also offers a 90-day usability warranty under which you can return the program if you are unhappy for exchange with any other program (you have to pay any difference in price).

TECHNICAL SUPPORT

Avagio: *Good*
Our calls were answered immediately. The technician (the same one handled all our calls) knew the basic product; when our questions went

beyond that knowledge, he asked a programmer for the details. He also stayed on the phone while we tried out his suggestions. However, he occasionally made minor mistakes in his statements.

Express Publisher: *SATISFACTORY*
We found the technicians to be knowledgeable but in some instances brusque. For example, technicians did not offer work-arounds to product limitations unless we persisted in seeking them. However, we did encounter one exception, when a technician spent 15 minutes to reproduce our environment to find the answer to our problem. We had no difficulty getting through to the support hot line. Because of the inconsistency of the technical support, we limited the score.

Finesse: *GOOD*
The support technicians answered questions readily and were clear on the program's limitations, offering work-arounds when available. The support lines were occasionally busy but not frustratingly so.

GEM Desktop Publisher: *SATISFACTORY*
Technicians were knowledgeable and answered our questions correctly. They were familiar with the product and typical user configurations, and made suggestions based on that knowledge. On several occasions, we could not get directly to a technician and had to leave a message, but technicians called us back promptly – always within a few hours.

PFS: First Publisher: *GOOD*
Technical-support staff was knowledgeable and answered our questions easily. Of the three technicians we spoke with, two anticipated further questions and volunteered helpful advice; the third needed to be asked obvious follow-up questions but knew the answers. Once we were put on hold for an extended time, and we were given the option of leaving a message after the first five minutes.

Publish It: *SATISFACTORY*
The quality of technical support was adequate, but technicians often did not gather enough detail to offer appropriate solutions to our problems. They also often had to ask colleagues for information. However, the technicians were willing to spend the time to see the solution through and were helpful in offering background and hints once the problem was identified. The support lines were occasionally busy, but we had no undue difficulty getting through.

VALUE

Avagio: *GOOD*
At $299.95, Avagio is the most expensive product in this comparison; however the strong graphics capabilities and nice layout features balance the price.

Express Publisher: *SATISFACTORY*
An inexpensive ($149.95) but feature-rich program, Express Publisher would be a good value if its flaws (awkward interface, extreme slowness, and difficult to learn) weren't so conspicuous and didn't affect so many basic operations.

Finesse: *SATISFACTORY*
At $179, Logitech is not bargain-priced, but neither is the price exorbitant for its features set. If your needs are simple, Finesse could be the product for you. Overall, Finesse is an adequate package.

GEM Desktop Publisher: *POOR*
At $299, GEM Desktop Publisher is the second-highest-priced low-end publisher. Added to that price is the cost of the import filter packs you will need. Its flaws and the lack of an update since fall 1988 – and the continued presence of bugs – diminish its value in a competitive market.

PFS: First Publisher: *POOR*
Although inexpensive ($149), First Publisher does not offer all of the features a low-end desktop publishing program should offer. It does have some impressive graphics features but the layout and typography features are weak.

Publish It: *VERY GOOD*
At $199.95, Publish It is well priced. The overall capabilities are strong, and the program is easy to learn and use. Version 1.2 of Publish It is scheduled to ship by the end of June, 1990. Several features are added or improved in the new version.

Product Summaries
Low-End Desktop Publishing Software

Avagio Version 1.1
Company: Unison World, 1321 Harbor Bay Parkway, Alameda, CA 94501; (800) 444-7553.
List Price: $299.95.
Requires: IBM PC, PS/2, or compatible; MS-DOS 2.1 or later; 640K of RAM; graphics card; hard disk; mouse.

Express Publisher Version 1.1
Company: Power-Up Software Corp., 2929 Campus Drive, San Mateo, CA 94403; (800) 223-1479 in CA, (800) 851-2917 outside CA.
List Price: $149.95.
Requires: IBM PC, PS/2, or compatible; MS-DOS 3.0 or later; 640K of RAM; graphics card; hard disk; mouse.

Finesse Version 3.1
Company: Logitech, 6505 Kaiser Drive, Fremont, CA 94555; (415) 795-8500.
List Price: $179.
Requires: IBM PC, PS/2, or compatible; MS-DOS 2.1 or later; GEM/3 operating environment (run-time version included); 640K of RAM; graphics card, hard disk; mouse.

GEM Desktop Publisher Version 2.0
Company: Digital Research Inc., 70 Garden Court, P.O. Box DRI, Monterey, CA 93942; (800) 443-4200.
List Price: $299.
Requires: IBM PC, PS/2, or compatible; MS-DOS 2.1 or later; GEM/3 operating environment (run-time version included); 640K of RAM; hard disk; graphics card; mouse recommended.

PFS: First Publisher Version 3.0
Company: Software Publishing Corp., 1901 Landings Drive, Mountain View, CA 94039; (415) 962-8910.
List Price: $149.
Requires: IBM PC, PS/2, or compatible; PC-/MS-DOS 2.1 or later; 512K of RAM (640K recommended); hard disk recommended; mouse recommended.

Publish It Version 1.12
Company: Timeworks Inc., 444 Lake Cook Road, Deerfield, IL 60015; (708) 948-9200.
List Price: $195.95.
Requires: IBM PC, PS/2, or compatible; MS-DOS 2.1 or later; GEM/3 operating environment (run-time version included); 640K of RAM; graphics card, hard disk recommended; mouse recommended.

Deciphering Desktop Publishing Terms Is Half the Battle

BY GALEN GRUMAN

Accessible desktop publishing tools have brought an arcane dialect to the masses. Not too long ago, only publishing professionals knew – or cared to know – what pica, kerning, crop, or PMS meant. Now almost anyone who wants to produce a nice-looking report or a simple newsletter comes across these terms in the layout programs' menus and manuals. Unfortunately, these terms are not always used correctly in manuals, or they are replaced with general terms meant to make nonprofessional users feel less threatened. Here is some of the basic terminology, grouped by publishing task – become familiar with them and you'll feel a lot more comfortable making desktop-publishing small talk.

TYPOGRAPHY CHARACTERS:

A *font* is a set of characters at a certain size, weight, and style (for example, 10-point Palatino Bold). It is now often used as a synonym for *typeface*, which is a set of characters at a certain style in all sizes, weights, and stylings (for example, Palatino). A *face* is a combination of a weight and styling at all sizes (for example, Palatino Bold Italic). A *font family* is a group of related typefaces (for example, the Franklin family includes Franklin Gothic, Franklin Heavy, and Franklin Compressed).

Weight describes a typeface's thickness. Typical weights, from thinnest to thickest, are ultralight, light, book, medium, demibold, bold, heavy, ultrabold, and ultraheavy. There are three basic stylings: *Roman* type is upright type; *oblique* type is slanted type; and *italic* type is both slanted and curved (to appear more like calligraphy than roman type). Type may also be expanded (widened), condensed (narrowed), or compressed (severely narrowed).

The *x-height* is the height of the average lowercase letter (based on the letter X); the greater the height, the bigger the letter looks compared to other letters in typefaces with a smaller x-height but the same point size. The *cap height* is the size of the average uppercase letter (based on the letter C).

A *descender* is the part of a letter that goes below the baseline (as in a q); an *ascender* is the part that goes above the x-height (as in a b). A *serif* is the horizontal stroke used in giving letters visual character, such as those used in the upper left and bottom of the letter p in a typeface such as Times. *Sans serif* means the typeface does not use these embellishments (such as Helvetica).

SPACING:

Leading/line spacing is the space from the base of one line (the baseline) to another. (Leading is named after the pieces of lead once used to space out lines).

Tracking/letter spacing is the overall space between letters within a word; if you increase tracking, space increases globally. Word spacing defines the preferred, minimum, and maximum spacing between words.

Kerning is an adjustment of the space between two letters to accommodate the letters' shapes. For example, you would have tighter kerning between TO than between OO because TOO looks better if the o fits partly under the t. Pair kerning is a table of letter pairs that you always want kerned by the program.

Justification adds space between words (and sometimes letters) so each line aligns at both the column's left and right margin. Ragged right and flush left both refer to text that aligns against a column's left margin but not right margin; ragged left and flush right text aligns against the right margin but not left margin. Centered text has equal space on both margins. Justification also means the type of spacing: justified, ragged right, centered, or ragged left.

Vertical justification adds space between paragraphs (and sometimes between lines) so that the tops and bottoms of each column on a page align. (This is often confused with *column balancing,* which ensures that each column has the same number of lines.) *Carding* is a vertical-justification method where the space added between paragraphs is in one-line increments. *Feathering* uses fractional-line spaces between paragraphs.

MEASUREMENT UNITS:

A *pica* is a measurement of column and page width and depth. A pica is just under one-sixth of an inch (it is usually rounded up to one-sixth). A *point* is a measurement of type size and space between lines. There are 12 points in a pica, so there are about 72.27 points to the inch (again, it is frequently rounded down to 72 points per inch).

An *em, en,* and *thin* space are, respectively, the horizontal space taken up by a capital M, capital N, and lowercase t. An em space is the same width as the current point size, an en half of that, and a thin space half again. In other words, for 12-point type, an em is 12 points wide, an en six, and a thin space three. A figure space is the width of a numeral (in most typefaces, all numerals are the same width to make tables align naturally), which is usually the same as an en.

PARAGRAPHS:

You typically mark a new paragraph with an *indent*, which adds space (an em space in newspapers and magazines) in front of the paragraph's first letter to set it off. An *outdent* moves the first character past the left margin and places the other lines at the left margin; it is typically used in lists. A *block indent* moves an entire paragraph in from the left margin, such as in a long quote. A *hanging indent* is like an outdent except that the first line begins at the left margin and all subsequent lines are indented.

A *bullet* is a character (often a filled circle) that shows a paragraph as one element of a list; it can be indented, outdented, or kept at the left margin. A *drop cap* is a large capital letter, used at the beginning of a section or story, that extends down several lines into the text (the rest of the text wraps around it). A *raised cap* is the same as a drop cap except that it does not extend down into the text; instead, it rests on the baseline of the first line.

Style sheets are named sets of attributes such as spacing, typeface, indent, leading, and justification that you can apply to your paragraphs. You *tag* each paragraph with the style-tag name you want to apply to it, and any formatting changes made to the style's definition are automatically reflected in all other paragraphs that have been tagged.

HYPHENATION:

A *hyphen* splits words at the end of a line and joins words that combine to modify another word. Hyphenation is determining where to place the hyphen in split words. Consecutive hyphenation determines how many lines in a row may end with a hyphen; more than three is considered bad typographic practice. *Hyphenation zone* defines how far from the right margin a hyphen may be inserted to split a word. An exception dictionary lists words with non-standard hyphenations; you can add words that the default dictionary does not know or override the default hyphenations for words like "project" that are hyphenated differently as a noun *(proj-ect)* than as a verb *(pro-ject)*. A *discretionary hyphen* in a word tells the program to hyphenate that word at that place if that word must be split; it affects only the word it is placed in.

LAYOUT ELEMENTS:

Layout is arranging the text and graphics elements on a page or series of pages. A *column* is a block of text. If there is more than one column side by side, there is a *gutter* of space (usually 1 or 2 picas in a newspaper or magazine) between them. The *margin* is the space between the edge of a page and the nearest standard block of text. For visual effect, text or graphics can intrude into the margin.

A *wrap* is a text cutout, where the column is intruded by graphics or other text. Rather than overprint the text, the column's margins are altered so the text goes around the graphic or other text. A wrap can be rectangular, polygonal, or curved, depending on what it is wrapping around and the layout program's capabilities.

A *folio* is the page number and identifying material (such as month or publication name) that appears at the bottom and/or top of every page.

White space is the part of the page left empty to create contrast with the text and graphics, providing visual relief and emphasizing the text and graphics.

A *frame* holds layout elements on the page. Most desktop publishing programs use frames for their elements. Using a mouse, you can select frames to delete, copy, resize, or otherwise manipulate them in your layout. You can create a template for repeat use by using empty frames and defining style tags in advance.

IMAGE MANIPULATION:

Cropping an image means selecting a part of it for use on the page. *Sizing/scaling* an image is determining the amount of reduction or enlargement of the image (or part thereof) used. With layout programs, you can often *distort* an image to size it differently horizontally than vertically, which achieves special effects such as compressing or stretching an image.

Reversing (also called *inverting* in some programs) exchanges black and white, which is like creating a photographic negative.

TOOLS:

Galleys are single columns of type. They are typically used to proof hyphenation and errors and to show the authors of books what the text will look like for correction before it is laid out.

A *grid* is the basic layout design, including standard positions of folios, text, graphics, bylines, and headlines. A layout artist adapts each story to the grid, modifying the grid when necessary to each layout. It is also called a *template*. A *dummy* is a hand-sketched layout of a particular story. *Guidelines* show where columns and margins typically are on the grid. In some programs, guidelines are nonprinting lines you can use to ensure that elements align.

An *overlay* is a piece of transparent paper or film laid over a board for overprinted material such as text or graphics and to indicate screens in a different color. Some programs have electronic equivalents.

PRODUCTION:

Registration marks tell a printer where each negative should be positioned relative to other negatives (the registration marks must line up when the negatives are superimposed). *Crop marks* tell a printer where to cut the negatives; nothing outside the crop marks is printed. Crop marks are used both on full pages to define the page size and on images to show which part of the image is to be kept.

A *screen* is an area to be printed at a particular percentage of a color (including black). For example, the border of a page may have a 20-percent black screen. 100-percent black would be solid black; zero-percent black would be white; a 20-percent black screen will look like a gray background, handy as a background for highlighting a boxed item such as a table.

Spot color is a single color applied at one or more places on a page, such as for a screen or as part of an illustration. You may have more than one spot color per page. Spot colors may be process or PMS colors. A *process* color is one of the four primary colors in publishing: black, yellow, magenta, and cyan. A *PMS* (Pantone Matching System) color is an industry standard for specifying a color; the printer uses a premixed ink based on the PMS number you specify; you look up these numbers in a table of colors. *Four-color* is the use of the four process colors in combination to produce most other colors; most magazines and newspapers use four-color. A *color separation* is a set of four photographic negatives – one filtered for each process color – shot from a color photograph or image that when overprinted will reproduce that image. A *build* is an attempt to simulate a PMS color by specifying the appropriate percentages of the four process colors and overprinting them.

How We Tested Low-End Desktop Publishing Software

Evaluating the Elements of Low-End Desktop Publishing Packages

To test these affordable packages, which are aimed at less-ambitious publishing projects rather than full-sized books and manuals, we created a four-page newsletter, "Fanning the Flames," that included a graphical logo (in IMG format); an oval cutout between two columns; a contents box with a drop shadow and screen; two self-contained stories; two stories that jump to subsequent pages; intercolumn rules; and folios (page number, publication name, and issue date). The layout included captions for the artwork to be entered by hand in the desktop publisher. Our newsletter's look was predefined so we could try to implement the same grid – its margins, column sizes, paragraph styles, and typeface choices – on all publications.

We used the built-in Helvetica typeface (or variants such as Bitstream's Swiss, depending on the program) for headlines, captions, folios, and continued lines.

We used WordPerfect and Microsoft Word for imported text, but not all programs supported Word. For those programs that did not support TIFF or PCX graphical formats for the art, we used other bit-mapped formats like IMG, generating them through Inset's Hijaak graphics translator.

We also created another newsletter for a bicycling club. This newsletter was more free-form so we could experiment with individual strengths and weaknesses to judge range and versatility. All tests were performed in the InfoWorld Test Center on a Compaq 386 20e with 4 megabytes of RAM and a 110-megabyte hard drive, VGA, and a Microsoft-compatible serial mouse.

Our evaluation was divided into the usual InfoWorld software review categories, with the performance category adjusted to meet the needs of desktop publishing users, based on InfoWorld reader surveys and previous comparisons.

PERFORMANCE:

The *layout* category measures the functions that handle the positioning and sizing of the publication's text and graphics elements, as well as related features such as text wrap, text flow, page numbering, page orientation, and page views. For a satisfactory score, the product should include the capability to lay out multiple columns of text, link text from column to column and page to page, and wrap text around graphics. We award bonus points for the automation of these layout features; the use of style sheets or similar mechanisms that implement formatting changes throughout a document; the capability to position and size layout elements by coordinate; snap-to guides; and rulers with user-selectable measurement units.

Word processing: This category covers both the program's inherent text-editing capabilities and the capability to import word processing files. Text editing basics include cut, paste, and insert, as well as formatting italics, boldface, and other character attributes. Other essential criteria for a satisfactory score include the capability to import text with basic formatting (boldface, italics, and underlines) retained for at least three of the following word processor formats: WordPerfect, Microsoft Word, DCA/RFT, and WordStar. We award bonuses for additional attribute support (like double underline and subscripts); import format support; automatic export of changes to either the original file or to a copy of it; search and replace; and word processing functions like spell checking, table of contents generation, and index generation.

Continued on page 222

Features
Low-End Desktop Publishing Software

■=Feature present □=Feature not present	Express Avagio Version 1.1	GEM Publisher Version 1.1	PFS: Finesse Version 3.1
Minimum RAM	640K	640K	640K
Hard disk space used	4.2MB[2]	1.8MB	350K[3]
Minimum MS-DOS Version	2.1	3.0	2.1
Layout			
Style sheets	■	■	□
Automatic text flow	■	□	□
Automatic wraparound	■	□[5]	■
Nonrectangular wrap	□	■	□
Position by coordinate	□	■	■
Working views	8	1	3
Facing pages	□[6]	□[6]	■
Rulers	■	■	■
Guidelines	■	□	■
Page numbering	■	■	■
Text			
Import formats (excludes ASCII)	4	4	5[7]
Microsoft Word	■	■	■
RFT/DCA	□	■	□
WordStar	■	■	■
WordPerfect	■	■	■

1 For higher resolution you need 640K with Publish It.
2 Avagio includes 2.8 megabytes of sample graphics files.
3 The GEM/3 operating environment takes an additional 500K.
4 Layout approximates a style-sheet capability.

Desktop Publisher Version 2.01	**First Publisher** Version 3.0	**Publish It** Version 1.12
640K	512K	512K[1]
750K[3]	2.6MB	1.6MB
2.1	2.1	2.1
■	■[4]	■
■	■	□
■	■	■
□	□	□
■	□	■
4	1	5
■	□	■
■	■	■
■	■	■
■	□	■
6[7]	10	7
■	■	■
■	■	□
■	■	■[7]
■	■	■

5 Wrap must be manually invoked for each frame in Express Publisher.
6 In Avagio and Express Publisher this is a preview mode only; you cannot edit in this mode.
7 Does not retain formatting such as boldface and italics with some imports.

InfoWorld Software Buyer's Guide

■=Feature present □=Feature not present	Express Avagio Version 1.1	GEM Publisher Version 1.1	PFS: Finesse Version 3.1
Quote conversion	□	□	□
Dash conversion	□	□	□
Exports edits	■	□	□
Hyphenation	■	■	■
Discretionary hyphens	■	■	■
Exception dictionary	□	□	□
Contents/index generation	□	□	□
Search and replace	■	■	■
Typography			
Supplied typefaces			
(HP Laserjet/Postscript)	5	3/12	5
Kerning	■	■	■
Tracking	□	■	□
Bullets, symbols	■	■	■
Automatic drop caps	□	□	□
Graphics Imports			
Bit map import formats	3	7	3
GEM IMG	□	■9	■
MacPaint	□	■9	□
Paintbrush PCX	■	■9	■
TIFF	■	■	■
Macintosh Pict	□	□	□
Graphics Editing			
Bit map editor	□	■	□12
Drawing (vector) input formats	3	1	1

Desktop Publisher Version 2.01	First Publisher Version 3.0	Publish It Version 1.12
□	□	□
□	□	□
■	■	□
■	□	■
■	□	■
■	□	■
□	□	□
□	□	■
9/11[8]	16	7/8
■	□	■
■	□	■
■	□	■
□	□	□
3	6	2
■	□	■
□	■	□
■[10]	■	■
■[10]	■[11]	□
□	□	□
□	□	■
4	0	2

■=Feature present □=Feature not present	**Express** **Avagio** Version 1.1	**GEM** **Publisher** Version 1.1	**PFS:** **Finesse** Version 3.1
Encapsulated Postscript (EPS)	■13	■	□
GEM Draw GEM	□	□	■
Lotus PIC	■	□	□
Windows Metafile	□	□	□
Drawing editor	■	■	■
Tools			
Basic (ellipses, lines, rectangles)	■	■	□
Advanced (polygons, curves, free-hand)	□	□	□
Scaling/resizing	■	■	■
Cropping	■	■14	■
Fill patterns	25	74	6
Gray-scale screens	100	14	8
Output			
HP Laserjet (PCL)	■	■	■
Postscript printers	■	■	■
Can use downloaded fonts	■	■17	■
Other			
On-line help	■	■	■
Undo	■	■	■

8 Symbol font must be installed manually in GEM Desktop Publisher.
9 Express Publisher, MacPaint, IMG, and GIF formats are limited to files using less than 64K of RAM.
10 GEM available through Digital Research. CGM and PXF also available ($15 each).
11 First Publisher does not support all common versions of this format.
12 In scanning mode with Finesse.
13 Avagio uses a conversion utility that supports limited formats.

	Desktop Publisher Version 2.01	First Publisher Version 3.0	Publish It Version 1.12
	☐	☐	☐
	■	☐	■
	■10	☐	■
	☐	☐	☐
	■	■	■
	■	■	■
	☐	■	■
	■	■	■
	■15	■16	■14
	0	0	36
	8	0	9
	■	■	■
	■	■	■
	■	■	☐
	☐18	■	■
	☐	■19	☐

14 Cropping not available for TIFF or EPS files in Express Publisher or for GEM or PIC formats in Publish It.

15 Not WYSIWYG with Desktop Publisher.

16 First Publisher works only with high-resolution artwork (more than 72 dpi).

17 Express Publisher is only for dot-matrix and HP Laserjet printers.

18 Desktop Publisher is limited to two screens of keyboard shortcuts.

19 For certain functions First Publisher is context sensitive.

InfoWorld Software Buyer's Guide

Continued from page 215

Typography covers the controls over character appearance. This is an area that few low-end programs excel in. The program must let you set sizing and spacing, including tracking, kerning, hyphenation, leading, indents, tab settings, and justification. We subtract points from programs that do not support style sheets or a similar global mechanism for implementing formatting changes. We award bonuses for the capability to set different attributes for different style tags; sophisticated hyphenation features such as exception dictionaries and discretionary hyphens; support for downloadable fonts; and support for special symbols such as typographic quotes and bullets.

The *graphic objects* category evaluates the program's capability to draw basic shapes such as circles and rectangles required during layout. It also examines the features available for drawing rules, placing screens over text, and boxes around text. The criteria for a satisfactory score include the capability to draw, move, and resize ellipses, rectangles, and lines, as well as placing gray screens over text and drawing boxes around text. We award bonuses for more sophisticated capabilities such as free-hand drawing, mirroring, and rotation.

The *graphic images* category evaluates the programs' capability to crop, scale, size, and manipulate imported images, as well as the range of supported formats for import. Important criteria for a satisfactory score include cropping; resizing that preserves the original image's aspect ratio; cut and paste; and support for at least two popular bit-map formats – for example, GEM IMG, Mac Paint, Paintbrush PCX, and TIFF – and at least one popular vector format such as GEM Draw, Encapsulated Postscript, Lotus PIC, Mac PICT, or Windows Metafile. We award bonuses for wider import support, bit-map editing, and the capability to distort an image during resizing. We subtract points for non-WYSIWYG implementations.

Speed: We scored speed by comparing the results of all the packages' performance in five basic tests: opening a document, jumping to the last page, redrawing the screen, save/continue, and placing a text file in an existing document. We weighted more heavily on functions that are used more frequently, such as change view and flow text.

Output quality measures the clarity and precision of the output compared to the screen and the printer's capabilities, as well as against the other programs in the comparison. InfoWorld editors and test center technicians compared output from the various packages printed on an HP Laserjet II. Special attention was given to output factors such as graphics placement and scaling, line accuracy and precision, headline placement, typography, and other features.

Other scoring categories follow our standard procedures.

CHAPTER SEVEN

Analyzing Relational Databases

InfoWorld measures nine well-known DOS multifile databases for the right mix of power and convenience.

BY NICHOLAS PETRELEY, CONTRIBUTING EDITOR,
WITH ZOREH BANAPOUR AND LINDA SLOVICK, TEST CENTER
AND JUDY DUNCAN, REVIEW BOARD

When InfoWorld began exhaustive comparisons of relational databases several years ago, a small group of competing products had begun to challenge, but not yet to shake, the strong hold that Ashton-Tate's dBASE held on the DOS personal computer market. Today, that hold is weakening, with interesting results.

In this comparison of single-user PC relational databases, we look at dBASE IV and eight other well-known packages that offer a variety of venues for building a powerful PC database. Broadly speaking, they fall into two groups: those intended strictly for development work, and those that are also appropriate for interactive use by everyday users without first requiring them to build an application.

Paradox and R:BASE are strong contenders for dBASE's market. Paradox takes a middle-of-the-road approach; equally suitable for novices and experts, it's the best all-around product for both interactive and development use.

R:BASE 3.0 boasts a well-rounded design for both building applications and interactive use, including the power of Structured Query Language (SQL) in an ANSI Level 2-compatible implementation. Unfortunately, MicroRim seems to have ignored Ashton-Tate's Dbase history lesson and has released R:BASE 3.0 before it is quite ready – though it adds some improvements and is not nearly as unstable as the original version of dBASE IV, R:BASE has its share of bugs. On the

223

bright side, R:BASE 3.0 is not nearly as slow as we originally feared.

This version of DataEase, touted primarily as an easy-to-use interactive product, offers noticeable improvements from previous versions, but DataEase is still quirky after all these years. It is basically a good product, evidenced by its capability of surviving in the market even with numerous ease-of-use glitches, but we won't be fully satisfied with DataEase until the edges are smoothed out.

FoxPro, the update of FoxBase Plus, is one of only two truly dBASE-compatible products in the group. FoxPro out-dBASEs dBASE in design, looks, and functionality, and produces the most dazzling programs of any interactive dBASE-compatible product. As with R:BASE, though, interactive features are not FoxPro's primary selling point.

Wordtech Systems' dBXL is the other dBASE-compatible product here and is priced at less than $250 – roughly a third of the cost of most of the others. A simple interpreter originally created to compete with dBASE III Plus, dBXL is no fancy dancer, but it has some unique advantages, such as the availability of a companion compiler product.

Informix's Smartware II Database, a separately offered component of the Smartware II integrated software package, is the unexpected gem of the bunch. Though we're not fond of the interface, which makes it one of the most difficult-to-use products here, Smartware has overall the most polished feel. This version boasts the most dramatic improvements and gets one of the biggest boosst in scoring.

Among the developer-only products, Clarion Professional Developer is capable of using dBASE data files directly, but it is not dBASE-language compatible. An extremely full-featured professional developer's environment, Clarion has the best set of tools for heavy-duty, data-heavy applications generation.

Informix-SQL, a minicomputer-heritage database system, sports the most plain-Jane interface, but it also gives you full SQL support for the most query power per line of code. Its stripped-down interface is built for speed – of creation, if not of execution.

We also include dBASE IV, version 1.1, the leading member of the family that continues to dominate the installed base of PC database applications. Much improved over its buggy, unreliable predecessor, version 1.1 ranks somewhere near FoxPro as an interactive development system.

Several of the products in this comparison are on the brink of updates or improvements that will have a major impact on value, according to the vendors; many will have been released by the time you read this book (the world of PC software moves quickly). For example, many of the glitches we complain about in R:BASE 3.0 will, its vendor says, be mended in Version 3.1, due out in November, 1990. dBXL just began bundling (but not in time for inclusion in our review) at no extra charge Concentric Data's R&R Relational Report Writer, a much-needed addition. A version of DataEase that will translate the program's query language commands into SQL will be available in mid-1990 as a front end for Microsoft-Sybase's SQL Server database server. Versions that will support Oracle and IBM servers and DB2 will follow, according to DataEase.

EXECUTIVE SUMMARY

As the bottom line, we found in this comparison quite a few top relational-database competitors that, while similar in many respects, offer a range of powerful and convenient production database environments suitable for different users.

This group of relational-database products represents the finest in the category. With this high-caliber lineup, you'll have to make your pick based almost entirely on need and personal preference. Notice, however, that it isn't always the products with the highest profile or the most comfortable laurels that are the best choice for reliable, quick database performance.

Paradox is the high scorer, and one of the highest-scoring products we've ever reviewed. Uniquely the volks database, for novice or expert, Paradox is the productivity choice for users who prefer an interactive environment. From a standing start, you'll get results from Paradox before other products finish plowing through their tutorials. Learning with Paradox slows to a more conventional pace only with the most complex, sophisticated applications. In any event, Paradox is capable of handling the most challenging tasks.

Close behind is **Clarion Professional Developer.**

While Paradox gets you out of the starting gate faster, Clarion will get you polished, flexible database applications more quickly, once you're over the learning curve. It's a comprehensive set of integrated development utilities that provides the shortest distance between you and an attractive, bulletproof database application. The utilities are superb; Clarion puts all other form designers to shame. Interactive users, please note: Clarion is for professional developers only.

FoxPro and Informix-SQL run neck and neck in our scoring. FoxBase Plus had an interface so lean it could inspire a benefit rock concert, but users won't even recognize that product in the new Fox-Pro, which features a brilliant mouse-driven windowing interface to the speediest dBASE-compatible package available. There are some exquisite features here, as well as a few limitations and shortcomings, but this is as good as dBASE compatibility gets, and then some.

Informix SQL offers industrial-strength query power. This power is integrated into a set of tools for building relational-database applications. You have to get your hands dirty in this production line; the tools are honed for relational power, not ease of use. Development takes on the steady pace and regularity of a factory, and the look of Informix applications have about as much charm.

The **Smartware II Database** pleasantly surprised us as one of the best overall offerings, with vast improvements over its old version in speed, relational power, and cosmetic flexibility. It is still a weaker product than many stand-alone relational database products, but not by much. The new features make it much better equipped to stand on its own, and make it worthy of consideration for developing solid relational database applications.

Though not as well-rounded as Smartware, **dBXL** also has some important capabilities. dBXL is the best deal for dBASE III Plus fans on a budget. dBXL is one of the dBASE-compatible products in the group. It's reasonably quick alone and offers the added attraction of being usable with a companion compiler product (Wordtech's Quicksilver).

R:BASE 3.0 is an outstanding blend of interactive SQL and SQL-based database applications development. As such, R:BASE teeters on the brink of being a remarkable product. It's all the more of a shame, then, that this version suffers from poor memory management and a number of bugs that have not yet been addressed. It needs some fine tuning. Our advice on this one is to wait until 3.1 comes out.

DataEase is one of the quickest ways to develop simple relational applications. Compared to similar products, though, DataEase still manages to fall short of the mark in some places. Its programming language is not as full-featured as R:BASE's, for example; and it has a rough feel to it, often behaving like a product that was seemingly written by programmers who bit off more code than they could chew. Though promising, DataEase needs an upgrade to take care of the problem areas before we can wholeheartedly recommend it.

dBASE IV is finally a viable product with version 1.1, but it is lagging behind in the very race it started nearly two years ago. At its introduction, dBASE IV 1.0 represented a major step in the evolution of the dBASE standard. To be sure, it was noticeably behind much of the other competition even then, but when it came to dBASE language and file compatibility, it was poised and ready to leap ahead of dBASE compatibles Foxbase, dBXL, and Clipper. Then the bugs, design flaws, and performance problems surfaced.

Ashton-Tate is calling dBASE IV 1.1 a smaller, faster, more reliable dBASE IV. Indeed, it is a faster product overall, and most of the problems have been fixed. But having been given a preview and then nearly two years lead time while Ashton-Tate was busy producing the working version, the competition is singing "Anything you can do I can do better" to Ashton-Tate's repeat performance of "I did it my way." FoxPro, a dBASE IV compatible product, has a template language, includes a far better forms and applications designer, and it is faster and easier to use. dBASE IV has the check-mark QBE facility, but Paradox does it much better. dBASE IV lets you use SQL on dBASE files, but Dquery does that much better, and so on.

The bottom line is, the fixes in version 1.1 make dBASE IV a reasonable option — but when it comes to features, performance, ease of use, and yes, even dBASE compatibility, there are better choices.

When it comes to relating information across tables, Paradox comes closest to combining SQL query power with ease of use, though the cost is space-eating answer tables from complex queries. R:BASE's SQL-flavored language lets you easily select data to the screen, but only for queries involving two tables at a time. The dBASE-compatible crowd is the most limited in this regard, because it can't do anything complex without first indexing the fields. And finally, everybody in this group runs faster than Informix, but no one can go as far in relational querying as Informix can.

INTRODUCTION

DataEase

A few years ago, when its simple relational capabilities and limited storage capacity compared well to competitors like Rapidfile and PFS:File, DataEase was in its glory. When it graduated to a heftier relational design and greater data handling capacity in Version 4.0, DataEase brought a unique simplicity to the world of multifile databases, even though it still had the feel of a more primitive product.

Report Card
Single-User Relational Databases

	Clarion Professional Developer 2.0	dBASE IV 1.1	FoxPro 1.0
Performance			
Relational data entry	Excellent	Poor	Excellent
Relational querying	Good	Good	Good
Relational reporting	Excellent	Very Good	Very Good
Programming language	Excellent	Very Good	Very Good
Speed of relational operations	Excellent	Good	Excellent
Documentation	Very Good	Very Good	Excellent
Ease of learning	Very Good	Very Good	Good
Ease of use	Excellent	Good	Very Good
Error Handling	Excellent	Good	Satifactory
Support			
Policies	Good	Very Good	Very Good
Technical Support	Good	Satifactory	Satifactory
Value	Excellent	Good	Very Good
Final scores	**9.0**	**6.3**	**7.7**

With Version 4.2, DataEase adds some important new features. However, some ease-of-use and reliability problems that plagued Version 4.0 remain.

With this version DataEase comes as two separate executable programs: one that uses expanded memory for menus and caching, and another that can take advantage of up to 16 megabytes of extended memory.

Clarion Professional Developer
An inventory of features included in the Clarion Professional Develop-

Informix-SQL 2.10.06	Paradox 3.0
Very Good	Excellent
Excellent	Excellent
Very Good	Excellent
Excellent	Excellent
Satifactory	Very Good
Excellent	Excellent
Very Good	Excellent
Good	Excellent
Very Good	Excellent
Satifactory	Very Good
Very Good	Very Good
Very Good	Excellent
7.6	**9.5**

er would read like a more ambitious version of the InfoWorld wish list we had for the original product. Clarion has exceeded all our expectations. Since we last looked at Clarion 2.0, updates of the product have resulted in several enhancements. We continue to be impressed by the Designer, an applications generator that generates code from the screens you draw. This is one hard-to-resist development package.

Clarion has every imaginable utility to accelerate the creation of an attractive, bulletproof database application. dBASE developers who have been looking for an excuse to find another programming environ-

Report Card
Single-User Relational Databases

	DataEase 4.2	dBXL 1.3
List Price	$750	$249
Performance		
Relational data entry	Very Good	Poor
Relational querying	Excellent	Satisfactory
Relational reporting	Very Good	Satisfactory
Programming language	Very Good	Very Good
Speed of relational operations	Very Good	Good
Documentation	Good	Very Good
Ease of learning	Excellent	Very Good
Ease of use	Satisfactory	Good
Error handling	Poor	Good
Support		
Support policies	Very Good	Good
Technical support	Poor	Satisfactory
Value	Good	Very Good
Final scores	**6.5**	**6.0**

ment need look no further. Clarion can read and write dBASE files directly if necessary. The Clarion file format is more robust, though, and Clarion provides a convert utility to make the switch.

One key to understanding Clarion is to appreciate the fact that it is entirely a development environment, not an interactive database package. It has no ad-hoc querying or reporting facilities. Everything you want to do, you generate code to do — and, if you're a developer, you enjoy every minute of it.

R:BASE 3.0	Smartware II Database 1.0
$725	$449
Excellent	Very Good
Very Good	Good
Excellent	Excellent
Excellent	Very Good
Satisfactory	Excellent
Excellent	Very Good
Excellent	Satisfactory
Very Good	Good
Satisfactory	Very Good
Very Good	Good
Satisfactory	Satisfactory
Good	Very Good
7.7	**7.5**

dBASE IV (1.1)

dBASE IV Version 1.0 was such an improvement over dBASE III Plus that its introduction was met mostly with enthusiasm. The Control Center was actually easy to use — a dBASE first. The query-by-example module that Paradox made so popular on the PC was a welcome move. dBASE IV introduced a more versatile screen and reports designer, and replaced an obscure utility with a real applications generator. The production index file was perhaps least visible but very significant. It was the first step taken by Ashton-Tate to eliminate the need for continual reindexing as a characteristic of dBASE applications.

As dBASE IV Version 1.0 received a more rigorous workout over

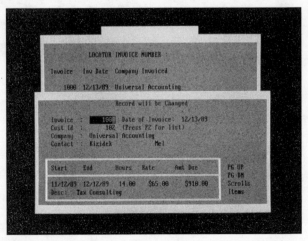

This Clarion application, with a looking screen linking two files and a three-file one -to-many relation data entry screen, was built within The Designer in less than an hour.

time, however, the importance of all these issues was undercut by a steady stream of glitches. In a few short months, owners of dBASE IV found themselves participants in one of the biggest unplanned beta-test project the software industry has ever seen.

After more than a year of waiting, dBASE IV, Version 1.1 finally arrived. Our evaluation shows that Ashton-Tate appears to have kept its promise to deliver a stable, working version of the product. As with any major new software product, we found minor glitches. But the basic product functionality that has been promised all along is here. The product must now withstand the tests of time and thousands of dBASE users.

A number of new features have been added to Version 1.1 in order to enhance its memory management and performance. dBASE IV now requires a minimum of 450K of free memory (down from 514K in Version 1.0). A new dynamic memory manager handles overlays better and releases more memory for application space. An optional integrated disk cache uses extended or expanded memory to cache data and overlays. Performance-tuning options allow users to balance memory requirements against speed.

Other improvements include conditional indexes, several new language commands, and removal of the limitations on user-defined functions and On commands.

For multiuser systems, a new command lets you check how long a record has been locked and who created the lock. The browse and edit screens now have access to the Organize menu, which allows you to build and select indexes as you work. The QBE module has been improved and printer support expanded. When using SQL (structured query language), users can now browse data tables and run reports or queries.

dBXL

dBXL offers some features that are unique in the world of dBASE-compatible interpreters. The most prominent of these is the capability of creating graphs from your data files. With a few simple menu selections you can display information from up to 40 records in a pie, bar, step, line, scatter, or regression line graph. dBXL also was the first dBASE-compatible product to provide text-based windowing support (followed by dBASE IV and FoxPro). You can define, display, and move up to 99 independent windows.

Most dBASE products offer either an interactive environment or compiler, but rarely both. You can use dBXL with Quicksilver, Wordtech's separately sold companion compiler product, to develop, debug, and compile your applications, a convenience offered by few dBASE products. Wordtech also just began bundling Concentric Data's R&R Relational Report Writer (not available at the time of our review) with dBXL, an addition that should alleviate some of dBXL's report writing limitations. Here we look only at dBXL.

FoxPro

FoxPro is the most sensational dBASE-compatible product we've ever seen. The core of the program is a character-based windowing system that Fox Software calls an "event-driven" interface because you can jump from any window to any menu or to any other window.

FoxPro also includes a set of development tools, including a well-rounded forms designer and applications generator called Foxview, which is based on a highly customizable template language. Also included is Foxdoc, a utility that will analyze your application and produce a document describing various aspects of the program, such as tree structure and data dictionary.

FoxPro can run in dBASE-compatible mode. We were able to run several dBASE IV programs with only a half-dozen changes, and FoxPro ran these programs without a hitch and consistently better than dBASE IV could. FoxPro unquestionably has the better design overall, but dBASE IV has a few advantages here and there. Most notably, FoxPro may be the only interactive relational database left that won't maintain your index files unless you specifically activate them.

It is virtually impossible to list all the new features in FoxPro. The top of our list would probably include full dBASE III Plus compatibility (Fox Software claims more even than dBASE IV), EMS support, the capability to run in 512K of memory, the debugging tools, the applications and document generator, the template language, and, of course, the new interface.

Informix-SQL

Informix-SQL is one of several interrelated database development products from Informix Software. Its companion package Informix-ESQL-C (reviewed along with Informix-SQL in our April 10, 1989, multiuser relational database product comparison, Page 65) is an embedded C product for C programmers who want to further customize their applications. There's also the Informix-4GL Rapid Development System-Interactive Debugger (reviewed April 18, 1988, Page

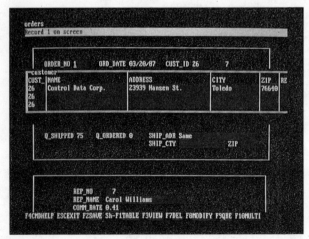

In DataEase you can reference related files during data entry by splitting the screen to show linked form.

37), a fourth-generation language database programmers' tool that uses nonprocedural statements to create a database. In this comparison we look at Informix-SQL.

Informix-SQL and its siblings are available on multiple operating systems (mostly flavors of Unix); one of its major selling points is that code developed on any platform can be run with little or no change on other platforms. An uninspired screen appearance is the price extracted for this universality. (The 4GL system produces applications that are a little more PC-like, with simple pop-up windows and limited key trapping.)

Though of the no-frills variety, the Informix-SQL development tools are powerful, and they do the job in a clean and straightforward way that we found a pleasure to use. The major utilities are integrated into the menu-driven program ISQL; the rest are accessible through the DOS command line. An interactive SQL module is provided to create, edit, execute, save, and retrieve SQL command files.

Paradox

Paradox 3.0 accomplishes one of the most impressive feats ever seen in the history of relational database products. It gives new users instant gratification. Better still, it has the staying power to keep you hooked and keep you busy until you've become an expert.

As a database development system, Paradox seems to have something for everyone; along with dBASE, and to some extent FoxPro, Paradox is useful for ad-hoc querying, but it still offers a strong language for the would-be programmer.

R:BASE 3

Historically a strong product that competes with Informix-SQL in SQL power, and with Paradox in PC interactive ease of use, R:BASE adds many worthwhile new features with Version 3.0. R:BASE now sports a fully ANSI Level 2-compatible SQL, a pull-down menu interface operable by mouse or keyboard, and a query-by-example (QBE) system. Otherwise, much of the rest of the original design is intact: Transaction processing is supported, and you still build tables, views, forms, reports, and applications pretty much the same way as before. Cross tabulations are possible, and the full range of what Microrim calls "super-math" functions are there.

R:BASE 3.0 is still rough around the edges – there are bugs, error handling is not up to par, and the program now requires 520K of free memory, up from 460K. However, MicroRim promises quick fixes with Version 3.1, due out in August (as we were going to press). This version will return memory requirements to approximately 460K and will remedy many of the other problems and bugs we mention here, according to the vendor.

Smartware II Database

The Smartware II Database is one module excised from Informix's Smartware II integrated software package, which includes spreadsheet, word processor, communications, and programming language (we reviewed the whole thing in *InfoWorld* August 14, 1989, Page 45.) The Smartware II Database (purchased separately) gives you the database module plus a simple text editor, the macro and programming language, communications, and a few extra goodies (such as a calculator).

Of all the products in this comparison, Smartware has grown the most since we last looked at it. Many of its inconveniences and severest limitations are gone. There are several new useful features, including some important relational capabilities. Smartware II handles memory management better than most of the other products compared here. It requires only 512K of RAM in a single-user configuration (though it performs better with 640K), and will take advantage of expanded memory.

Smartware lacks a true database applications language, and is still a little weak in its implementation of some of its relational capabilities, but it is a more refined and useful database product than ever before.

Performance

DATA ENTRY

Clarion Professional Developer: *EXCELLENT*

The way you create a data entry screen in Clarion will vary, depending on whether you're writing the code yourself or using the Designer to build an application. If you program it yourself, you create the data entry screen by pressing a special key from within the editor. If the definition for a screen does not exist at the cursor location, a new one will be created. At this point, the screen becomes a canvas for designing a data entry form. When you're done with the design, you are returned to the source file, where Clarion has already interpreted your work into equivalent source code.

You can access as many database files as you want in a Clarion form. The Designer will let you specify up to three files in addition to the master used for the form. The Designer is surprisingly friendly for creating links and lookup fields, and offers appropriate choice lists of fields and index keys. If you're not using the Designer, there are no limits to the number of files you can include in a form, but you'll have to write all the code that links the files.

When you add or edit a field, you interact with a pop-up window where you specify all the field's attributes. Field types include but are not limited to display fields, data entry fields, and repeat fields for easy access to arrays. You can even embed menus within a data entry form.

The range of customization available in form design is truly phenomenal. Even when you look just at the field level, much of what you'd have to code into a database program is specified in the form. This is even more so if you're using the Designer. Variable name, field name, field color, color when selected, and picture format are mere child's play in Clarion.

You can also specify a help screen; determine which field will be selected when you back up; how the field will react when you fill it; and even whether the Num Lock key should become active when you enter the field.

Once you use the Clarion Screener, no other form-design utility ever looks the same. This is as good as it gets. We rate Clarion an enthusiastic excellent in relational data entry.

DataEase: *VERY GOOD*

Data tables and data entry forms are created with equal utility in DataEase. When you create a form, DataEase creates the necessary data files and index files. This is a compact process that lets you define data files, data entry forms, data validation criteria, and index specifications all in one step.

After all the data files are created, relationships can be established to tie the files together. DataEase has a variety of methods for entering data in multiple tables. You can embed in a main form a number of subforms, which will reference data in related files according to the relationships you establish. If you don't set up subforms, you can still reference related files during data entry in a handy, though visually unappealing, ad hoc fashion: When you press the appropriate key, the data entry screen will split, and a linked form will appear within the open space. You can also bring up a linked table as a list from which you choose the entry for the current field.

You enter the criteria for data validation when you create or edit the field on the form. You can have the form offer a list of predefined entries when you fill in a field. If you wish to browse through data via the data entry forms, you simply type the criteria you want DataEase to use right into the data entry fields.

DataEase allows you to set search criteria in a data entry form, and then view and edit a matching record in the form, or view and edit all the matching records in a table. The one thing DataEase won't do is allow you to place formulas, even simple ones, in fields of the form.

(You can place formulas in fields on the form as search criteria when using the query-by-example, or QBE, feature; however, you cannot edit the resulting records.)

DataEase has added features to enhance data entry, and has cured many of the bugs that plagued it in our previous review; however, there still are a number of loose ends, including problems caused by altering values in lookup fields (see ease of use category).

dBASE IV 1.1: *Poor*

dBASE IV will not allow you to enter data into more than one file at a time without writing custom programs to do so. Using the screen designer, you can create read or write forms and forms for multifile views, but if you relate two or more files, then the forms will be read-only.

Data-entry control is quite extensive, with a large collection of formatting templates and functions. Edit options let you specify a prompt, error message, range, and validation for each field. A rather unusual option lets you specify under what conditions a field can be edited. Calculated screen fields can be defined, but the formula cannot reference another calculated field – a severe limitation. Calculated fields are not updated until the record change is complete.

The screen painter has most of the common features for boxes, lines, and color control required to create attractive data entry forms. We found screen manipulation to be somewhat awkward and sometimes frustrating. Area moves are performed by pressing F6 to select the area and then F7 to move it. The area remains selected after the move is completed. Pressing the delete key when the cursor is in the currently selected area will delete the area – quite a surprise when you were just trying to delete a character. Similarly, if you press the delete key when the cursor is on a calculated field, the field is removed from the screen and the field's definition is also deleted.

The whole point of using a relational database is to have relational capabilities. We find the continuing lack of nonprogrammed multifile data entry a disappointment. Relational data entry receives the same score as Version 1.0: poor.

dBXL: *Poor*

For the most part, dBXL matches piece for piece the facilities offered by dBASE III Plus. The one feature you don't get is the capability to draw screens and create the corresponding format files. (Format files are used to present a visually appealing screen design when the user adds or edits records in interactive mode.) dBXL will use and support format files, but you will have to program the contents of the files by

R:BASE 3.0 offers a "Browse" view of data in its query-by-example system, but you cannot save the layout.

hand or use a third-party product to create them.

You can design a format file with a multidatabase view to browse related files. The contents of up to 10 related database files can be displayed. However, if a one-to-many relationship exists, only the first matching record will be displayed.

Format files can also update the contents of more than one file, but this type of use is not advised, as there are no controls to ensure that related files are updated properly.

dBXL does not completely ignore screen creation. One utility allows you to create and modify window screen image files, and another command will retrieve the saved image and display it on the screen. However, this facility is most useful in programming and does not affect interactive data entry.

dBXL's browse mode operates the same as it does in all the dBASE clones, with some added unique frills. The No Append command prevents you from adding records; No Modify disallows changes; and No Follow keeps the cursor in place when a record is reindexed (instead of allowing the cursor to follow the changed record).

Although all of its limitations can be overcome with programming, dBXL has little to offer in interactive relational data entry.

FoxPro: *EXCELLENT*

The Foxview forms designer is light years ahead of the dBASE IV equivalent. You can specify up to 10 related files, and define all the relationships, index files, and index specifications from within Foxview. When the application is generated, the appropriate Set Relation To statements will be written for you. You can also create and use a format file that will build the commands to display a relational data entry form, and even add a few maintenance features in the programming if you like.

There are a couple of specifications that have not yet been implemented to change the way code is generated. For example, Foxview lets you specify the relationship as one-to-one or one-to-many, but this setting has no effect on the code produced. This is an intentional omission and is documented as such.

There are some really nice touches in Foxview that make the dBASE IV forms designer thoroughly obsolete by comparison. Not only are you free to use fields and objects that aren't already defined, but you can use the form design you create as the basis for a database file to be created by Foxview. This is especially useful for those developers who build on their ideas at design time. Bad programmers can get into a lot of trouble here if they neglect a few steps, but a programmer will never feel hemmed in by the imposed limitations.

The Foxview forms designer is somewhat object-oriented. Forms are created from text, field, and variable objects that can be moved around the screen individually or in groups. Each field becomes an entry in a table where they are assigned various controlling and formatting attributes. These attributes specify the validation checks, field formatting, and even user-defined functions to be performed on the field.

FoxPro pulls out all the stops in dBASE form design. It imposes none of the traditional dBASE data entry limitations. Building a relational data entry form for dBASE files has never been so easy, nor have there been so many features for doing so.

Informix-SQL: *VERY GOOD*

Informix-SQL handles data entry through a program called Perform. Data entry forms are all do-it-yourself, and what they look like will depend on the capabilities of your text editor (no text editor is included). There is a new feature that lets you choose from seven foreground colors (eight minus the background) for field text. As limited as this sounds, it's more color than you'll get anywhere else in Informix.

The form descriptions consist of several segments that describe the different aspects of the form. These include the database used, the tables, a text representation of the actual screen image, the field definitions and their attributes, and any special instructions on handling data entry. Despite the unglamorous nature of this approach, it does make forms self-documenting. You can glance at a form description and see everything from field validation checks to the table relationships used

— and even what should happen to data before and after an update operation.

The attributes segment is where fields are assigned table and column names. You also place data lookup instructions, validation, and format instructions here. The instruction segment includes the commands that control the flow of data entry, including data validation and some error handling.

Once the form is compiled, the Perform module turns it into a query-by-forms program. Here is where you find a set of rows to edit, add rows, or delete rows. The only real weakness in Perform is that it requires you to edit each table on a multitable form separately. Perform indicates which table is active by placing brackets around its fields, and by displaying the table name and its position in the order of tables.

The form definition is a simple yet robust means of directing data entry for a multitable form. Editing complex forms can be keystroke intensive, as both form creation and use will require frequent trips through menus. The best part is that once you know the format and syntax it is very easy to combine related tables into a form.

Paradox: *EXCELLENT*

Paradox offers all the features you'll need to build an attractive data entry screen. It's no Clarion, but it does have a few things that go beyond the basic. There is a really nice feature available to add multirow fields to a form. This creates a minitable within a form, which can be used as the "many" side of a one-to-many relationship.

Most of the time you don't design one data entry form that includes all the fields from related tables. Instead, you design a smaller form for each of the tables involved and then link the forms into the one for the master table. At data entry, you see all the forms combined into one screen, but you edit the fields for each table separately. While this sounds like the same inconvenience you find in Informix, there are important differences. Unlike Informix, Paradox forces a visual grouping of fields by table. Moving through tables and rows is just a one-key operation in Paradox, whereas you'll have to jump back and forth between the data entry screen and menu in Informix.

Another way Paradox can perform multitable data entry is through a method often associated with set-oriented SQL. Instead of editing data in the various tables in real time, you create one big temporary table with all the fields you need. You can fill this table with data, or just use the structure to add new data. Either way, when you're finished working with the table, you distribute the changed or added data back to the original tables. Using the menus, the whole process takes several steps the first time you do it, fewer after that. If you use the Personal Programmer to set this up, some steps will be automatic.

Paradox has what it takes at every level. It makes relational data entry easy whether you're putting together a simple form, or designing a way to automate relational data distribution using imported files.

R:BASE 3: *EXCELLENT*

R:BASE lets you edit single tables using the QBE module, but the best way to edit multiple tables is through R:BASE forms. The R:BASE forms editor is not our favorite, but it is about the easiest way to get a combination of linked tables on-screen for editing. Even setting up one-to-many relationships is a breeze.

New to R:BASE 3 forms are pop-up submenus that allow you to select the data to be entered into a field. You go to the form field, press the proper key, and a menu will display some subset of the data for that column in the table. If you preprogram a SQL Where clause, the data will appear automatically. If you don't, the word Where will prompt you to type in a Where clause to narrow the search before the data appears. These menus are not as flexible as we'd like; they don't allow you to define data that isn't already in the database. They are convenient, however, because they don't require any programming.

Editing data through R:BASE forms has always entailed a slightly different procedure than with other products. You usually select the records you want to edit before displaying the form. You can move forward or backward one record at a time, but you can't jump to the beginning or the end of a subset of data. If you want to jump directly to any given record from within a form, you must complete your edit session and begin the whole process again. This technique imposes no real limitations on the data you can edit; however, it is now slower than ever.

R:BASE 3 now supports auto-refresh for multiuser applications, which automatically updates your screen with the most current data input by other users. R:BASE 3 also can now automatically number your rows of data, and descriptions can now be associated with columns.

All things considered, R:BASE 3 still has all the data entry capabilities of its predecessor. The new interface isn't as responsive, but at the same time there are a few additional goodies included in this version.

Smartware II Database: *VERY GOOD*

As with DataEase, you create the data file structure in Smartware by creating a form, and you specify the field validation and display criteria when you create the field. You can control the order of the fields at data entry.

Creating the data entry screen is a little convoluted when compared to most products, but this is mostly a side effect of the Smartware database being designed primarily for use in an integrated product environment. You have to go through a few more steps than usual to create a data entry screen, and a few extra steps to activate it later on.

There is a lot of flexibility for multifile data entry, though the methods for designing a screen are not very intuitive. Smartware is a multiwindow product, with each window containing a view of your data. A view can display data from one or more data files. You can place fields from multiple files in a single view and then link those files, or you can link a number of windows that are simultaneously on-screen, with each window containing its own view of data. Either way, the relationships can be one to one or one to many. A one-to-many relationship within a single view is cleaner than linking windows, since using a browse window for the "many" side will cause Smartware to display more data than you really want to see (you will see the related records, plus whatever follows those records).

Smartware now includes some features that add to data integrity control. You can define a rule for each field, which consists of a formula to check the contents of a field. You also can define a pop-up value selection menu for a field. This version has some additional cosmetic flexibility as well. For instance, you can set individual field colors, or paint all the fields at once.

Though it's not as streamlined as it could be, we like Smartware's multifile data entry capability, and the new convenience features are helpful. Smartware has come a long way from its original score of poor.

Performance

QUERYING

Clarion Professional Developer: *Good*

The table lookup capability of the Designer is a very powerful method of finding a record in one file or a set of related files. One of the simplest means of finding a record is also one of the most elegant. If you include a Locator field on the table, the highlight bar will home in on matching records as you type, displaying a closer match with each additional keystroke. You can design a table to include an entry field and use that information to search for a record.

You can also write more powerful lookup queries right in the table definition. The table can be designed to take data entered by the user and place it in a conditional statement. The conditional statement will evaluate true or false, and the result determines which of two query statements will get the data for the table.

Still, complex queries will usually have to be hand-coded. Fortunately, the language is streamlined for flexible data retrieval. Memory tables and indexes can be created as well. These features afford much greater control over data handling than you can get out of a query language or query-by-example technique, but you pay for it in programming.

Clarion is not an interactive product, but the language gives you excellent tools at the level of detail for which Clarion is designed. We discovered that the lookup table has more going for it than our prior comparison gave it credit for. It isn't a relational query machine, but the lookup table could be an important link to such queries.

DataEase: *EXCELLENT*

DataEase handles querying with little trouble. Once you set up your relationships between forms, DataEase pulls data from just about anywhere you like. Even if you do not have an established relationship, DataEase can handle ad hoc relationships within queries, and can even look up data in unrelated files.

When it comes to viewing data in read-only fashion, DataEase relies on its reporting features: You simply reroute the output of the report to the screen, instead of the printer.

There are several different ways to build queries through reports. DataEase's QBE mode allows you to fill out a form with a search specification and print the results to the screen or printer. For more complex queries, there's the DataEase Query Language (DQL). Results from DQL programs are also routed through the report specifications, and can be viewed on-screen or printed. The formatting of data for viewing is more print-oriented than screen-oriented, but a little fudging here and there will produce attractive screen presentations of data.

Despite the occasional quirk and limitation (see Ease of Use) we still like the wide range of methods used to query data in DataEase.

dBASE IV 1.1: *GOOD*

Relational Querying: dBASE IV's query facility implements a query-by-example (QBE) interface similar to the one so popular with Paradox users. Up to eight files can be related and queried by pointing to fields in a diagram. To link files, you specify by placing matching labels in the common fields of the files to be related. A file can be related to itself to perform a self-join.

dBASE IV does not include an optimizing query engine. To perform a query, it writes a program. If an index does not exist for a linking field, one will automatically be created. The index is created when the query is saved. If you are working with large files, this means it can take a surprisingly long time to do the initial save of the query, even if it is not executed. This index tag is not removed when the query is deleted. As we observed in our earlier reviews, these indexes will be maintained unless you manually remove them (to prevent performance degradation).

The QBE interface lets you easily control which fields are included in the resulting view. Filtering operators provide comparisons, Soundex searches, pattern matches, and aggregate functions. The Group By operator lets you group records for summary information. Up to 20 calculated fields can be defined per view. The results of a query can be saved to a new database if desired.

Queries involving multiple files cannot update data. However, the update query lets users perform global file updates on a single file to replace, mark or unmark for deletion, or append a group of records specified by the query conditions. The append update is particularly appealing since it lets you easily transfer data from a target to a source file when the field names do not match.

We used dBASE IV's SQL interpreter to run several test queries. Although it performed most of them correctly, it returned invalid results for a correlated subquery. (Changing the default to Set Exact On will solve this.) Version 1.1's relational querying capability is much improved over 1.0's.

dBXL: *SATISFACTORY*

dBXL can perform queries through the menu-driven Intro module or in command mode. In the Intro module, you are limited to a single related file. You can specify a filter on the master file and choose fields to display from either the master or the related file.

In command mode, you can open and relate up to 10 database files. The Set Relation Additive command lets you relate more than one child file to a given parent file. The information displayed during a query is controlled by the Set Filter and Set Fields commands. The filter lets you specify the conditions that a record must meet to be included in a query. The fields specification controls which fields are displayed for any of the list commands. The Create Query command provides a menu-driven environment to specify filter conditions and save them in a file for later use. Once the files, relations, and filter are established, you can save the entire setup in a view file with the Create View From Environment command.

As with relational data entry, when a one-to-many relationship exists, only the first record that matches the parent file's key field will be retrieved during a query. To obtain all of the detail records, you will have to turn the relationship around so that the file with many records for the same key is the parent and the file with a single record per key is the child.

The dBASE environment has never been very good for performing relational queries, and dBXL hasn't done much to improve it. The interactive filter construction provided by Create Query is a useful aid, but its capabilities do not begin to compare to products like Paradox, R:BASE, and Informix-SQL.

FoxPro: *Good*

FoxPro is not a query machine. It doesn't support even the dBASE IV query-by-example system, so queries will have to be coded individually. Like dBASE IV, a different Set Filter can be applied to each open database, which helps. Filters can also be set as a part of the indexing scheme.

The FoxPro interface is a very friendly way of setting up several database files and establishing relationships between them. The mouse-driven features will also let you set filters for each of the files. You can build the equivalent of queries this way, but it will take a lot more know-how and work than in Paradox or R:BASE.

We would go so far as improving the score over dBASE III Plus due to the additional features in the interface and Foxview. But relational queries aren't up to what dBASE IV introduced in the QBE module.

Informix-SQL: *Excellent*

Multiple table queries can be made through the Perform module. You enter conditions to filter the data in the fields on a form. Perform does a few impressive tricks here using designated characters to denote special conditions like highest and lowest values. Once the data is in, you can then step through the rows that are retrieved and edit them using the same form.

In addition, you can write your own brand of SQL in Informix using the interactive SQL facility. This module lets you test the queries and then save them as command files when you're happy with them. The command files can later be integrated into an application or an Ace report.

All of the power of SQL is present here; the complex outer joins, nested query statements, correlated subqueries — the works. Informix has none of its competitors' limitations; in fact, the test procedures are child's play compared to the query possibilities. The test queries and much more complex queries can be performed in one Select statement, with or without indexed fields, and with or without saving the results for later use.

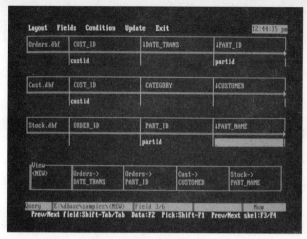

A Paradox-like QBE table query system is available in dBASE IV. Results of its queries, though, cannot be edited and redistributed to related tables.

SQL is not as easy to use as query by example, by any means. When it comes to sheer range and depth of query power, though, Informix is the clear winner in this group. Add the capability of Perform queries to the power of the Informix-SQL, and that equals a relational querying score of excellent.

Paradox: EXCELLENT

Queries are of the query-by-example variety. You create them by placing check marks, examples, and instructions in an Ask table. The queries will perform updates on existing tables or, in the case of a question, produce an answer table.

Paradox has it all over the competition when it comes to the ease with which a multitable query can be built. The distance between creating a two-, three-, and four-table query is little more than a few keystrokes in Paradox. R:BASE can only handle two tables at a time; more involved queries must be handled in several steps. When it comes to sheer query power, though, we haven't gone deeply enough into either to say, but Informix-SQL seems to have the edge.

Paradox can do some pretty impressive tricks with queries, though, and they can get equally tricky to construct. Queries can start sounding like calculus word problems; for example, ``In one step, how do you get the names of only those customers who have ordered parts that cost over $1,000, when the prices are in one table, the customer's orders are in another, and the customer names are in another?'' This is actually quite easy in Paradox if you know what to do. An SQL afficionado will also find it to be a simple task, one that's made easier, some might argue, due to the closer resemblance SQL has to the language of the question. We're not aware of how you'd do it in one step using R:BASE, and we're confident you couldn't come close using the dBASE language.

Paradox will take some getting used to if you're planning on very complex queries, but it is one of the few that can handle them with such finesse.

R:BASE 3: *VERY GOOD*

R:BASE 3 offers a variety of ways to query data. First and foremost, there is the new SQL capability. If you know enough SQL to get started, R:BASE 3 will usually take up the slack, even on complex queries. For example, if you type the queries yourself, R:BASE 3 has a function to list the table and column names if you forget them, and then type the ones you want into your query or program. This is a valuable convenience feature.

R:BASE 3 continues to support read-only multitable views (a limitation of ANSI Level 2 SQL). Paradox stays one step ahead of R:BASE 3 in this respect by letting you combine multiple tables, edit the merged data, then redistribute the updates to the proper source tables.

Microrim has faithfully followed the current trend by including a new QBE system. The Browse function has been integrated into the QBE system. You can also format columns that appear in the browse table, and lock, resize, hide, and rearrange them.

The only thing you cannot do is save the layout once you're happy with it. If you know in advance how you want the table to appear, you can record your changes in a script, but replaying that script gets to be tedious when you have to run it every time you want to browse a table in the desired layout. (The capability to save a layout is a planned enhancement, according to Microrim.)

Also due to be fixed is a bug in Rbdefine that will sometimes abort your queries if you perform secondary indexes from that module.

With the implementation of ANSI Level 2 SQL, R:BASE 3 has raised its query power one more step. The QBE module is a welcome addition, and except for the oversight in being able to save the layouts, we like using it.

Smartware II Database: Score: *GOOD*

Smartware isn't the obvious product to pick for complex ad hoc queries, but much of the power is there if you are willing to uncover it. We created two- and three-table queries by opening a window for each table, linking the windows, and then constructing the queries as reports that used the relationships set by the linked windows. You probably won't see this technique anywhere else, but it works quite well.

Smartware also can perform union, intersection, nonintersection, and subtraction queries by placing the results of the queries in a new table. This more complex query process is somewhat confusing when compared to an easy-to-use product such as Paradox, but it can be mastered in time.

Smartware isn't without its occasional design glitch. When you perform a Relate command, Smartware often insists that you provide alternate names for duplicate field names in queries, even when there really is no obvious duplicate. The program has enough information to skip this step; however, the designers simply chose not to use it. (Version 1.02, released during this comparison, fixes this problem, according to the vendor.)

We're not satisfied with every aspect of the Smartware interface when it comes to querying, but Informix has greatly expanded its query capabilities and power.

Performance
REPORTING

Clarion Professional Developer: *EXCELLENT*
Clarion handles relational reports in the same way it does relational data entry. When you create reports from within a source-code file, the Reporter takes over. You place fields and draw tracks much like you would in the Screener. Here, too, Clarion gives you extraordinary control over customization. Control sequences can be sent to the printer before and after virtually every field that appears in the report.

There's no limit to the number of files you can access in a report. If you use the Designer, you can include things like printing by groups in key order without having to write code. If you create a report from within the editor, the Reporter module is used for the visual design of the report. You'll have to do the rest of the programming that controls the sort order and groups.

The Designer will take control of high-level report tasks if you like, but if you'd rather code it yourself, Clarion has all the tools you'll need to create an attractive report in the Reporter module.

DataEase: *VERY GOOD*
You can create a quick report on an ad hoc basis, or program a more complex report using the DataEase Query Language (DQL). Reporting is so closely tied to querying in DataEase that most of the criteria we use to score one can be applied to the other. The primary difference is

the wider range of print formatting you get when sending the output of a query to a printer.

The DataEase language does not support the elimination of duplicate values in queries; however, you can trick the program into displaying your answers as "distinct." You do this by cutting out all of the normal "detail" field items that comprise a report. Instead, place the fields you want to view in the summary area (which DataEase calls the group trailer), normally used to display subtotals and the like for a group of records. This undocumented technique will get DataEase to print only one item for each set of duplicates.

DataEase does the job at reporting, though it is somewhat uneven. Sometimes it is extraordinarily easy to produce brilliant results, and sometimes you have to use extra ingenuity and effort (as with making query results distinct) just to get a simple report.

dBASE IV 1.1: *VERY GOOD*

dBASE IV's report writer and label facilities let users create almost any type of output by painting the design on-screen and making menu choices. Reports can access multiple related files by using views created with the query facility. The band-oriented report writer is used for columnar, form-oriented, or mail-merge reports. Labels are created with a separate module.

You can add calculated fields to your report using any expression including previously defined memory variables. There are four types of calculated fields: named, hidden, summary, or unnamed; named calculated fields can be referred to in the formulas for other calculated fields. The calculation type and field position affect the order of evalu-

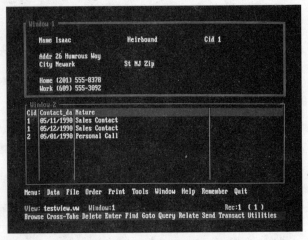

Smartware II Database lets you link data entry windows in a one-to-many relationship.

250

ation. You can put page breaks in any band. Groups can be based upon field contents or created every n records — unusual, but very useful.

dBASE IV uses printer drivers and therefore supports several print styles and up to five user-specified fonts. A special output function lets you write control codes directly to the printer when necessary without affecting row and column counts. Printer option selections can be saved to a file for easy reuse. Users may find that the report writer alone justifies dBASE IV's purchase.

dBXL: *SATISFACTORY*

dBXL offers columnar reporting almost identical to that in Dbase III Plus. You can specify groups and subgroups with the choice of totaling numeric fields on group breaks. Data from up to 10 related database files can be presented. File relations and filters must be established external to the report definition. The user is responsible for restoring the appropriate file settings before running the report. As with relational querying, in order to get the detail records from a one-to-many relationship, you will need to make the file containing the detail records into the master for the report.

Report specification in dBXL improves somewhat on dBASE III Plus; its on-screen diagram defines various parts of the report, such as group headers and how they will appear. Field placement is controlled solely by the specified column width. For anything more elaborate than a simple columnar report, you'll have to write a program or resort to third-party products (such as the R&R Relational Report Writer).

FoxPro: *VERY GOOD*

FoxPro offers the same basic ingredients for its report designer as are offered by the other products reviewed here. Separate visual sections in the report designer include header, footer, and detail; you have various tools to place your fields and define groups and calculations. Beyond the visual layout, the programs differ from each other to a greater degree. FoxPro is more menu and pop-up oriented than the rest, which is sometimes useful, sometimes tedious.

FoxPro carries over to the report designer some of the object-oriented text and field handling of Foxview. The concepts you learn in one will save you time in the other, but that's the closest the two modules ever get to being similar. Foxview doesn't use the menus or the mouse, and the report designer doesn't use the function keys. One real plus exists for Foxbase users. Conversion is done automatically when you retrieve an old Foxbase report.

You have the same range of file relations in the report as anywhere else. Up to 10 files can be linked, and filters can be activated for any combination of files. FoxPro requires that you set file relations and fil-

ters external to the report designer. The FoxPro interface makes it easy
to do, because you can jump to the view window without exiting the
report design.

Programmers and even interactive users are responsible for saving
this view and also for activating it before printing the report. Defining
such views can get tricky in reports. You'll have to account for details
such as how relationships are handled when a child record cannot be
found for a master record. Otherwise, when you print the report the
fields in the report that are derived from the child file will be incorrect.

FoxPro makes relational reports as easy as they can get using the
dBASE file formats, views, and filters. This isn't always the smoothest
path to a relational report, but smart programmers will find everything
they need here without having to play too many tricks.

Informix-SQL: *VERY GOOD*
Reporting is handled through the Ace report writer. An Ace report is
more like a stand-alone program than perhaps any other aspect of
Informix-SQL. You can generate a primitive default report program,
but other than that, reports have to be coded from scratch. For this,
Informix provides all the needed report writer building blocks and then
some. (A stand-alone DOS report writerwill be released in mid-1990.)
A full range of print formatting commands are available for everything
from defining headers to grouping and subgrouping data.

The language supports SQL-style Select statements, which gives
Ace all the impressive relational characteristics of SQL. You'll also
find traditional programming structures like If, For, and While. Variables can be defined, interactive prompts can be used, and several date
functions are added to those normally available. Ace calls the groups
of functions that summarize information in a report aggregates. These
calculate a count of rows, totals, averages, and the like.

Informix has the advantage in queries and reports of being an SQL-
based system. The Select statement and all its permutations make for a
powerful query tool to build on. All the means are provided to format
the selected data into a printed report. Being a programming language
of sorts, a lot of flexibility is built in, but that means more work than
with a WYSIWYG report painter.

Paradox: *EXCELLENT*
Relational reports in Paradox are very easy to generate. The simplest
way to get an ad hoc relational report is to execute a relational query
and then print the default report of the answer table. That won't always
do, and there are more elegant alternatives. Paradox has all the basic

elements of a WYSIWYG report painter, as do R:BASE, Clarion, dBASE, and FoxPro.

You can design around the master table to get a relational report. A blank report or a default report would be the canvas, and you build on it from there. Fields are menu-selectable for placement. When you need fields from a related table, you specify the name of the table and the link field. After that, the fields for that table become available for the report. A nice touch here is how Paradox keeps the field names separated by table. When you bring up a menu of available fields, the names of any related tables you've chosen appear along with the fields, but in brackets. The fields for the related tables are accessed via these submenus.

Calculated and lookup fields can be used in a report. Grouping by field is also easily accomplished, and groups can be sorted. Summary fields can be calculated as totals and/or by group. You can also make calculations based on summary fields.

There aren't any visible holes in Paradox's relational reporting features, and reports are as easy to create as we could imagine.

R:BASE 3: *EXCELLENT*

The report module in R:BASE 3.0 is for the most part unchanged, except for some additional features and a few corrections to the design. You can now produce "Quick reports" through the Reports Create and Modify menu, rather than having to wait until you're developing an application. Short versions of the reports can also be previewed on-screen or printed out before you print the full report.

One of the nicest enhancements is the new menu-selectable set of

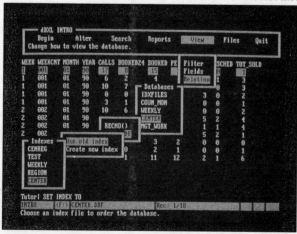

dBXL's Intro module prompts you through each step of an operation with a series of pull down menus.

253

special printer effects. You can now create a report using all the special features of your printer, including italics, compression, boldface, and underlining.

R:BASE 3 continues to support variables and math functions within reports. Break points can be set, and information can be grouped according to need. Thanks to the new interface, most of the report functions are a little easier to access. Information about the database also is more accessible through the series of pop-up menus that list all of your data elements.

Smartware II Database: *EXCELLENT*

Smartware has a good repertoire of report features for a module in an integrated package. The report can have a columnar or printed form type of format, or you can combine the two formats into one report. The combination approach is good for formats such as invoices, where you want addresses to appear in a formlike block and items listed in a columnar format with totals.

Smartware can handle multiple break points with subcalculations with no trouble. A degree of font control and limited line drawing is also available.

You can create a multifile report based on linked windows when the order of the output data is driven by a field in the master window. If the driving field is in a slave window and it is the "one" side of a many-to-one relationship, you must use the Relate command (intersection, etc.) to create a temporary result table before running the report.

This version of Smartware employs handy reporting capabilities, the speed of which are all the more impressive in light of the extra steps you must often take.

Performance
PROGRAMMING LANGUAGE

Clarion Professional Developer: *EXCELLENT*

The Designer is a template-driven stand-alone applications generator that will impress even the skeptics who think real programmers don't let software write software. You create menus, lookup tables, data entry screens, and reports right from the Designer. You can also link in source-code modules you've already written, or even use binary modules written in Assembler or C.

The template used by the Designer is a Clarion language file that the Designer uses as a model to build your applications. You can customize the template so the Designer will generate the kind of application you like, but it is already set up to do some neat tricks. It is built to precede data entry screens with a lookup table. In addition to its record-finding functions, the lookup table is also where you insert, delete, and change records (actually, the edit form pops up, allowing editing).

Even with the Designer, programmers will be drawn to writing in Clarion's structured high-level database applications language. It can be semi-compiled and used with the supplied run-time module, or converted to object modules and linked into a stand-alone DOS executable file. The language is more comparable to C or Pascal than dBASE, yet Clarion makes many of the trickiest operations in any of these languages a breeze. You'd have to write custom functions in other database languages to detect keystrokes that are considered standard in Clarion.

Clarion is a robust and feature-rich programming language. Whether you write the code yourself, use the Designer, or both, Clarion delivers in areas others don't even address. Its programming language rates an unequivocal excellent.

DataEase: *VERY GOOD*

The DataEase Query Language has been expanded in this version to include several new commands. It is more like a structured language than ever, though it still doesn't compare to most other database languages. It includes most control structures such as If . . . Then . . . Else, While, and Case, and can launch any module available in DataEase; however, it has some odd limitations. It is the only language we know of in which you cannot use an If statement to choose between working with records directly and launching another program.

Applications building is centered around filling out a set of data entry forms. DataEase will build menus from the information in these forms, and the menus will run various modules within DataEase, including data entry forms, queries, reports, and other DQL functions and procedures. You don't have much control over the look and feel of your application this way, but it is about the simplest means of building an application.

DataEase has a unique program editor that writes your code for you as you select menu options. Some of the bugs we found in the editor's automatic modes are gone, but there are still operational quirks (see Ease of Use).

The convenience of DataEase's method of creating applications combined with the expanded query language is enough to boost the score one grade.

dBASE IV 1.1: *Very Good*

dBASE IV contains over 440 commands and functions, more than 300 of them new since dBASE III Plus. The language now includes most of the enhancements that are available in other dBASE-language products. Simple creation of pop-up picklists, lightbar menus, and windows lets you design the interfaces that today's users have come to expect. Version 1.1 includes some major improvements, one of the most significant being the removal of most restrictions on user-defined functions, especially in Valid clauses. The capability to replace record contents from arrays, stuff character strings into the keyboard buffer, and create conditional indexes are welcome additions. A pseudo-compiler speeds execution of operations. When an application is complete, you can distribute it with the free run-time module included in the package.

The applications generator allows the nonprogrammer to glue all of the objects produced by the report, query, and form designers into a cohesive turnkey system. You can create bar and pop-up menus, selection lists of files, fields, or values with a series of menu selections. Actions assigned to menu options can include file manipulations, browse or form data entry, reports, labels, macro playbacks, or batch processes. When working with the interactive application front end, you can directly enter up to 19 lines of dBASE code into a batch process.

Although powerful, the applications generator holds many traps. Error checking is minimal. An application will be generated without any checking to see if the forms and reports that are referred to exist. In this case, the generation and compile process will work flawlessly, but the resulting application won't run correctly because many of the necessary components don't exist.

For those willing to write their own templates (programs that write programs), the template language is quite powerful. It can even be used in a stand-alone mode to create programs in other languages. We found it to be thorough, but not as complete as other stand-alone template products. Combining the extensive language with the template and code generator facilities, we rate dBASE IV's programming language very good.

dBXL: *Very Good*

dBXL's programming language is where it really shines. There is no applications generator or template language, but dBXL's implementation of dBASE is chock-full of seemingly minor enhancements that combine to create a language that's a pleasure to work with.

The windowing commands make elaborate screen manipulations a breeze. The Automem features cut down on repetitive lines of code. In addition to Set Function To and Set Key To commands, dBXL adds the unique Set Event and On Event commands. These let you specify a procedure that should be automatically implemented whenever the specified condition occurs. Writing code that interfaces smoothly to the hardware is facilitated by several commands that let you execute a DOS interrupt, directly load the machine registers, do bit testing, and input or output directly to an I/O port.

For debugging, dBXL implements the standard Dbase Set Step, Set Echo, and Set History commands. The suspend, cancel, and ignore options that are offered at a break point are enhanced with a fix option that automatically calls the editor, loads the source file that is executing, and points to the current line. The Generate command eliminates the time-consuming chore of filling a database with test data.

dBXL's programming language is a real pleasure, with surprising bonuses.

FoxPro: *VERY GOOD*
Of the applications generators, FoxPro's uses a technique most similar to dBASE IV for generating an application. The Foxview template has its own set of instructions to direct how an application is built. A full

Benchmarks
Single-User Relational Databases

	DataEase Version 4.2	dBXL Version 1.3	R:BASE Version 3.0
100,000-record ASCII file import	1:25:39	4:36	13:47
Create index	0:53	0:13	0:07
Indexed report	3:43	6:04	3:13
Select from one table	0:01	0:01	0:01
Select from intersection of two tables	0:04	0:35	0:40
Select from intersection of three tables	0:53	7:11	8:18

Times shown in hours:minutes:seconds.

explanation of how all of this works would require a lengthy tutorial, but Foxview is a major achievement, offering as feature-rich a means of building custom applications as you'll ever find. It suffers from the same lack of consistency that dBASE IV does, so its code cannot be as tight as that of non-dBASE-language competitors.

On the plus side, you don't have to learn the template language to use it. Foxview will offer a choice of templates when you get to the point of creating an application. The applications Foxview creates are the sleekest-looking we've ever seen in the dBASE language. There are some things we'd change immediately, but it is obvious that Foxview makes it possible to do everything you'd ever want in a user interface. You'll have to write your own help files, but the way the help system works in the final application is surpassed only by Clarion.

The Advanced Application template will generate a fairly complete relational database application. It doesn't handle the file relationships adequately on its own, though. When you get to a field on the form that is derived from a related file, the application you create will not have what it takes to cope with the error. Any relational data integrity handling will have to be handled by programming it in yourself.

Benchmarks
Single-User Relational Databases

	Clarion Professional Developer Version 2.0	dBASE IV Version 1.1
100,000 ASCII file import	1:27:49	41:14
Create index	0:07	0:09
Indexed report	0:31	1:04
Select from one table	0:01	Immediate
Select from intersection of two tables	0:01	0:11
Select from intersection of three tables	0:04	1:38

System configuration: Compaq Deskpro 386/20e running at 20 MHz using a 40-megabyte hard disk and 4 megabytes of RAM.
Times shown in hours:minutes:seconds.

With only a few exceptions, the FoxPro language supports the entire dBASE IV command set. All the menu and pop-up commands are available. Applications written for dBASE IV do run faster in Fox-Pro, but not as much as you'd expect. Certain techniques — such as embedding a browse window into a form for the "many" side of a one-to-many relationship — hold back both systems noticeably, slowing dBASE down to a crawl and FoxPro to a minor annoyance. Surprisingly, FoxPro programs written strictly in FoxPro language syntax usually run a lot faster than dBASE IV programs, even when they also include the trimmings of an easy-to-use application.

Fox Software claims the FoxPro language offers more than 140 extensions and enhancements that are lacking in dBASE IV. We'll take their word on it. The FoxPro language is certainly as robust and feature-rich as any dBASE programmer would wish for, and it creates the most attractive dBASE file-compatible applications we've ever seen.

Informix-SQL: *EXCELLENT*

Building an Informix-SQL menu-driven application is not like writing an application in a procedural language, neither is it like anything else we can imagine. We're not recommending this as a programming strat-

FoxPro Version 1.0	Informix-SQL Version 2.10.06	Paradox Version 3.0	Smartware II Database Version 1.0
3:03	28:33	12:34	10:12
0:05	0:47	0:08	0:42
0:12	2:02	0:12	1:03
Immediate	0:03	Immediate	0:02
0:02	1:01	0:07	0:04
0:22	2:44	0:50	0:17

See "How We Tested and Scored Single-User Databases" in this chapter for description of tables used. Tables are 25, 1,000, and 5,000 records.

egy, but here's how we can best describe the way an application comes together: You do most of your work with Perform, Ace, and the interactive SQL facility. When you're finished, you have a heap of disconnected modules, including forms, reports, and SQL functions. You arrange these into an application by launching appropriate modules or command files from menu selections. Paradox is similar in this respect, though Paradox is far more likely to be useful to beginners before this point is reached.

You don't design menus in the traditional sense. The menu selections are defined in a system table. The fields in the table determine what the selection text will say, the number it gets when the menu is displayed, and what happens when you make the selection. Menu selections can perform one of six actions: run a form, run a report, call a submenu, run an SQL command file, execute a script menu, or run a DOS command. The "script menu" is not a visible menu, but a means of performing a batch of the other actions. For example, one script menu can run a form, run an SQL command file, and then run a report.

This kind of applications development forces you to design self-contained modules and command files. It doesn't afford the kind of customization and flexibility you might get from a package like Clarion, but it isn't likely to be considered by the same programmers.

The only other "language" is the Informix brand of SQL. This implementation has some nice extensions and no obvious limitations. It supports nested, compound, and complex queries. It is also supplemented by some nice mini-utilities like Dblink, which allows you to import and export Lotus 1-2-3, dBASE, and ASCII files.

The relational power of SQL is undeniable. Informix puts it to good use and helps you bypass some of the tedious programming.

Paradox: *EXCELLENT*

Paradox may be the interactive users' choice, and for these people scripts, saved queries, and the Personal Programmer will be more than enough. If they ever find themselves getting the urge to make coffee, order pizza, and stay up until four in the morning chasing insignificant bugs, Paradox will accommodate them there, too. There is a robust programming language, the Paradox Application Language (PAL), and a debugger that you can use on PAL programs and recorded scripts.

The programming language is astoundingly full-featured. The list of commands and functions is truly awe-inspiring, including as obscure a function as one that tells you what kind of link exists between two tables — one-to-one or one-to-many. Practically the only thing Paradox doesn't do is tell you what you ate for breakfast. Similarly, the commands are varied enough to be useful in complex programs or in clever tricks you can play using keyboard macros.

Finally, the Data Entry Toolkit is a library of prewritten routines to spruce up applications. The toolkit is a sort of prefab means of getting many ease-of-use features that would be difficult to program from scratch. For example, it could be used to specify that when the cursor gets to a field, a list of appropriate choices pops up.

There is a high-level and low-level function for almost everything in Paradox. For the seemingly endless list of resources for the database programmer, we rate the programming language excellent.

R:BASE 3: *EXCELLENT*

R:BASE 3 has a richer set of language extensions than any other SQL-based product for the PC that we know. This is because, unlike most other SQL-based products for the PC, R:BASE started with the proce-dural language first, then added SQL. As the R:BASE query language has always been similar to SQL anyway, this is an asset.

Like any compatible SQL implementation, R:BASE 3.0 still has its own peculiarities. For example, when commands span more than one line (which most SQL commands do), each incomplete line must have a plus sign at the end.

Some of the holes in the R:BASE language have been filled. R:BASE 3.0 supports the "Switch. . .Case" structure, which replaces the cumbersome "If. . .Then. . .Else" structure.

We're still fond of R:BASE's applications generator, which has been enhanced somewhat. More menu types are available, reports are better integrated, and at least one inconvenience has been ironed out — you can now rename a database on which an application has been based. (Previously, you could rename a database, but the application would neither recognize it nor run it.)

Overall, R:BASE 3 still rates as one of the best means of generating a relational database application.

Smartware II Database: *VERY GOOD*

Smartware's Project Development Language (PDL) is actually an expanded script language with some surprising capabilities, such as being able to tap into DOS interrupts.

PDL is not a fine-tuned database application development language and it has limitations typical of a language with roots in an integrated environment (an exception to this rule is the Open Access inte- grated system, which includes a powerful development language). Neverthe-less, you can program Smartware to do just about anything the compe-tition can do, even if it requires a few detours where another language would offer a straight path.

You can record project files macro-style, or by coding them long-hand into a text file, or using some combination of the two techniques.

Programs written in PDL are compiled to a tokenized form before running, which may explain Smartware's speedy execution.

Performance

SPEED OF RELATIONAL OPERATIONS

Clarion Professional Developer: *EXCELLENT*

The Clarion language has commands to place different portions of data file keys (indexes) in memory for the fastest possible access to a data record. This allows it to blow the top off the rest of the products in all the select tests.

DataEase: *VERY GOOD*

Except for the second lengthiest import time and largest index creation, DataEase performed quite well, once we manually applied secondary indexes to our two- and three-table queries.

The only exceptions were in relatively less important areas: in import time, where DataEase was second slowest, and in index creation, where it was slowest in our 100,000-record test (though it still took under a minute).

dBASE IV 1.1: *GOOD*

dBASE IV's overall operation shows a marked improvement in speed, particularly if you use the included Dbcache disk cache. Vastly improved memory management has greatly reduced the amount of disk churning as overlays are swapped in and out of memory. In addition, more system parameters have been added to let users tune system performance.

Our benchmarks show the ASCII import and indexing to be about the same as in Version 1.0. The indexed report is actually a little slower, but query speeds are radically improved, particularly the three-table select. Overall, the dBASE IV benchmarks show much slower performance than FoxPro, and are still a bit slower than Paradox, for a net score of good.

dBXL: Score: *GOOD*

dBXL is a middle-of-the-road performer in our benchmarks. It was the slowest of the products at creating an indexed report, and turned in midrange times for the two- and three-table intersections, but it blazed through the 100,000-record ASCII file in less than five minutes.

FoxPro: *EXCELLENT*

FoxPro is fastest or second-fastest to Clarion in all our relational tests, and close enough to allow us to rate FoxPro excellent in speed.

Informix-SQL: *SATISFACTORY*

Informix doesn't seem to optimize its SQL at all, or if it does, it must be using the world's sorriest algorithm. Simply switching the order of the tables listed in the From portion of the Select statement made all the difference in the world in three-table joins; we tried three or four variations, dropping the time from 33 minutes (for a query phrased as we had presented it to the other packages) to just under three minutes, depending on how the query was structured. Although this second time is faster than Rbase's, we can't give full credit for this hunt-and-peck approach to performance. We rate Informix satisfactory in speed of relational operations.

Paradox: *VERY GOOD*

We were impressed by how fast Paradox was; with all that friendly-interface stuff to lug around, we kind of expected it to earn a gentle-man's C. But instead, it's good even at the three-table join, lagging only a bit behind the less casual-user-friendly Clarion and FoxPro. We rate Paradox very good in speed of relational operations.

R:BASE 3: *SATISFACTORY*

Provided with secondary indexes on two of our test tables, R:BASE 3.0 performs acceptably. Though we wish R:BASE 3.0 handled secondary indexes differently (either automatically creating them or not depending so heavily on them for speed), the steps one must take to implement them are not onerous.

Smartware II Database: *EXCELLENT*

Despite being the oddball product in this comparison, Smartware made an impressive showing in our benchmark tests. Our two-table indexed report required a temporary table to work properly (because the order of the data displayed was driven by a field in a secondary table, not the master); however, this had little effect on performance, since Smartware clocked in as one of the fastest products in this test. It performed the three-table intersection in only 17 seconds, once we programmed in a velocity number that would scroll results to the screen as quickly as possible.

DOCUMENTATION

Clarion Professional Developer: *VERY GOOD*

Clarion's documentation has improved tremendously with more thorough and better arranged writing. Clarion has the kind of flexibility that makes some things almost impossible to discover except by example and experimentation. The help screens also are extremely useful, often placing on-line just what you need to avoid having to reach for the manual.

Included with the on-line tutorial is a language tutorial, a first for us. Nobody else we know of has a language tutorial, let alone one this extensive. As a whole, we rate Clarion's documentation very good.

DataEase: *GOOD*

The documentation is laid out logically, and if you're using DataEase for simple office applications, you probably won't have any difficulties in finding what you need. As DataEase becomes a moderately powerful relational tool, however, the complex portions of the product are more likely to get used, and these features are not as well documented as the basic operations. For instance, we could find nothing in the documentation to help us construct our three-table benchmark query. Also missing is how to tweak DataEase into giving distinct query results. The documentation claims incorrectly that DataEase will convert the layout of a Paradox form to a DataEase form.

If you're using DataEase for larger or more complex jobs, the documentation falls short.

dBASE IV 1.1: *VERY GOOD*

You'll need a large desk to hold all the manuals that come with dBASE IV. The documentation is of high quality and well written. Our only complaint is that there are a dozen pieces. After you've learned the product, you will probably reduce the number that you use on a regular basis to two or three. Each individual book has good indexing, but there is no global index across all manuals.

The product also includes on-line help with a contents directory, keyboard templates, and a quick-reference guide.

dBXL: *VERY GOOD*

dBXL's documentation is one large volume, broken into sections by tabbed dividers. The material is presented in clear, concise language and the organization is outstanding. The introduction and tutorial serve to get the beginner going. The reference, command, and function sections contain all the meat for the experienced user. The index is outstanding, an all-too-rare occurrence in software documentation. Your use of the manual will be reduced once you discover how complete the on-line help manual and help system is.

FoxPro: *EXCELLENT*

FoxPro's documentation includes a manual for the tutorial, commands and functions, user's guide, and a manual for Foxview and associated utilities. There are also a couple of smaller manuals: one quick-reference for the DOS filer utility and one for installation.

All of the documentation is well-written and couched in a personal and friendly manner. It's almost impossible to reach for the wrong manual, and once you grab the one you need, the information is moments away.

The help screens are normally context-sensitive, but you can also find information through an index or ask for help on a topic from the command line. A neat feature is being able to cut and paste from the help window into another window.

Informix-SQL: *EXCELLENT*

The Informix-SQL documentation is a marvel. Informix-SQL is split into two manuals, a user's guide and a reference manual. The organization of information is thoroughly logical. We rarely, if ever, went even to the wrong manual for information. The writing is top-notch — tutorial quality in many places.

Paradox: *EXCELLENT*

The Paradox documentation, six manuals ranging from a user's guide to a booklet on how to generate reports, is among the best we've seen. It is personal in approach, and of a tutorial quality in many cases. We particularly like how recommendations are made on how best to use a feature, such as the type of query to use or when to use a method of updating tables.

Paradox provides both context-sensitive help and an indexed help system. As a whole, the documentation both written and on-line is well-written, well-organized, and the information within is easily accessible.

R:BASE 3: *EXCELLENT*

The R:BASE manuals are still top-notch, and have improved even over the previous version. Documentation is composed primarily of two large manuals: a user's manual and a reference guide. A smaller introduction manual and an installation guide also are included. An R:BASE for R:BASE Users guide is included in upgrade packages of R:BASE 3.0. In addition, you get a quick-reference guide.

R:BASE 3 also includes the first part of an on-line, three-part tutorial written by American Training International (the other two installments are available at an extra cost). The 187-page introduction manual features five tutorial lessons.

All of the manuals are well written and thorough. There is little R:BASE 3 could do to improve its documentation.

Smartware II Database: VERY GOOD

The Smartware documentation has improved significantly since our last review. It consists of nine manuals in all, including one for the database, project processing (programming), software system (user's manual), formula reference, communications guide, installation guide, quick reference, and a pamphlet on the appointment manager. There is an update guide as well.

An on-line tutorial in the form of a script-driven program can be run from within Smartware. There is now a multilevel help index and on-line table of contents, which resolves our main complaint. There are better examples of how to perform tasks. If you are going to tackle a full-blown application, the Smartware manuals still come up a little short. For light to moderate database use, however, the documentation serves its purpose.

EASE OF LEARNING

Clarion Professional Developer: VERY GOOD

Clarion is a lot to learn, but it isn't difficult to learn, thanks to several features. The annotated examples and the help screens really make the job easier. The help screens are completely accessible from the same Clarion Helper utility you use to create help for your applications. The ones provided are more than adequate, but it's a simple matter to change or add help screens if you want to build in your own helpful reminders.

Since we last looked at it, Clarion has added a handful of sample Designer applications files. In addition, a model file shows you how to change the templates for the Designer.

A more subtle aid to learning is in the language itself. Clarion is more forgiving than most structured languages. Programmers won't spend as much time learning complex data-type conversions and the like. Clarion figures most things out on its own.

You won't get the instant productivity of a Paradox, but for the kind of complex development environment Clarion offers, it is surprisingly easy to learn.

DataEase: *EXCELLENT*

For the most part, DataEase is a cinch to learn, and it has gotten easier as it has grown. There is a good tutorial manual that teaches you the basic moves, and a fancy demonstration program to show off what you can do with DataEase.

The most difficult part of learning DataEase is picking up the syntax of DQL. Many casual users can get away with using DataEase without ever having to deal with DQL. However, those who want to put together applications will need to learn the various tricks you need to play in order to get DataEase to perform much like other packages.

Overall, however, DataEase continues to be a product with which you can master the basics in a minimum of time.

dBASE IV 1.1: *VERY GOOD*

dBASE IV 1.1 comes with an improved installation facility that provides options for quick, full, and menu-driven installation of the single or multiuser versions. The program will take from 3 megabytes to 6.4 megabytes of space on your hard drive, depending on options. We found that if you install dBASE in a subdirectory with a name other than dBASE, the SQL module can't find the sample SQL database.

For the novice, a series of learning tools move from a very basic on-line tutorial to a more extensive set of lessons in the Learning manual. One of the environmental settings, Instruct, can be set to cause additional instructive menus to pop up at various points in the program.

Ashton-Tate has remained consistent with its dBASE III Plus interface, which provides a status bar, navigation message, and active-key prompt at the bottom of the screen. This may be fortunate for migrating dBASE III Plus users, but we have never found this to be a very intuitive design for novices.

Pull-down menus at the top of the screen and dialog boxes in the center are new. Overall we found dBASE IV's ease of learning considerably improved.

dBXL: *VERY GOOD*

dBASE has always required a long haul for novices trying to learn what a database is and how to use the commands at the same time. dBXL provides a friendly interactive environment for new users. The Intro module is a tremendous improvement over the dBASE III Plus Assist, offering a layout and prompts that are much more intuitive.

Once you're past the capabilities of Intro, you're faced with dBXL's version of the dot prompt. You can configure the prompt in a manner similar to the DOS prompt, but in its default form, the prompt displays the current work area and file name if one is open. dBXL's excellent help system and on-line manual are a big help here. The tutorial in the manual not only takes you through general interactive use, it includes an extensive discussion of programming.

FoxPro: *GOOD*

The FoxPro tutorial is a collection of files and assignments. This truly hands-on approach is actually preferable to the "press spacebar to see next screen" variety for a product as complex as FoxPro. It is also one of the most thorough tutorials we've seen, arranging learning sessions from prep school to senior. By the time you're a senior you'll be tackling memory variables, relations, and views.

The designers of Foxview may have heard rumors about the FoxPro interface, but that's about the extent of their similarity. Once you start Foxview, you're at the command line — no mouse, no menus, nothing. Many of the commands are a synthesis of DOS and the FoxPro/dBASE language. You'll find the menus when you get to the forms designer, but by this time you'll realize there's no getting anywhere without studying the manual and examining the help screens.

FoxPro's only drawbacks are the limitations imposed by the original design. dBASE file handling poses so many different ways to access data incorrectly, you just need to know more about how to handle relationships, filters, index files, and numerous details on how to build proper queries to get anywhere useful. Many of these details are easier to learn or even automatic in Paradox or Rbase. Overall, however, we rate FoxPro's ease of learning good.

Informix-SQL: *VERY GOOD*

To call the Informix-SQL user interface an economy in design would be accurate only if the economy were in a state of severe depression. The documentation lists as new features the capability to use Insert and Delete keys during editing. While it's difficult not to be impressed by such bold flirtations with state-of-the-art ergonomics, note also that Informix-SQL doesn't yet recognize keys like Home, End, Page Up, and Page Down. You needn't plan on a steep learning curve when it comes to keystrokes.

The documentation is an oasis in a desert of learning aids for ISQL. Only by studying the manuals will you learn things like how to create and use menus. The SQL language is sufficiently complex, and you'll have two other languages to cover: forms definition and report writing. The good news is that there is a good deal of overlap in the languages. Most of the rest is easy to pick up. Obviously, no help is available when writing reports or creating forms, because you must use an external editor at that time. If you can suffer with the ISQL editor for writing the interactive SQL facility command files, the Help key will list simple SQL syntax diagrams.

If Informix-SQL is anything, it is not foɪ sissies. There is no fancy on-line tutorial, no hypertext help system. In spite of this, the excellent documentation and the modular design makes it surprisingly easy for its audience of developers to learn.

Paradox: *EXCELLENT*

The biggest obstacle that lies between a new Paradox user and flat-file use is creating the first table — that's all. Once you create the table, you need only learn two keys to get a default form or report. It's more difficult to figure out how to change directories.

A more difficult step would be to learn how to put together the first relational data-entry screen. This is the first place you'll have to depart from the defaults and strike out on your own. Building a linked form isn't very difficult, but everything is so easy up to this point, it will seem like a giant leap. The last real hurdle will be learning how to build a relational query and report. The reports are very easily learned. Those who are new to data management probably won't find the queries a problem, because the query table is intuitive to the unprejudiced (non-dBASE-oriented) mind.

Between this point and the first application, most of the new material you learn will be things like how to speed up operation, how to create and make use of shortcuts, how to improve the look of reports and forms, and so on. These are all useful and, sooner or later, necessary. What we like about Paradox is that it keeps you actively productive in the meantime.

Where Paradox has a clear edge is between the first successful query and the first complex relational application; at this point, R:BASE and Clarion are at an advantage in teaching how to build a well-oiled relational database application.

We know of no other relational database that requires less learning to be productive at the interactive level. The ones who need the power of PAL or the Data Entry Toolkit will be the ones who have what it takes to learn them. The rest can go on using Paradox unconcerned.

R:BASE 3: *EXCELLENT*

R:BASE 3's on-line tutorial serves as a fairly complete learning aid. If you're computer literate, you can skip the tutorial and begin working with the sample exercises in the user's manual. All of the manuals are so well written that they are good tutorials in themselves.

R:BASE users and SQL buffs will have no problem at all adapting to this new version. The transition from the older, more limited syntax to this adaptation of ANSI Level 2 SQL should be painless, since the SQL command set is a natural extension of the original R:BASE language.

Version 3.0 also brings some welcome improvements to R:BASE's help system. There is a better help index, with hypertextlike menus providing deeper degrees of information. Help is available at the R: prompt or inside the program for context-sensitive assistance.

Smartware II Database: SATISFACTORY

The mere fact that Smartware is menu driven does little to aid you in learning or using it. Smartware ranks behind only Knowledgeman as the product with the most inefficient and unintuitive menu system we have ever seen. For example, should you choose to go through the menus to position the record pointer, you will find yourself hunting through the selections Data, Goto, Record, and Record-Number, after which you type the record number and press Enter. Fortunately, there usually are speed keys (Goto, for example) available to bypass such odd paths in the menu tree.

The help screens have improved since our last look, with the addition of a help index. Smartware's documentation aids the learning process, and the on-line tutorial is a good way to master the basics. (You'll have to run it from the beginning, because it isn't obvious how to move around within the tutorial if you jump in at the middle.) Although it's not an on-line version of the manual, on-line help contains just about everything in the manuals.

The unintuitive nature of many of the operations can impede learning, and though features have been added to make this version of Smartware easier to learn, this is balanced by the fact that Smartware is now more robust with more features to master.

EASE OF USE

Clarion Professional Developer: EXCELLENT

Clarion offers a shortcut for almost every operation. It makes smart choices wherever possible. When it comes to things like designing an attractive help screen or form, Clarion is to the competition as Word Perfect is to Edlin.

Clarion's free-form "track" mode for line drawing goes beyond any other line-drawing feature we've seen, allowing you to use virtually any character in the IBM set and intersect the popular variety of box and line characters with no problem. The free-form draw approach is usually more dangerous than the "pick a corner, pick the other" approach, but Clarion handles it with finesse. You can even use the

Backspace key to restore anything you've overwritten.

An elegant development tool called the Scanner will allow you to examine and change data in virtually any type of file. If the file is anything other than a Clarion data file, the Scanner automatically takes on the characteristics of a text/hexadecimal file editor utility.

The Clarion help-screen designer has to be experienced to be believed. It is thoroughly without rival. Help windows share some attributes of the screen designer, including track drawing and paint features. They also have the same placement options. You can predefine where the window will pop up, or let Clarion place it at run time so it won't hide the field that is active when you press the Help key. Help windows can automatically advance to any other, and they can include menus with selections that lead to other help windows. Help windows can be any size, and a window can even be made to appear in any shape or combinations of shapes. You can "cut" holes in the help screen by using transparent paint to let parts of the application screen show through. A cleverly designed help screen can include a graphic diagram pointing to and explaining the items that show through.

From the DOS file manager to the utility that generates a cross-reference of variables and procedures, Clarion gives you the feeling that every possible measure has been taken to make development a pleasurable experience.

DataEase: *SATISFACTORY*

DataEase remains one of the easiest products for building a simple relational application — in concept. If you interact with it on a daily basis you will find it is still beset with quirks. First of all, the interface is simply too rigid. DataEase may be the only product in which the table view will not scroll data one line at a time. The forms editor cannot perform true block cut-and-paste. Also, DataEase does not allow for piecemeal work. If you try to leave an incomplete or incorrect program with the intention of coming back to it, DataEase will refuse to let you exit or will discard your incomplete work, unless you take the time and trouble to "comment off" each line.

If your relationships between data files are at all complex, DataEase can behave unpredictably. For example, if an ad hoc subform (related file) is related by a lookup field in the main form, DataEase will not find the correct record in the ad hoc form if you make a change that alters the value in the lookup field. The only solution we found to this was using the multiuser option Auto-Refresh.

The DQL program editor could be less quirky. If you reposition the cursor, it can get confused about syntax and write unwanted instructions over existing code.

As much as we like the basic DataEase concepts, the little problems that need to be cleaned up prevent us from rating it any higher.

dBASE IV 1.1: *GOOD*

The flaws that marred Version 1.0's generally good user interface seem to have been mostly removed, resulting in an easy-to-use and productive product. We think even die-hard dot prompt users will find the Control Center a great convenience once they give it a try. Consistency of function-key use across modules is very strong. The use of Alt plus first-letter combinations for menu selections lets experienced users navigate quickly from module to module without stopping to read the menus. The macro recorder lets you automate repetitive functions even further.

dBASE IV automatically compiles programs, forms, and queries whenever you exit a design module, assuming you save your changes. Although this is necessary to keep the compiled versions up to date, it can be irritating if you make no changes or only minor comment changes. It would be nice to have the capability to disable this when desired. (You can turn off code generation in the Developer's Edition.) All of this compiling means that for every object you create there is a design file and a compiled file — your disk fills quickly as you work. In addition, we found several zero-byte work files left in the dBASE directory that are not cleaned up by the system.

The dBASE IV editor is a massive improvement over dBASE III Plus, but still constitutes only an adequate facility. Although you can set margins for report word wrap bands, the right margin for memo fields and program files is fixed at 65 and 1,024 characters, respectively. Many of the original Wordstar Ctrl-key combinations have survived. If you dislike the editor, you can replace both the program and memo field editors with your editor of choice by settings in the CONFIG.DB configuration file.

dBXL: *GOOD*

dBXL is a command-driven product for the most part, waiting patiently at the prompt for your directions. The Intro, query, report, label, and graph modules are menu-driven with easy-to-use pull-down menus, but the rest of the time you need to know what you're doing. You can get guidance at any time from the help and on-line manual by pressing the F1 key.

The History buffer records commands as they are issued. You can recall previous commands without typing by simply pressing the up arrow keys. After recalling a command, you can edit its contents before pressing Enter to reissue it. The Intro program allows you to record a series of menu selections into a macro. In command mode you can store frequently used commands to a function key.

dBXL lets you store multiple images (such as windows you paint on-screen) in one handy library file, a feature we appreciate. We also like the way dBXL handles memo fields: Instead of requiring you to go into a full-screen editor to edit a memo field, dBXL lets you store its contents to an array of strings. This enables you to use all the available string-handling and validation routines with a memo field, and lets you develop creative editing alternatives, such as reading the strings in a pop-up window.

FoxPro: *VERY GOOD*

You can use the keyboard for any operation in FoxPro, but use a mouse — you won't believe your eyes.

One of the best things about FoxPro's new interface is that you are never forced to exit one utility to do the necessary housekeeping you may have forgotten to do in another. FoxPro also is unique among these packages in that it offers a calculator, ASCII table, calendar/diary, and, to be funny, a scramble puzzle.

FoxPro doesn't give you the cosmetic control of Clarion, but it is the only other product that makes it so easy to modify the content of the regular help screens, and add new topics.

The program editor puts everyone but Clarion to shame. The edit features carry over to other modules, as well. You can cut, copy, and paste with or without the mouse at the command line, in a report, and in a program file, to name a few.

Foxview, the forms and applications designer, is not very difficult to use, but it is a culture shock after you've been using FoxPro. The object-oriented nature is definitely a plus, but working with fields using the function keys takes some getting used to after the point-and-click FoxPro.

In ease of use, FoxPro is mixed. For all its pop-ups, pull-downs, and submenus ad infinitum, this is still no relational database to be taken lightly. Everything you can do in the dBASE language is made easier because the interface has improved. But, in the end, you're just taking the same steps with a mouse that you would at the command line. The FoxPro interface is light years ahead of dBASE IV in many ways, but even dBASE IV makes things like queries easier than FoxPro. On balance, we rate FoxPro very good in ease of use.

Informix-SQL: *GOOD*

In our review of Informix ESQL-C as a multiuser product (April 10, 1989, Page 65), we praised it for the ease with which you could embed SQL into C programs. We still do. But Informix-SQL is a different frame of reference. We're not talking about making things easy for a C programmer, we're talking about making applications development easy for someone accustomed to Clarion or R:BASE.

When you don't bother to address the cosmetic side of presenting data, you cut out a lot of ease-of-use issues. Informix does have its own way of creating and maintaining menus, which is both a blessing and a curse. The way to edit a menu table is to use Perform, and Perform is definitely lacking in ease of use. It's not that easy to build a forms, reports, or SQL query, nor is it terribly difficult. But there are no screen painters and no WYSIWYG report generators to make easy. This is a different style of development.

In the end, we don't penalize Informix-SQL for sending you to your text editor, but we can't praise it like we do Clarion's screen designer. What we do credit it for is how it handles the files that you create in your editor. ISQL calls your text editor right from the menu system. When the forms compiler finds problems at compile time, error messages are inserted into the text-file definition. The problems are easy to find and correct when you go back to edit the form. Best of all, the error messages are automatically deleted from your text file when you recompile.

Finally, the data entry involved in putting together a set of menus isn't made friendly, but the modular design that allows you to do it this way speeds up applications development. This isn't a pinnacle of user-friendliness, but what it needs to do, Informix does well enough.

Paradox: *EXCELLENT*

Paradox could easily be the most usable relational database, if not the easiest to use. Everything seems to have a default just a keystroke away. You can successfully avoid dealing with anything remotely challenging and still make use of most of the features in Paradox.

The capabilities of Paradox are uniquely cumulative among the products in this comparison. Everything you create as you go about your business can be used when you move to the next skill level. The relational query you use for producing reports can later be used to generate a map for multitable data entry. When you learn how to record keystrokes into scripts and play them back, you can automate the process of picking a table, choosing the right form, and even the series of keystrokes required to send mapped data to the right tables. The scripts can later be integrated into a menu-driven application written by the Personal Programmer. Not a single line of programming was required to get to this point.

Paradox isn't without its share of wasted keystrokes and unfriendly operations. Some of the oddest things, like changing directories, are more difficult than they have to be. In the low tradition of database management, the Paradox editor surpasses only the interactive SQL facility editor in Informix SQL, a questionable honor.

There is no question that Paradox has the most in the plus column for ease of use. There are the numerous defaults, the way Paradox often anticipates your selections, and the clarity of the table query design. There is also the ease with which you can create a form, query, report, or graph. And, we haven't even begun to address things like how easy it is to import data directly from the menu and then distribute it to a set of related tables. Clearly, Paradox rates an unqualified excellent in ease of use.

R:BASE 3: *VERY GOOD*
R:BASE 3's new menu interface lags behind your selections, most noticeably when you use the mouse. Like Paradox, R:BASE requires you to remember path names; there is no disk navigation system. (The next version of R:BASE 3 will correct both of these problems, according to Microrim.)

Regardless of where you are in R:BASE, you can use the F3 key to pop up lists of data elements, a valuable new convenience feature. This alone provides a good reminder of the database structure when you need it; R:BASE also lets you use the menus to save typing.

You can now get a context-sensitive list of the valid keystrokes in your current operating mode. Databases, tables, columns, and the rest of the database elements in R:BASE 3 appear as menu selections when appropriate. Unfortunately, this selection technique imposes limits on the usefulness of R:BASE's scripting capability. Scripts in R:BASE 3 record only keystrokes, and because data elements are in the menus, the keystrokes you use to select any given element will change frequently. If a script picks the wrong element, it could wreak havoc.

Though it has grown and improved in many respects, R:BASE 3.0 0has become more tedious to use, due primarily to its lack of responsiveness. For this reason, we drop its score for ease of use.

Smartware II Database: *GOOD*
Like DataEase, Smartware suffers from a few minor ease-of-use problems, but most of them stem from the design of the interface. For example, keyboard operation can be inconsistent — of five places where you can point to a selection, the available keys to do so are all different.

You will want to use macros (or scripting) if you regularly perform queries in Smartware that create what you want to be a temporary table. Unlike Paradox, Smartware does not support automatically created and deleted temporary answer tables, so you must delete an old table each time you begin a fresh query.

Fortunately, Smartware handles macros more intelligently than R:BASE. In addition to being able to save the keystrokes, you can save the actual instructions that result from the keystrokes (such as the name of the file selected). This allows you to perform operations any way you choose without fearing that the keystrokes will have a different meaning if the list of files changes.

Smartware offers some nice ease-of-use features for designing data entry screens, including automatic assignment of field labels. Smartware successfully overcomes many of the problems of the complex menu structure by offering alternative keystrokes. Overall the package has improved, but the interface still could be easier to use.

ERROR HANDLING

Clarion Professional Developer: *EXCELLENT*

Clarion provides a utility that will repair a data file and reindex the key files. Fortunately, this won't often be necessary, since Clarion automatically maintains the key files.

Some safety and maintenance features are also built into the language. A database can be defined so that Clarion will reuse the space taken by deleted records, or leave deleted records alone so that later restoration is possible. There is a command that allows you to bypass normal buffering and write data immediately to disk. Clarion has transaction logging and rollback. Files can be encrypted and password protected, even to the point where the Scanner utility will not reveal the file structure.

Clarion makes a backup of Designer applications, which gives you the equivalent of a single-level Undo to any changes you make with the Designer. The debugger also now has a couple of additional pop-up screens for instant display of useful information for debugging programs.

Clarion boasts an impressive roundup of error-handling features and automatic error-handling capabilities in its applications; we rate it excellent.

DataEase: *POOR*

DataEase adds important new relational integrity options in this version: Null, Restrict, and Cascade, which control the effects on data when you make a change to a parent record in a parent/child form relationship.

On the down side, which is pretty steep, DataEase often lets you make grievous errors that could be easily trapped or prevented. For example, if you change a field's data type from string to numeric, but you neglect to define the kind of number you want (integer, floating, or fixed point), it will let you save this incomplete field type and even the form. Saving the form in this state destroys all your data for that field because it creates a damaged field in its place.

DataEase rebuilds indexes when you run a process called "reorganizing a form." For the most part, DataEase will reorganize a form automatically when you change its structure. The program is not consistent, however. DataEase often executes the lengthy process of index rebuilding when it is not necessary, or conversely, neglects to rebuild index files when it should.

DataEase is inconsistent in the way it is designed to handle operational errors — severely limiting your actions at one moment, the next moment allowing you to make serious mistakes without so much as a warning.

dBASE IV 1.1: *Good*

dBASE IV provides a wide assortment of features for error handling, including log-in security, file protection, data encryption, and transaction processing. SQL Grant and Revoke options are included in the SQL module. The log-in security system lets you create groups of users and assign security rights based upon group membership.

Transaction processing is available on both single and multiuser systems. You can use the Rollback command to recover from a catastrophe during a major file update. Set Autosave On bypasses the usual buffers and writes directly to the hard disk for single-record updates, but it doesn't work for global replaces. If you're running single user, the direct hard-write option in Dbcache is the most effective method to commit to updates. This reduces the performance boost of Dbcache but also reduces the chance of data corruption in the event of a system crash. The decision to use these security features will have implications on performance and flexibility, as is true with other products. Use of Protect, encryption, and SQL Grant/ Revoke options places restrictions on some operations.

The source code debugger is an excellent tool, allowing you to set break points, check variable contents, and view and edit source code. Unfortunately, the debugger window takes up a full screen. You can use the F9 key to toggle between the debugger screen and the program display. This is not as convenient as FoxPro's movable window debugger, but it is still highly functional.

Overall data in the dBASE IV environment is much more secure than it was in dBASE III. The automatic maintenance of the production MDX file with up to 47 index tags removes one of the most often criticized dBASE data integrity issues. The removal of the massive

The Informix form definition is a combination of screen design (using your own editor, in this case Qedit, to draw the lines and boxes), and field definitions.

bug infestation in Version 1.0 results in an environment in which it is difficult to accidentally lose data. In the short time we've had to test Version 1.1, it appears to be much more robust than the first version. Most of the remaining bugs we have found have been relatively minor, and Ashton-Tate has vowed to respond to new problems quickly.

dBXL: GOOD

dBXL does an adequate job of preventing accidental data deletion or corruption. When Set Safety is on, dBXL requires confirmation before overwriting or clearing a file. (This feature can be turned off for use in programs.) Like most dBASE products, abnormal termination of a program in dBXL will frequently result in damaged index files, but they are easily rebuilt.

Several commands are provided to facilitate error handling within a program. On Error lets you specify a procedure to execute whenever a dBXL error occurs, while other commands let you control the appearance of error messages. dBXL, like Dbase and most clones, can mark records for deletion, then recall them until the file is packed.

There is no password protection and no commit or rollback functions. When an error occurs during program execution, you are given the chance to ignore the error, cancel the program, fix the program, or suspend its operation and examine the environment status for the source of problems.

FoxPro: *SATISFACTORY*

It sometimes seems like no one is fully adept at screen handling when using the dBASE/FoxPro language. Both products have their share of problems in the sample programs. The sample template file for Foxview is buggy enough to have given us fits for quite a while before we realized the bugs were in the template file, not in Foxview or FoxPro. Prodemo, a third-party program distributed with FoxPro, is mostly error-free, but some error messages will get hidden, and others will cause the data entry screen to scroll and become muddled.

FoxPro, like dBASE, will not necessarily reset the color schemes to the default upon returning from an application that changed them. Nor will it always close windows if the application fails. (In some cases this is a good thing, since you can examine how things ended up when the application failed.)

FoxPro comes with a debugger. The multiwindowing interface really comes in handy here since you can keep track of several things at once. There is no password protection in FoxPro, nor is there data encryption or transaction logging.

Needless to say, dBASE IV users can find refuge in FoxPro. Other than that, FoxPro does well with what it has but lacks some data integrity features found in all the other packages.

Informix-SQL: *VERY GOOD*

There is much to be touted about Informix-SQL error handling. The attributes section of the form definition makes it easy to create prompts that guide users through data entry. There is a Verify attribute that forces users to enter data twice, which is useful when accuracy is critical. The instruction section is a real plus for including data validation commands, even those that perform some degree of referential integrity checks. On the down side, the default data entry error message is thoroughly meaningless. Any invalid character, whether a letter in a money field or a decimal point in an integer field, will induce the same response: "Error in field."

Informix-SQL has nice transaction logging features with roll back and roll forward, extremely useful for maintaining data integrity. You can decrypt the password file using a hex calculator, but this will be too much trouble for most. You can't just delete the password file to get access, as you can in dBASE IV. Informix-SQL will force you to reinstall the product if you do.

Any problems we encountered were inconsequential, having mostly to do with the screen and keyboard handling. To cite a couple of examples, nearly every Alt-key combination and many Control-key combinations mysteriously toggle insert mode if they have no other function.

For another, when you print a list of forms during data entry and interrupt the report, the data entry screen scrolls up one line, upsetting the form until another query operation is performed. All the pluses in error handling add up, and offset by far the few quirks.

Paradox: *EXCELLENT*

Paradox has a lot of built-in safety checks for data entry. Paradox will not let you delete a row in the master table from a multitable form if by doing so you cause it to abandon rows in the child tables.

Paradox also protects you from losing data during behind-the-scenes operations. If you add data to tables by any other means than the keyboard, there's always the potential that rows won't make it into a table when they create duplicate keys. Paradox puts these rows in a key violations table. This accomplishes the twofold goal of letting you know what didn't make it and giving you the chance to fix errors and update the tables. Add these features to the incremental undo, and the capability to edit the transaction log from within the PAL language, and you have a great lineup of error-handling features.

R:BASE: *SATISFACTORY*

R:BASE 3 provides the SQL commands Grant and Revoke, which are used to assign data selection, updating, insertion, and deletion privileges. R:BASE 3 also supports transaction processing with rollback. Version 3.0 adds to table (or browse) mode automatic concurrency capabilities for multiuser configurations. R:BASE still employs "rules" for data validation.

R:BASE 3.0 seemed to trap most, but not all, errors in our limited use. Some missed errors can develop into more serious problems. If you mistype your password, for example, R:BASE 3.0 will not stop you, but will simply assume that a password for a new user is being created. If you go on to create a table under the mistyped password, exit the program, and then type your password in correctly the next time, you won't be able to access the table you created.

We also experienced various printer-related errors. For instance, if you print a report that involves a table with restricted access, R:BASE 3.0 correctly provides a "no access" error message — if you print to the screen. If you send the report to the printer, it will print the error message on the printer but not on the screen.

Fortunately, the transaction processing, privilege assignments, and rule processing all help the score.

Smartware II Database: *VERY GOOD*

We couldn't catch Smartware off guard by creating error situations. The program is unfazed by problems such as disconnected printers.

Smartware has a "help on error" feature that allows you to enter the error number you received, for which Smartware will print the appropriate error message. In addition, the project processing manual lists system error messages and their numbers.

Smartware has a feature it calls transactions, though this is not the same as "transaction processing" in other products — it is more like a referential integrity feature that updates a related file when a master file is changed. An audit trail log is kept, a feature more in keeping with real transaction logging, but there are no rollback or roll-forward capabilities. Data files and views can be password protected, and data files can be encrypted if passwords are assigned. However, there is no means of recovering an encrypted file if a password is forgotten.

Smartware has a file-fix option available at the menu, which will rebuild a file if it is damaged. Keys can be maintained automatically, but you can rebuild them at the menu as well.

Smartware comes very close to matching the security features found in more robust competitors.

SUPPORT POLICIES

Clarion Professional Developer: *GOOD*
Clarion offers 90 days of support on a non-toll-free line. The company also provides support through fax and an electronic bulletin board service, extended corporate support plans, and extended support hours (8:30 a.m. to 8 p.m. Eastern time) to customers on the West coast.

DataEase: *VERY GOOD*
DataEase provides unlimited free support over a non-toll-free line, private electronic bulletin board service, and fax. There are also extended support hours (9 a.m. to 8 p.m. Eastern time) and corporate extended support plans.

dBASE IV 1.1: *VERY GOOD*
Ashton-Tate offers unlimited free support, and offers fax, private BBS, and CompuServe and Genie services. There are extended support plans available. Support hours are weekdays from 6 a.m. to 4:30 p.m. Pacific time (Thursdays from 6 a.m. to 4 p.m.). We rate support policies very good.

dBXL: *GOOD*
Wordtech offers one hour of free support over a non-toll-free line, private electronic bulletin board, and fax. Extended corporate support plans and a 30-day money-back guarantee also are available.

FoxPro: *VERY GOOD*

Fox Software offers unlimited support on a non-toll-free line, a 30-day money-back guarantee from the dealer from which FoxPro is purchased, and support through Compuserve and fax.

Informix-SQL: *SATISFACTORY*

Informix offers 90 days of free support, including updates, support through fax, and extended corporate support plans.

Paradox: *VERY GOOD*

Borland offers unlimited free support on a non-toll-free line to registered Paradox users. It also offers a 60-day money-back guarantee, fax support, and corporate extended support plans.

R:BASE 3: *VERY GOOD*

Microrim offers 30 days of toll-free support for R:BASE, beginning with the first telephone call. There also is support over a private electronic bulletin board and fax, and a 90-day money-back guarantee. The 3.1 update will be free to current users, Microrim said.

Smartware II Database: *SATISFACTORY*

Informix offers unlimited free support for Smartware over a non-toll-free line, private electronic bulletin board, and fax. Score: Good

TECHNICAL SUPPORT

Clarion Professional Developer: *GOOD*

We have received immediate top-notch technical support in the past, but this seems to have changed a little as Clarion has grown. After a few bouts with a busy signal, we spent a few minutes on hold this time around. The person we spoke with was knowledgeable about the main product, but had to do some searching for answers about the language extension modules, though no callback was necessary.

DataEase: *POOR*

After encountering several busy signals, we got through to technical support, only to wait on hold — with the receptionist checking us every few minutes —before leaving a message. We received a callback within the hour. Support personnel were eager to help, researching questions while we waited on hold, but we were given one inaccurate answer.

dBASE IV 1.1: *SATISFACTORY*

We ran into some busy signals when trying to contact Ashton-Tate, but when we did get through we were able to talk with a technician within moments. If all the support lines are busy, the call-routing system lets you know approximately how many calls are in front of you in the queue. The technicians we spoke with were still learning the nuances of the new version. When in doubt, they were quite willing to consult with other staff to arrive at an answer.

dBXL: *SATISFACTORY*
We were able to get through immediately each time we called Wordtech. The technicians we spoke with were friendly and courteous, although not overly eager to supply the answers we needed.

FoxPro: *SATISFACTORY*
We were always able to get through to technical support, but the support person usually needed to research our question and call back. It took four days to get one question answered. We get the impression that support personnel are knowledgeable but overwhelmed by requests.

Informix-SQL: *VERY GOOD*
We usually had to wait on hold to get through to technical support, then leave a message. When we received a callback, the support person was professional and had an answer for every question without needing to research it. Because of the high level of expertise, we like the technical support. But the wait-and-call-back arrangement reduces the final score.

Paradox: *VERY GOOD*
We had to wind our way through a network of voice mail to reach technical support, but once we got through, we received accurate and immediate answers to our questions.

R:BASE 3: *SATISFACTORY*
We got through immediately to Microrim support each time we called; help was quick and accurate.

Smartware II Database: *SATISFACTORY*
We got through immediately each time we called technical support. Support personnel had to put us on hold in order to research each question we asked, but we received correct answers within a few minutes each time.
We tested technical support during December, 1989, May, 1990, and July, 1990.

VALUE

Clarion Professional Developer: *EXCELLENT*

At $695, Clarion Professional Developer gives you a tremendous amount of applications development muscle. Clarion applications have the most potential for being the easiest to use, the most visually appealing, and the easiest to customize. Once you get the hang of it, Clarion could also be the fastest means of developing bulletproof applications.

You can distribute the run-time Clarion with your programs, or you can choose to translate your programs into DOS-executable files. There are no distribution or licensing fees. This translates into the best database applications development cost/performance ratio of the group. Clarion is an exceptional development environment.

DataEase: *SATISFACTORY*

As other relational database products break into a gallop, DataEase continues to lumber along, resistant to change. DataEase is a terrific idea, but it suffers from a number of glitches, design flaws, and oversights, most of which are minor. The real mystery is why so many simple oversights remain unchanged version after version.

Quirks aside, the biggest drawback is DataEase's lack of speed when used with multiple files. We do not recommend it for manipulating large quantities of data, or even using moderate amounts of data in a complex way.

At $750, DataEase remains an uneven product with a lot of unfulfilled potential. However, if your needs are light, you don't mind a few annoyances in the design, and you want one of the simplest means of building a multifile application, DataEase is a viable choice.

dBASE IV 1.1: *GOOD*

Ashton-Tate appears to have finally created a stable dBASE IV environment with Version 1.1. (Updates are free to registered users of Version 1.0.) The Control Center, query facility, and report designers provide powerful tools for interactive manipulation of data. The improvements to the programming language should remove the barriers to producing functional advanced applications.

While we don't think professional developers who have moved on to other environments will find enough features to bring them back, for the large pool of users who need both a highly functional interactive environment and turn-key custom programs, dBASE IV can be attractive. The biggest drawback is the lack of multifile data entry capabilities in interactive mode. The SQL module is still unreliable, as well.

The Developer's Edition comes with the template-language source code, two extra LAN keys for multiuser program testing, and a royalty-free unlimited run-time license for $1,295. The competition is tough, with Paradox, FoxPro, and R:BASE offering comparable capabilities; but this version of dBASE IV can stand up to these products. With all the improvements, we now rate dBASE IV a good value.

dBXL: *VERY GOOD*

dBXL lists for $249. Wordtech also sells dBXL/LAN, which supports an unlimited number of users, for $599; and Networker Plus, a server utility, for $259. Wordtech sells Oracle Server front-end versions of both dBXL (dBXL/Oracle) and Quicksilver (Quicksilver/SQL) and a front-end version of Quicksilver for Gupta's SQL-Base database server.

It may not be as fast and glitzy as some other Dbase-compatible products like Foxpro, but dBXL offers a surprisingly capable Dbase environment at a bargain-basement price. In addition, it's got some features that others lack, such as graphics, windows, and an interpretive environment that is compatible with a compiler from the same vendor.

FoxPro: *VERY GOOD*

Every time you fire up FoxPro it presents one of the most delightful and flexible character-based interfaces available. It gives you easier access to all the steps you're used to making but doesn't cut away enough fat to compare to products like Paradox and R:BASE.

It has power to spare in its template language and applications generator. FoxPro also removes many of the limitations imposed in the dBASE IV forms design, and it still supports almost the full range of dBASE IV commands. It is missing some important features you'll find in dBASE IV. There are no query-by-example module or production index files, and it is missing a few data integrity features.

At $795 (costing $195 to upgrade from Foxbase Plus), FoxPro has enough going for it to win over a large segment of disgruntled dBASE users. It has the speed, user interface, applications generator, multitable forms, and much more in its favor — all of which add up to a very good value.

Informix-SQL: *VERY GOOD*

Informix-SQL is robust in data management features. For $795, it has all you need to create a menu-driven application that won't balk at the most heavy-duty tasks. This is the stuff of mainframes, and it both looks and acts the part.

For the Informix addicts who won't want to stop at Informix-SQL, the Informix 4GL-RDS-ID ($1,095, $295 for run time) has more to offer in portable tools, and the ESQL-C package ($595, $150 for run time) produces a more customized application. Informix-SQL alone, however, is more than worth its price.

Paradox: *EXCELLENT*

Expert database programmers or novices who see themselves as future experts can pick Paradox without hesitation. Paradox is so appealing for its instant productivity, some other treasures often remain unnoticed. For example, it may be one of the better programs for importing data from other systems or other products. Add Quattro to the picture, and you've got a seamless data path between database and spreadsheet.

This is a no-risk investment from novice to expert. It remains our favorite combination interactive relational database and applications development environment.

R:BASE 3: *GOOD*

R:BASE and Dbase have competed for so long, it's surprising that Microrim would fall into the same trap that has given Ashton-Tate so much trouble — releasing a product before it's ready.

Though capable of much faster queries than we originally thought, R:BASE 3.0 has a number of bugs and an unfinished feel. However, it probably does not have nearly the amount of serious anomalies as dBASE IV. R:BASE also continues to benefit from a conceptual unity that dBASE lacks. R:BASE 3 was bumped in price from $725 to $795 with this version. Users of Version 2.11 can upgrade to 3.0 for $175. The R:BASE compiler ($895) does not yet work with Version 3.0, but will eventually, according to the company. It could use some fine-tuning, but with its new interface and many new features, R:BASE 3.0 has a lot to offer.

Smartware II Database: *VERY GOOD*

Version 1.0 catapults the Smartware II Database from its former position of "barely useful" for multifile requirements to well into the ranks of respectable relational database products. It's still not quite at the level of a stand-alone product, and it wouldn't be our preferred choice for a development tool (its interface makes it best for light applications), but Smartware handles large quantities of data admirably, better than many large-scale competitors. Such a capability cannot hurt its usefulness as part of an integrated system either.

At $449, the new and improved Smartware, which we previously rated a poor value, makes a dramatic climb.

Product Summaries
Data Bases

Clarion Professional Developer Version 2.0
Company: Clarion Software, 150 E. Sample Road, Pompano Beach, FL 33064; (305) 785-4555, (800) 354-5444.
List Price: $695 single user and multiuser, including run time and compiler (translator). Optional graphics, communications, financial, and dBASE III language extensions available.
Requires: IBM PC, XT, AT, PS/2, or compatible; PC- or MS-DOS 2.0 or later; 512K of RAM (640K recommended); hard disk drive.

DataEase Version 4.2
Company: Dataease International, 7 Cambridge Drive, Trumbull, CT 06611; (203) 374-8000, (800) 243-5123, fax: (203) 374-3374.
List Price: $750, single user; $750 for three additional users; $1,000 for five additional users.
Requires: IBM PC, PS/2, or compatible; 640K of RAM; MS-DOS 3.1 or later; hard disk. Uses expanded or extended memory.

dBASE IV Version 1.1
Company: Ashton-Tate Corp., 20101 Hamilton Ave., Torrance, CA 90509-9972; (213) 329-8000.
List Price:$1,295 for Developer's Edition (with unlimited run time); $795 for Standard Edition; $995 for Lanpack, (five users). Upgrade from 1.0 is free.
Requires: IBM PC, PS/2, or compatible; PC- or MS-DOS 2.1 or later; 450K of RAM; hard disk drive.

dBXL Version 1.3
Company: Wordtech Systems, P.O. Box 1747, Orinda, CA 94563; (415) 254-0900, (800) 228-3295, fax: (415) 254-0288.
List Price: $249; Dbxl/LAN for unlimited number of users, $599; Quicksilver compiler 1.3, $599.
Requires: IBM PC, PS/2, or compatible; 512K of RAM; MS-DOS 2.0 or later; two floppy drives (hard drive recommended); capable of using up to 64K of expanded memory. **FoxPro** Version 1.0
Company: Fox Software, 134 W. South Boundary, Perrysburg, OH 43551; (419) 874-0162.
List Price: $795; $195 to upgrade from Foxbase Plus. ($1,095 unlimited use version and $500 run-time version available first quarter 1990.)
Requires: IBM PC, XT, AT, PS/2, or compatible; 512K of RAM; PC- or MS-DOS 2.0 or later; hard disk. Supports expanded memory.

Informix-SQL Version 2.10.06
Company: Informix Software Inc., 4100 Bohannon Drive,
Menlo Park, CA 94025; (415) 926-6300.
List Price: $795; $195 run time. (LAN package starting at
$1,995 for four users).
Requires: IBM PC, XT, AT, PS/2, or compatible; 640K of RAM;
PC- or MS-DOS 3.0 or later; hard disk recommended. Supports
extended memory up to 16 megabytes. Also available on Unix,
VMS, MVS, and OS/2 operating systems.

Paradox Version 3.0
Company: Borland International, 1800 Green Hills Road, Scotts
Valley, CA 95066; (408) 438-8400.
List Price: $725. Run time: $29.95 each; $995 LAN Pack for five
additional users.
Requires: IBM PC, XT, AT, PS/2, or compatible; 512K of RAM;
PC- or MS-DOS 2.0 or later; hard disk recommended (supports
both expanded and extended memory); also available on OS/2
operating system.

Smartware II Database Version 1.0
Company: Informix Software, 4100 Bohannon Drive, Menlo Park,
CA 94025; (800) 331-1763.
List Price: $449; $699 for Smartware II integrated package; net-
work node pack for one additional user, $249; five-user pack,
$999; 12-user pack, $1,999.
Requires: PC, PS/2, or compatible; 512K of RAM; MS-DOS 3.1
or later; hard disk (uses expanded memory).

How We Tested and Scored
Single-User Databases

All products in this product comparison were benchmarked on a Compaq Deskpro 386 running at 20 MHz, and using a 40-megabyte hard disk and 4 megabytes of RAM.

The products are scored according to the criteria listed below. The individual product write-ups cite specific elements that influence the final score but are not an exhaustive listing of the positive and negative aspects that were evaluated. Our weightings are derived from surveys of readers of InfoWorld involved in buying and using relational database products. You can customize these weightings on the Report Card to reflect your own requirements.

We score all categories from the perspective of a corporate or independent database developer, rather than a casual user, because that's who these products are intended for. Convenience features are also valued; PC database developers often find themselves making use of a number of data-handling products, so accessibility to power is often as important as the power itself.

PERFORMANCE: We separated performance grading into five categories, including one grade for speed.

Relational data entry: To test the capability to enter data into more than one table at a time, we created a data entry form designed to enter data into both tables. The data entry score reflects how well each product handled this task. All of the products tested are capable of such an operation, but some make it easier than others. A product earns a satisfactory score if it requires only that you specify fields from various tables, and the links between the tables, when you create the form. Higher scores go to those that can easily handle both one-to-one relationships and one-to-many relationships. In every case, the more the product distances the chore from the user without limiting the design, the better the score. We also considered the convenience of editing features during data entry, including choices for cursor handling, correcting, and deleting. Also credited were screen painting features and the capability to decide in which order data can be entered in fields on the screen.

Relational querying: This score rates the facility with which the product allows you to draw data from two or more tables. Most of the products we have reviewed offer query languages or fourth-generation query facilities (such as query by example, or QBE) that help to make this operation easy. Such facilities earn bonuses in this category. Because of its power, flexibility, and completeness for database use, SQL earns a substantial bonus where present, as does the capability to make SQL more usable. If the product is not interactive and lacks a query language, the usability of the programming language and associated tools for building queries is considered. Such languages must be powerful enough to support complex query operations, with an easy syntax that won't discourage programming.

Relational reporting: To test relational reporting, we generated reports drawing data from two related tables. Relational reports are usually created via a report painter or a report writer/ language. If the product supports only a report writer, the language must have some advantage in power or flexibility to justify the added burden of programming.

Programming language: We looked for a robust programming language capable of handling the demands of serious database programming. The full set of flow control statements (IF..THEN, DO..WHILE) must be present, and higher scores go to those with appropriate built-in functions for math, string handling, statistics, date translation, and functions that report the state of various elements in the system (such as one that might tell you a field is numeric and not string type). No credit is given for a command or function that simply compensates for a design flaw. Bonus points go to those products with the best debugging and error-handling features. We also credit products that offer a compiler or tokenizer.

Speed of relational operations: PC-based single-user relational and multifile database products are inching closer to their mainframe cousins in complexity and power. With this in mind, we decided to test how well each product could select records from an increasingly complex chain of relations.

In each language, we created three tables: a salesperson table of 25 records, a customer table of 1,000 records, and an orders table of 5,000 records. We modeled our code on the queries below. (In each case, the results were sent to the screen; the time reported is time required to produce the complete result. All necessary indexes were created beforehand.)

Indexed report: Generate a report to the screen listing the names of all sales representatives and their customers in alphabetical order.

Select from one table: List each sales rep's number and name in rep number order.

Select from intersection of two tables: List the number and name of each sales rep who represents a customer.

Select from intersection of three tables: List the number and name of each sales rep representing a customer who currently has an order on file.

Each query was phrased in natural order (approximately as described above), rather than in the order that would be best for obtaining the quickest results. Consequently, products with optimizers (which can rephrase queries if necessary to speed things up) can be expected to better handle more-complex queries. Most of the products did well in all three tests even without optimizers, but hand-recoding for optimal performance would improve the scores of some of the packages tested here.

After initial publication in *InfoWorld* of part of this product comparison, we reworked the two- and three-table select test to ensure that all products were selecting a "distinct" record, so their results would be comparable.

The Distinct command in SQL (or its equivalent in other languages) limits query results to one instance of an answer, eliminating superfluous information. For instance, by making our three-table query distinct we are able to produce results listing the name of each sales representative only once – instead of repeating the rep's name for each customer who has an order. For consistency, all of the products in this comparison also were tested for distinct query results.

The Distinct command may slow down or speed up benchmark results, depending on how the program handles the background work to perform the command. Our retest of Dbase and Foxpro three-table queries resulted in a minor slowdown; Paradox was speeded up considerably overall, though not enough to change its previous speed score. Clarion and Informix results were already "distinct." The changed results are indicated in the benchmark table by an asterisk. The changed timings did not affect speed scores.

We did not index-link fields for any of the products unless it was required to perform the test (other products may be creating temporary indexes). We made an exception for R:BASE 3.0, which does not require secondary indexes but will not perform reasonably without them.

Our benchmark table also includes the timings for creating indexes and for executing the necessary ASCII import into our 100,000-record file. These results, along with the products' import/export capabilities in general, are largely unremarkable; however, we were impressed with the fact that Clarion's DOS file structure makes it possible to define virtually any known file format and import data from it.

To grade speed, we awarded the highest scores to products that came closest to matching Clarion, the overall best performer. We also rewarded products that performed the more complex intersections the most quickly.

ERROR HANDLING: We give bonuses for data-recovery utilities, multilevel security (password) features, data-encryption features, and extended data-validation features, especially when the data validation is programmable. Products that allow easy methods of bypassing security or, conversely, with the potential for using security features to sabotage the system, score poorly.

Other features valued in error handling include automatic record locking; transaction logging that allows rollbacks and/or rollforwards in case of major problems; on-screen updating of modified data; and SQL security and access-control features.

All other items are scored according to our standard procedures, except that the products were rated from the perspective of the professional database user. We paid special attention to depth of information, and features or shortcuts that make the user's or developer's life easier. If a product is interactive, interactive ease of use is a prime consideration. If it is strictly a developer's tool, ease of development is scored. If it is both, both aspects are considered in the scoring.

CHAPTER EIGHT

Microsoft Windows 3.0: The Graphics Interface Grows up

Its graphics, memory management, and third-party support may take the industry by storm.

BY SERGE TIMACHEFF, SPECIAL EDITIONS EDITOR
AND MICHAEL J. MILLER, EDITOR-IN-CHIEF

Windows 3.0 is more than an update; in many respects, it's an entirely new environment that will provide users with many of the features they've wanted for years but thought they would have to switch to OS/2 or Unix to get. The environment uses the protected-mode features of the 286 and higher CPUs, providing access to extended memory, better multitasking, and more powerful applications. Windows 3.0 sports a much improved user interface, including better-looking icons and buttons, more colors on-screen, and new icon-based ways of launching applications and managing files. As a result, many users will now be able to use Windows as their primary operating environment for running both Windows-based and traditional DOS-based applications.

Crucial to the success of Windows are Windows-based applications, which are blossoming like wildflowers. While Windows contains a number of lower-end "accessory" applications such as a communications package, a calendar program, and a basic word processor, literally hundreds of other applications are being upgraded to run under Windows 3.0 or are being released specifically for this version.

FEATURES:

Memory management: The most transparent yet significant feature of Windows 3.0 is its advanced memory management capabilities.

From a technical standpoint, the biggest change is the support of protected mode and extended memory on 286-, 386-, or 486-based systems. Windows 3.0 can run in one of three modes. Real mode runs much like Windows did before; standard mode requires a 286 and at least 1 megabyte of memory and takes advantage of extended/protected memory; and a 386 enhanced mode (which requires a 386 with at least 2 megabytes of RAM) lets the system act as if it had more memory than it really does (by swapping to disk). Enhanced mode allows you to run multiple non-Windows applications — each in its own "virtual machine" (to the DOS application, the DOS window looks like an 8086 computer).

In standard or 386 enhanced mode, you get access to protected-mode memory, which gives Windows improved memory management features. Protected mode allows Windows 3.0 applications to use "extended memory" — the memory above 1 megabyte that only exists on a 286 or higher. The protected mode support should allow for both larger applications, and faster large applications, because extended memory data does not have to be swapped in and out of "conventional" memory in segments like expanded memory.

Windows runs in the mode it deems most appropriate for the computer it is installed on, or you can force it to run in any of the modes possible on your computer. Many older Windows programs that will not work in protected mode (standard or 386 enhanced) can run in real mode.

Interface: The most obvious change is a better three-dimensional look to buttons and controls. And gone are the days of navigating through subdirectory listings to find the .EXE file of the program you want to run. The old MS-DOS Executive has been replaced by three new applications: The Program Manager, the File Manager, and a Task List. You start applications from the Program Manager, which displays windows, or "program groups" of icons that represent your applications. You start applications by simply double-clicking on the icon for each program or the File Manager listing.

Within Program Manager you can create and arrange windows (Program Groups) that contain applications. These windows can be automatically tiled or cascaded using the program manager, and moving applications between windows can be accomplished by merely dragging the icon to another window.

The File Manager lets you find a particular file, create a directory, or move, copy, delete, or rename files. It shows the tree structure of each of your disks or partitions. You can expand or collapse different parts of the tree to show or hide subdirectories, and by double-clicking

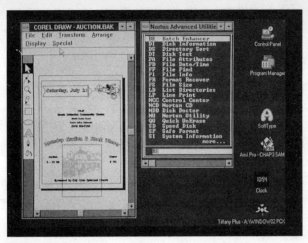

Microsoft Windows *3 - Handsomer, but also more powerful, faster, and more capable.*

you can see the contents of a directory.

The Task List window lists all active applications and lets you immediately switch between or arrange applications; the Task List is available by double-clicking on any blank screen space.

Native applications: With a few notable additions and changes, the same native accessories exist as from previous versions of Windows. Notepad, Write, Cardfile, and Calendar have changed little.

Paintbrush is a color painting/drawing program that is a great improvement on the old black-and-white Windows Paint. The Calculator includes a simple arithmetic machine as before, but there's also a new model with statistical, scientific, and programming capabilities. The Clock looks the same in analog mode, but now there's also a digital mode. Terminal has been substantially revamped with new communications capabilities (another related change: Four COM ports are now supported).

The PIF (Program Information File) editor has been expanded to cover the memory management and multitasking capabilities of Windows 3.0. Also new is the Recorder, which lets you capture keystrokes and mouse movements, and save them as macros. You can play them back at any time, and your macros can span applications.

The Spooler has been replaced by the Print Manager, which very nicely tells you which file is currently printing and what percentage of it is completed; it also lets you pause or terminate printing, and alter the priority of local printing jobs.

Installation and customization: One of the hair-tearing frustrations

Report Card

OPERATING ENVIRONMENT
Microsoft Windows Version 3.0

Performance		
Memory handling	(125)	Very Good
User interface	(75)	Very Good
Multitasking capabilities	(100)	Good
Speed	(75)	Good
Compatibility	(75)	Very Good
Data integration	(75)	Very Good
Other features	(50)	Excellent
Documentation	(50)	Very Good
Ease of setup	(50)	Very Good
Ease of learning	(50)	Very Good
Ease of use	(125)	Very Good
Error handling	(25)	Very Good
Support		
Support policies	(25)	Good
Technical support	(50)	Poor
Value	(50)	Excellent
Final score	**7.2**	

PRODUCT SUMMARY

Company: Microsoft Corp., 16011 N.E. 36th Way, P.O. Box 97017, Redmond, WA 98073; (206) 882-8080.

List Price: $149; $50 upgrade from any previous release or run-time version of Windows.

Requires: IBM PC AT, PS/2, or compatible; 640K of RAM (256K of extended memory recommended); hard drive; graphics support; MS-/PC-DOS 3.1 or later; mouse optional but recommended.

Pros: Great improvements; new interface; very customizable; effective memory management for multiple applications; numerous third-party applications available.

Cons: No notable speed improvements; technical support can be hard to reach currently; most old versions of Windows applications only run in real mode.

Summary: Windows 3.0 is a phenomenal improvement over previous versions of Windows. It is an effective graphical user interface for everyday use.

of previous Windows versions was that you had to reinstall the entire system to change a monitor, keyboard, or mouse, — from the orginal floppy disks. Finally, Windows has a Setup program that can be run within Windows to update your configuration. Unfortunately, if you have a nonsupported hardware device that typically comes with its own Windows driver (such as a large-screen, high-resolution monitor, for example, or a digitizing tablet), you'll still have to resort to changing your SYSTEM.INI file.

Windows has greatly improved customization; most features are accessible through the Control Panel icon, under which icons for all the various capabilities are found. You can alter colors, and Windows now supports 16 colors (or more, depending on the video adapter

Benchmarks
Microsoft Windows 3.0

	Windows 3.0 386 Enhanced	Windows 3.0 Standard Mode	Windows 3.0 Real Mode[1]	Windows/286 Version 2.11[1]
Microsoft Excel				
Open 297K file	0:13	0:12	0:13	0:13
Recalc	0:05	0:05	0:05	0:0
View 24K graph	0:11	0:10	0:12	0:09
Open 202K file	0:20	0:20	0:26	0:25
Swap windows	<0:01	<0:01	0:01	<0:01
Close 297K file	0:04	0:04	0:04	0:04
Micrografx Designer				
Load 46K drawing	0:45	0:40	0:44	0:36
Redraw	0:37	0:35	0:33	0:28
Zoom all pages	0:17	0:16	0:17	0:11
"Save as"	0:07	0:05	0:07	0:06
Multitasking,				
Excel and Designer	**0:21**	**0:24**	**0:23**	**0:29**

[1]Windows 3.0 in real mode and Windows/286 2.11 were both run using Qualitas' 386 Max memory manager.

you're using) instead of the old eight. There are a number of customizable, predefined desktop palettes, which contain pleasing combinations of colors for various types of windows, menu bars, and so forth. You can also select from a variety of predesigned background screens, called "wallpaper," to decorate your working area. You can also create and import your own background images.

Font installation and support has not changed dramatically. You have a few new niceties, such as a font viewer, but for the most part it is the same as in Windows 2.11. The configuration and setup screens for printers has been enhanced a little; the one very nice change is that more than one printer can be assigned to a port; you merely specify which is to be active. Also, you can specify paths to networked printers.

Networking: This release handles networks much better than the previous version. You don't have to exit Windows to perform common tasks such as attaching to a server or changing drive mappings. In the File Manager, specially marked icons designate network drives.

Microsoft includes network connectivity out of the box for industry-standard networks such as Novell Netware, Banyan Vines, 3Com 3+Open and 3+Share, IBM PC LAN, and LAN Manager and MS-Net derivatives. During installation on a workstation, Windows recognizes the existence of a network driver and installs the correct utilities on users' systems. A command-line option to the Setup command provides for running Windows off a network — it copies the core files to the server and user preference files to workstation disks.

Help: A final addition to the Windows features set is the new Help facility. This hypertextlike system provides indexes and in-depth topical discussions on virtually all Windows capabilities. However, it is not context-sensitive.

PERFORMANCE:

Previously, we have scored Microsoft Windows as a multitasking operating environment for running both Windows and non-Windows applications, in comparison with programs such as Desqview and VM/386. However, users can now choose from a full complement of Windows applications, so we are scoring Windows 3.0 on a new report card for graphical operating environments, and looking at its performance running on top of DOS compared with alternatives such as the Macintosh operating system with Multifinder; OS/2 with Presentation Manager; and Unix with the Motif, Open Look, or Next Step user interfaces.

Memory handling: One of the biggest changes in Windows 3.0 is its new memory-management features, including running applications in

Protected Mode on a 286 or 386, and supporting extended memory. This feature allows for applications to be larger than the 640K limit under current versions of DOS, and lets you run multiple large applications simultaneously on a 286 or higher.

Because Windows 3.0 exploits protected mode, a crash in a single Windows application is less likely to bring down the entire environment. This is particularly true in 386 enhanced mode, where even non-Windows applications run in their own "virtual machines." This isn't to say that the environment never crashes, however. We have seen several situations where a crashing program hurts the environment seriously; however, we usually received error messages telling us of the problems — and usually had enough time to save work in any other open applications before restarting Windows. Also, in 386 enhanced mode, Windows 3.0 implements "virtual memory," using a swap file on disk to act as additional RAM, letting you run multiple applications that would otherwise be too large to fit in memory.

The memory-handling features are limited somewhat by running on top of DOS, which after all was designed as a single-tasking, non-graphical environment. As a result, Windows does not have the memory management features of OS/2 or Unix. Still, Windows 3.0 is a big step in the right direction for DOS users, and we suspect anyone accustomed to DOS will be quite satisfied with the larger memory space, access to extended memory, protected mode operation, and virtual memory features. As a result, we rate Windows 3.0 very good in memory handling.

User interface: Windows 3.0 represents a giant step forward in user interface from Windows 2.11. The Program Manager makes it easier to start applications; the File Manager makes it easier to find your files; and the Task List makes it simple to switch among running applications. Many of the little details seem right, such as the shading or 3-D effects, which make it easier to tell when you've depressed a button.

Yet there's still room for improvement. The File Manager lacks several features that would be nice, including the capability to view the directories from two disks at once. Most Windows applications do not have as many consistent shortcuts as do most Macintosh applications, and the shortcuts that do exist across Windows applications for Cut (Shift-Delete), Copy (Control-Insert), and Paste (Shift-Insert) can take a little getting used to. Overall, though, it is quite nice — and certainly the push to Windows applications with a consistent user interface should help reduce training and support costs. We rate the Windows

3.0 user interface very good.

Multitasking capabilities: Particularly in 386 enhanced mode, Windows 3.0 now offers much improved multitasking capabilities, letting you run multiple Windows or non-Windows applications simultaneously. In this mode, you can use the PIF editor to assign application priorities and foreground and background settings, enhancing multitasking performance significantly.

One weakness compared with environments such as DESQview and VM/386 is that Windows does not actually run non-Windows graphics-based applications in the background. You can load such applications, and switch back to them, but their operation is normally suspended while displaying graphics.

Finally, presumably because it is built on top of DOS, Windows does not have the multitasking features of the more sophisticated operating systems, such as OS/2. Notably, it doesn't have pre-emptive multitasking (where applications can intelligently request CPU cycles) and multithreaded applications (where an application runs as if it were several independent parts).

Balancing the very good job it does when running character-based, non-Windows applications against its limits with graphics programs, we rate Windows good in multitasking capabilities.

Speed: How you will perceive speed in Windows is largely a function of what you expect, and what mode you are running Windows in. In many cases, Windows 3.0 is somewhat slower running individual Windows applications than Windows 2.11. This is particularly true running graphics applications in 386 enhanced mode, where taking advantage of the 386's "virtual mode" means additional overhead in storing video information. You'll normally see better graphics performance running a single application in real mode or standard mode.

However, where Windows really shines is in running multiple Windows applications. The new memory management features and protected mode support allow multiple Windows to actually run much faster, particularly if you have applications attempting to complete tasks while running in the background. Balancing the slower performance running a single application against the better performance running multiple applications, we rate Windows good in speed.

Compatibility: In general, Windows 3.0 does a fine job of running both applications designed specifically for that environment, as well as most non-Windows applications — even relatively large applications. On our test 386 running the Novell Netware shell, DOS applications running under Windows still had about 450K of free space. Windows 3.0, however, will not let you load device drivers into high memory; large network and other device drivers will subtract from the maximum size of the DOS programs you can run. (Windows applications do not need to run in conventional RAM, so this limitation does not apply to them.)

Some programs that use "DOS extenders" to access extended memory, notably Lotus 1-2-3, Release 3, do not run under Windows in the 386 enhanced mode. Such programs can be run under standard or real modes; and you can expect their vendors to quickly update them to 386 mode. Also, you will receive an error message if you try to run programs designed for Windows 2.11 that have not been "marked" to run under Windows 3.0. In general, such programs do not run well in either standard or 386 modes; you can still run them under real mode. In most cases, the vendors of these programs either already have updates available or plan to shortly. We rate overall compatibility very good.

Data integration: Windows continues to offer terrific data integration capabilities. Using the Clipboard, you can cut and paste data between applications; this extends to copying text to and from non-Windows applications. You can even copy graphics from non-Windows applications into Windows applications. Furthermore, a growing number of Windows applications now support Dynamic Data Exchange (DDE), which lets you create hot links between files so that when you change information in one file, the change will be reflected in the other file.

Although it doesn't offer quite the communications features between applications of OS/2 or the planned Mac System 7, nor the capability to encapsulate other applications within an application, like HP's New Wave, Windows clearly offers very good data integration features.

Other features: Network and printer support have been substantially enhanced in Windows 3.0. You can now easily attach or detach a server from within Windows, search a network drive, or start a network utility. Third-party additions undoubtedly improve on these network features, but it's good to have the basics built into the environment. Printer support is very nice, including a new Print Manager that lets you view files being spooled in various queues, change priorities or pause individual files; and view various network queues. Most dot-matrix, ink-jet, and laser printers (including PostScript) are supported directly by Windows, although individual applications often come with some more unusual output drivers; e.g., word processors may support daisy-wheel printers and graphics programs may support film recorders or slide-making services.

Windows 3.0 comes with a nice set of bundled applications. Write is an adequate — although not exciting — word processor; Paintbrush is a quite nice painting program; and Terminal is a surprisingly full-featured communications package, mainly lacking the programming features and some of the protocols of its stand-alone brethren. Other accessories include Notepad, Clock, Calculator, and a useful Macro recorder that captures your keystrokes and mouse movements. Windows 3.0 also comes with Daybook, a very visual personal information manager written in Asymetrix Tool Book (although Daybook's usefulness is somewhat limited, and it is very slow unless you run it on a fast 386 with plenty of RAM).

It's tough to imagine how a basic operating environment could be expected to include any more tools. We rate Windows excellent in other features.

DOCUMENTATION:

The Windows Users' Guide has been overhauled. It is no longer one volume divided into separate "books" addressing Windows and its accessories, but one logically organized book that clearly adresses all of the topics in an orderly fashion. It covers all of Windows' features, its operation and accessories, and is complemented by a number of useful advanced sections on system optimization, networking, and memory management.

A further addition to Windows' documentation is the on-line help system, which, although it is not context-sensitive, is a decent implementation of a hypertext-style help system. Help is organized by topics and, for included Windows applications, each help file includes a comprehensive index. There is also a keyword search feature to help you jump from topic to topic, and a "bookmark" feature helps you get to frequently referenced help screens. Sometimes Windows' help system is a little difficult to use when you're trying to find a feature that isn't on any menu, in which case resorting to the manual's index is a good idea.

The error messages generated in Windows are clearly explained in lay terms, with plenty of information to help you navigate out of most problems.

Windows 3.0's manual is clear, concise, and useful. However, context-sensitive help would be a great addition. We rate documentation very good.

EASE OF SETUP:

Installing Windows has been exceptionally streamlined, to the point that it reads the information it needs directly from your system; swapping disks and answering basic questions are about all you have to do. The only downside is that applications for previous Windows versions may not run. If this happens, you'll have to get upgrades or run them in real mode.

The Setup application starts from the DOS prompt and works in character mode while the core of Windows is installed; then it launches Windows and finishes installation itself. Unlike the previous versions of Windows, you don't have to reload the entire system from floppy disks when you want to install a new keyboard, video driver, or similar peripherals. Ease of setup is very good.

EASE OF LEARNING:

There's no doubt that approaching Windows 3.0 for the first time can be a little intimidating. If you've never seen a graphical user interface before, there's a lot to learn and see. Yet Microsoft has done much to improve intuitiveness, and navigating through the various windows has been optimized with the addition of the Program Manager and File Manager. It's much easier to launch applications when you see them all as icons in one or two windows instead of having to wallow through subdirectory listings in search of one elusive .EXE file.

If you don't have a mouse, you can run Windows with the keyboard, but it's hardly advisable.

Overall, Windows is very easy to learn given its size and complexity. We rate ease of learning very good.

EASE OF USE:

The extensive face-lift Windows has undergone results in significant ease-of-use benefits. The changes in the interface make it easier to jump between applications; the installation/setup options make it easier to add or change equipment; and the memory management prevents you from constantly bumping into memory "ceilings" or conflicts. Other little additions, like a Move command that lets you move files from one place to another, and the capability to click on and drag application icons to other windows or file names to other drives, make for much easier use. The macro Recorder and the numerous shortcut keys available also enhance ease of use, making it easy to automate various steps.

While you can automatically organize windows, by cascading or tiling them or straightening out unruly icons, it could be a tad better. The icons, for example, when organized, always default to the bottom of the window; it would be easier if they would remain in the same general area in the window.

The changes in Windows are more than welcome — they were necessary for its success. We find them very effective and rate ease of use very good.

ERROR HANDLING:

Unlike Windows' previous iterations, it's tough to hang this system. With Windows 2.11, users were accustomed to running out of memory and having the system quit entirely. The biggest problems nowadays occur when trying to run previous Windows applications under Version 3.0 in the full-bore standard or 386 enhanced mode. While virtually all older applications will run in real mode, it's anybody's guess whether or not you'll hit a conflict if you try to run them in standard or enhanced mode. Most of our unruly applications brought up a warning and let us save data in other applications before Windows gave up and dumped us out of the system. Windows does an admirable job of protecting applications from each other — much better than Apple's current Multifinder, in fact.

Windows is not completely bug-free, of course. We noticed a little snag with Write's automatic time/date stamp feature: It correctly inserts the date, but leaves out the time. This will presumably be fixed in a maintenance release.

Given its improvement in stability and memory management, we rate Windows' error handling very good.

SUPPORT:

Microsoft offers unlimited, free technical support on a toll line, as well as BBS support. Phone lines are open Monday through Friday from 6 a.m. to 6 p.m. Pacific time. We rate support policies good.

The technical support lines were quite busy during our test period (right after Windows 3.0 was released). We were able to get through to the toll support line a few times, however, although we had to hold for five minutes or more almost every time. The support staff was adequately helpful and provided sufficient answers to our questions. Due to the repeated waits for technical support, however, we rate technical support poor.

VALUE:

Windows costs $149, and it is $50 to upgrade from any previous version or run-time version of Windows. Windows has always been relatively inexpensive (previously, the full version was $99 for the 286 and $195 for the 386 versions), and it continues this trend. Your real cost will come in upgrading your applications; while some are free and others are inexpensive, if you are managing many installed users or a number of applications, you should be prepared to pay for the new versions. Also, the vast majority of applications won't ship with run-time Windows anymore, so if you've been running programs in that mode you will have to buy Windows to get the benefits of Version 3.0. To really take advantage of Windows, you'll want either a fast 286 or a 386 machine, preferably with at least 2 megabytes of extended memory.

While there is a toll-free number you can call to get upgrade information for Windows applications ([800] 323-3577), we never managed to make it through the busy signals.

Considering the price of Windows 3.0, its performance and capabilities make it an excellent value.

Also reviewed in this book are the following Windows products:
Ami Professional
Word for Windows - word processor
Excel for Windows - spreadsheet
PageMaker for Windows - DTP high end

APPENDIX A
Glossary of Computer Terms

General Computer Terms

286 system - A moderately fast IBM PC-compatible computer system which uses an Intel 80286 chip as its main processor. Also known as an "AT," after IBM's first such model, it runs three to five times faster than an IBM XT-compatible computer system. (*See* XT-class system.)

386 system - A very fast IBM PC-compatible computer system which uses an Intel 80386 chip as its main processor. It runs five to twenty-five times faster than an IBM XT-compatible computer system.

486 system - The fastest class of IBM PC-compatible computer system; it uses an Intel 80486 chip as its main processor. (The Intel 80586 is not due for another year or two.) The 25-MHz model runs about 50 times faster than an IBM XT-compatible system.

640K system - A computer with 640K of RAM, or user memory, the maximum DOS can normally use (without going to EMS); the minimum you should demand in your XT or 286 system (a 386 or 486 should start with at least one megabyte of RAM).

ASCII - A standard format or code system PCs use for storing text data. Some programs store their own data in slightly modified ASCII, others store it in their own proprietary format. (A data format is simply a code for data; for example, that eight bits arranged in a specific way will stand for the letter "A," and arranged in a different way will stand for the letter "B.") Since most programs can read or write "plain ASCII" data, it is sometimes used as an intermediate format for transferring data between programs. However, in a word processing file stored as ASCII loses its special word processing formats such as boldfacing and font choices; and a spreadsheet stored as ASCII loses its formulas, so ASCII is a lowest-common-denominator format.

Assembly language - Computers use "machine code" for internal operations, but since it's just zeros and ones, humans find it hard to decipher. Assembly language is a "low level" programming language which substitutes short words for specific machine operations to make programming easier. A "compiler" converts the assembly-language code to machine code for execution. Assembly language can be very efficient and fast, though hard to use. "High-level languages" from BASIC to COBOL substitute short words for more complex operations, which makes them easier to use but also less efficient and therefore slower in operation.

AUTOEXEC.BAT - An optional startup batch file containing various MS-DOS commands that automatically execute when the system is turned on or restarted.

BASIC - A personal computer programming language originally made popular by its ease of learning. Best-known brands are Microsoft products: MS-BASIC, GW-BASIC, and Quick BASIC. Microsoft is introducing it as an advanced macro language for Microsoft Windows users.

C - A popular computer language; programs written in C run almost as fast as those written in assembly language, but are much easier to program. There are versions of C available on almost every kind of computer from microcomputer to mainframe computer, so you can port (translate) a program written in C to other systems.

Cold boot - Restarting your computer by first turning off the power (or pressing a power interrupt switch). You might do this after a severe program error causes the computer to "hang," or freeze and refuse to respond to the keyboard. *See also* "warm boot."

CONFIG.SYS - A startup configuration file your computer uses during system startup to configure certain aspects of the hardware and operating system.

Customizing - Modifying a standard hardware or software product to meet your specific needs.

DDE - Dynamic Data Exchange. A feature of Microsoft Windows (*see* Windows) that lets two different kinds of programs (a spreadsheet and a word processor, for instance) share information automatically and dynamically.

Debugger - A utility program you use to help you locate and remove errors (bugs) from a program or macro you've written.

DESQview - A nongraphical windowing, multitasking software package for the IBM PC and compatibles that allows you to run several programs at the same time and switch between them. Since it is not a graphical interface, DESQview requires less powerful computers than does Microsoft Windows (*see* Windows).

Dialogue box - A small box or window that appears on screen so a program can ask the user a question, get more data, or offer some options. Once the question is answered, the window disappears.

DOS - An acronym for Disk Operating System, the underlying software that applications (programs like word processors and spreadsheets) use to manage and interact with the computer's hardware, such as the disk drives and the monitor. MS-DOS (from MicroSoft) or PC-DOS (from IBM) are used on IBM PC compatibles; the Macintosh, Apple II, Amiga, Atari, and other families of personal computers each have their own operating systems, as do minicomputers and mainframe computers. *See also* OS/2, Unix.

EGA - A popular type of high-resolution computer display; better quality than CGA, but not as good as VGA.

EMS (Expanded Memory Specification) - a form of RAM. IBM PC compatibles are usually limited by the operation system (MS-DOS or PC-DOS) to using 640K of RAM (called "conventional RAM") for programs and data. The EMS specification (sometimes called EEMS or LIM specification) is a workaround that makes it possible to use memory beyond that limit, up to about 16 megabytes. Programs capable of using EMS can store data, and some program code, in this extra memory. Your computer automatically has EMS memory if it is a 386-based computer with a megabyte or more of RAM and an EMS software driver such as Quarterdeck's QEMM, Compaq's CEMM, Microsoft's Windows Hi-Mem, or 386-Max; or if you have an EMS memory board in your computer.

File compression - Squeezing down the size of one or more files using a compression program; done to save disk space or to reduce the time required to send files by modem.

File Format - The code a program uses to store data; different programs use different formats, some of them proprietary (so other programs can't read the data). Some formats act as *interchange*, or common file formats where one program can export the data to that format and another can import it. Examples of common formats are ASCII for text, DCA for formatted word processing, SYLK or DIF for spreadsheets, CSV (or comma separated values) for databases, and WKS for Lotus spreadsheets (which most other programs can import).

Function keys - Keys labeled F1 through F10 or F12 on the IBM PC and PS/2 keyboards. Their function depends on the software being run, but generally they perform special functions or shortcuts.

GUI (Graphical User Interface) - *See* Interface. The Macintosh and Microsoft Windows both use a graphical user interface — their screen displays are drawn dot-by-dot and can be changed dot-by-dot, like a painting or graphic. GUIs generally show icons, or small pictures, which you select by clicking on them with the mouse, which saves on the need for typing. Text interfaces, by contrast, show only text and have very limited graphical capabilities. (Text interfaces, too, are capable of displaying icons and offering mouse-selectable commands and operations; FoxPro is an example. But most people think of icon interfaces as being GUI.) GUIs offer flexibility and beauty, but they demand the fastest possible computer with lots of RAM and disk storage.

Hard Disk - A rigid magnetic disk, usually built into a computer, used to store data and programs; sometimes called a fixed disk, in contrast to a floppy disk which is flexible and can be removed and stored externally. Hard disk capacity is measured in megabytes, or millions of bytes (characters) of storage. Hard disks also operate faster than floppy disks. Forty, 60 and 90 megabyte hard drives are most common for business personal computers.

Hardware - The physical elements of a computer system such as integrated circuits, wires, and terminals. *See also* Software.

High end - a term applied to products that are priced higher than average; they are usually intended to be far more powerful and are aimed at users with specific needs that justify paying a premium to get extra capability.

Icon - A picture on a computer screen that represents a particular object, command, or operation. For example, on a Macintosh computer, the picture of a trash can represents a "delete" command. Using a mouse to drag a file to the trash can will result in the file being deleted.

Interface - The method by which a machine or program interacts with the user. In a computer program, an interface is the way the program looks,

how its menus are activated and used, whether it uses graphics and color
to dramatize what is going on, and anything else you use to get the program to do something. In hardware, the interface is the control panels,
buttons, lights, and keyboard you use to give orders and see results.

Keyboard terms: Several keys on the keyboard have special functions. The
Alt and Ctrl keys are used in conjunction with other keys (in the same
manner as a shift key) to issue a command to the computer. This effectively increases the number of commands (or command shortcuts) available when using a program.

Kilobyte (K) - A unit of information storage; it equals 1,024, or about one
thousand, bytes or characters. A typewritten, double-spaced page contains
about 2K of data.

Low-end - a term applied to products that are priced at the lower end of the
market; typically (but not always) they are designed to be less complicated, less powerful, and less ambitious than standard products. Low-end
products are typically aimed at novice users, or those with limited needs.

Macro - A sequence of keystrokes or commands that are recorded and stored
so they can be played back automatically. You might have a macro in a
spreadsheet that automatically sets the printer parameters and prints the
end-of-the-month report, for example. Macros are made available in many
programs.

Megabyte (M) - A unit of information storage, typically with reference to
disk drives or RAM. One megabyte equals 1,048,576 bytes, or about a
million bytes or characters. It's also a thousand Kilobytes.

Memory-resident (RAM-resident or TSR) programs (TSR is an acronym
for the technical term Terminate-and-Stay-Resident) - A program that is
loaded into background memory, so it can be called up in the middle of
another program. These programs provide "pop-up" functions, such as a
calendar or calculator, which can be called up and exited in the middle of
a program.

On-line help - Helpful information about an application, which resides within the application and can be readily called up by hitting the "help" key.

OS/2 - A next-generation operating system IBM developed as a replacement
for PC-DOS and the MS-DOS operating systems..

Pascal - A popular personal computer programming language, originally
designed to teach students how to write well-structured programs.

PIM - Personal Information Manager, a category of software that lets you
organize miscellaneous daily information.

Platform - The kind of hardware/operating system combination on which
software can run; for instance, a word processor may have versions on
Unix, MS-DOS, and Sun "platforms." Also used to refer to a level of
hardware performance: a program developed for "high-performance platforms" will require the fastest computer you can find.

Pop-up menus - A box that "pops up" and contains a menu listing options.

Presentation Manager - *See* Interface. A graphical user interface for OS/2;
it makes OS/2 look similar to Microsoft Windows.

Printer driver - A short file containing details of how a specific printer works. Application programs use them to look up printer codes for functions like printing boldfaced or changing fonts, codes for which vary from printer brand to printer brand.

Pull-down menus - Menu boxes that "pull down" from a menu bar at the top of the screen.

RAM - A (now-meaningless) acronym for Random Access Memory. A computer's RAM is its main, active memory from which programs and data are run. Generally, RAM loses its data when the computer is shut off. Disk drives, by contrast, are longer-term storage for programs and data, which must be loaded into RAM before they can be used. The amount of RAM (measured in K or Kilobytes, thousands of characters) is one measure of a computer's capacity (the other is the size of its disk drive). The more RAM, the larger the programs that can load, and the faster they can run.

SAA (Systems Application Architecture) - A proposed interface standard IBM intends to implement across all its computers from PCs to mainframes. The most visible element to the average person is the use of pulldown menus from which one can select program commands.

Silicon disk - Memory chips used as if they were disk drives; unlike RAM chips, these are capable of retaining data even when the power is off.

Software - Instructions that make computer go, and the data the computer uses or produces. Software is usually in the form of programs (called utilities or applications, depending on use). Software (programs) can be stored on disk prior to being loaded into the computer's memory for execution; so such disks and their documentation and packaging are loosely referred to as software also.

Support (technical support) - Aid provided by a product vendor to help buyers install, configure, or solve problems with the product. The aid is usually provided by phone, fax, or an online service like CompuServe.

System reboot - Restarting your computer.

UNIX - An operating system (which manages computer hardware for the application programs) which is available on a variety of computer platforms, including IBM PC compatibles, the Macintosh, and most minicomputers. Unix is most popular in universities and among engineers and scientists.

VGA - A form of super-high-resolution computer display, the highest resolution commonly seen on IBM PC compatibles these days.

Warm boot - Restarting your computer without turning off the power, by pressing a special series of keys (Ctrl-Alt-Delete) to force it to reload the operating system. You might do this after a program error hangs or freezes a program, but the computer still responds to the keyboard. A warm booting takes less time than cold boot because the computer doesn't have to go through a RAM test cycle first.

Windows (Microsoft Windows) - A windowing, multitasking software package which creates a graphical working environment for programs on the IBM PC similar to that of the Apple Macintosh, and lets you run several programs at the same time and switch between them.

Windows (on screen) - Boxed areas on the screen; they might contain separate programs you can switch among, or special information within a program.

XT-class system - An older, slower IBM PC-compatible computer system which uses an Intel 8088 or 8086 chip as its main processor.

Spreadsheet terms

3D/Three-dimensional spreadsheet - A spreadsheet composed of a stack of several similar worksheets; for example, a corporate quarterly report composed of several worksheets each containing the quarterly report for one division. A spreadsheet program that can consolidate the data on all these worksheets into a master worksheet is said to be a three-dimensional spreadsheet. (Three-dimensional graphs, on the other hand, are graphic displays on the screen which look three-dimensional.)

@functions - A set of special commands that can be entered in a spreadsheet cell, which can perform advanced calculations and provide the resulting value.

Add-In Manager (Lotus 1-2-3) A Lotus utility that allows you to "add in" after-the-product features to the application where the feature actually becomes part of Lotus, using its code unlike other "add-on" features which do not and are therefore, less efficient.

Auditing - It's easy to make mistakes in creating a complex spreadsheet; it's not so easy to spot the errors. An auditing feature reviews your spreadsheets and looks for problems, such as circular references, formulas that refer to to cells that don't have anything in them, or data cells in the middle of a block of formula cells (often a mistake), for example.

Background recalc - When the spreadsheet performs its calculations in the background, so you can continue entering data in the primary area of the computer screen.

consolidation - An operation that permits you to collect specific data from a series of spreadsheets, or what's known as a divisional roll-up, where spreadsheets from many divisions in a company can be consolidated into one, for instance.

DIF, SYLK, CSV, WK1, WKS, WR1, WK3 - Various formats for storing spreadsheet data. The ones that begin with "WK" are used by different versions of Lotus 1-2-3. *See* File format under "General Computer Terms".

Goal-seeking - A type of spreadsheet model in which you list your beginning point (such as this month's sales), and your desired goal (such as sales in the sixth month) and the program calculates the intermediate steps (such as how much sales have to grow each month to meet this goal), to give a simplistic example.

Linking - The ability to pass information between spreadsheets.

Page preview - A command that allows you to view a document as it will look when printed out.

Point-and-shoot - The ability to point cursor at a selection (one you want) and choose it; characteristic of an interface style.

Slash key - Commands in Lotus 1-2-3, and in some of its competitors, are accessed by typing the slash key on the keyboard; this causes a menu to appear or become active. This is referred to as the Lotus interface.

Strings - Text characters, as opposed to calculatable numbers or formulas.

Turn-key application - A program that has been set up for you and is ready to run; you need do nothing but "turn the key."

User-defined functions - The capability to create your own spreadsheet functions (usually by combining several built-in functions and assigning them a name).

What-if scenario - Repeatedly changing various assumptions in your spreadsheet to see what will happen under different circumstances. For example, "What if the Northwest region sales grew at 2% per month instead of 1.5%?"

Worksheet; organized in lettered columns and numbered rows. - The standard organization for a spreadsheet form where cells are arranged both vertically and horizontally.

WYSIWYG - An acronym for "What You See Is What You Get". The term refers to the status of the printout of a screen image. If a program is said to be WYSIWYG, it means that whatever is seen on the screen will look exactly the same when printed out.

Word Processing terms

Character-based - as opposed to graphical (like Windows or the Macintosh)

Clip art - Artwork created by others, but which can be freely reproduced by anyone. Several clip art collections are available on disk which can be used in a variety of programs.

Clipboard - An area to which information can be copied in order to transfer it from one application program to another. For example, the clipboard can be used to transfer text from a word processor into a drawing program.

DCA - *See* File format. A universal format for exchanging formatted word processing files between different programs without losing any of the formatting.

DCA/RFT - A specific element of the DCA exchange format.

Electronic outlining - A feature in some word processing programs that allows you to create an outline as well as regular text.

Export - the ability to store data in the format used by another program.

Formatting - The act of imposing a basic structure on a medium, such as setting sector boundaries on a magnetic disk.

Global replacement - Changing a sequence of characters throughout an entire document

Imports - the ability to bring in data created in another program.

Label support - The ability to print labels easily.

Mail merge - A command that allows you to merge large volumes of addresses from an application into one mailing list ready for printing out on to labels, for instance.

PCL - An acronym for Printer Control Language. A printer language used by the Hewlett-Packard family of plotters.

PostScript - A page-description language used to send fonts and graphics from a computer to a printer (or other display or output device) in a manner that allows the printer to print the image at the highest quality of which it is capable.

Printer font - The shape, size, and style of a particular typeface used by any machine that can produce printed copy.

Screen-capture program - A program which is able to "capture" whatever is on the screen and save it on a disk as a picture. Many technical publications use such a program to illustrate how a screen should look when a certain command is carried out.

Soft font - A font you can download from your computer to your laser printer when you need it, as opposed to fonts on cartridges that are inserted into the printer.

Spreadsheet import - the ability to bring in data created by a spreadsheet program.

Style tag - A shortcut method of assigning styles to documents. A style tag consists of some characters you use to mark heads, subheads, and paragraphs in your word processing document so that your desktop publishing program will recognize it and apply predefined styles to the text automatically. For example, if you created a tag in Quark Express for the main chapter head called <HEAD1> and typed that in front of the heading, "CHAPTER 1," in your word processing document , then in quark defined HEAD1 as 24 point Times bold centered with 3 picas following, the result when you imported the word processing file into Quark Express would be the words, "CHAPTER 1," in large type centered on your screen.

Style sheet - A sheet created in an application to set the style for the particular document being worked on. Style considerations include fonts, spelling, heads, subheads, etc.

Table generation - Features that make it easy to create and enter data into tables (rows and columns, like spreadsheets).

Template - A specification of a structure which allows programs to declare their own data types.

Wrap - The way in which text automatically moves, or "wraps" to the next line when it reaches the margin limits of each line.

Database terms

ANSI Level 2-compatible SQL - A standards-setting board; Level 2 is a basic standard database vendors are trying to follow in implementing Structured Query Language(*see* SQL) in their products.

Applications generator - A feature in database management programs that lets the user create a database application (such as a customer database), complete with data entry screens and reports, without writing program code.

Foreign keys - A "key" is the main indexed field, or column that a database management program uses to keep track of the data. A foreign key is an indexed field in another data file that can be matched to a corresponding field in the current file so matching data can be retrieved from two separate data files.

Object-oriented - Programming using objects as opposed to characters.

One-to-many - *See* relational database. A relational database term in which fields in one data file are linked to fields in several other database files. A database that can't handle one-to-many relationships can't be used to create certain kinds of databases (such as banking database in which each customer might have several separate bank accounts.

Prompt-by-example - An easy-to-use method of querying a database by filling out a form.

QBE - Query By Example, another easy-to-use method of querying a database by filling out a form.

Relational database - Technically, a table-oriented database system following the rules of relational math. The relational method is very powerful and most database vendors are trying to implement it in their existing databases. Any database that can link or "relate" two data files through a common field might be called a "relational" database in order to enjoy the cachet of this term, even though they don't follow the most basic rules of relational databases (a good example is the dBASE family, which is record-oriented rather than table-oriented.)

SQL - Structured Query Language: a database "query language" designed by IBM, SQL lets a moderately trained computer user extract basic information from a relational database. It is becoming a standard by which database products are supposed to be able to access data maintained by databases from rival vendors – if the vendors can ever agree on the details of implementation.

Template language - In databases, a template is a partially written application that contains stock information, definitions, settings, and other design elements that always remains the same in all your similar applications. For example, if you always use a sign-on screen with your business name and address, you can put that in your template so you don't have to enter it every time you start creating a new application. An applications generator that uses your templates reduces development time.

Desktop publishing terms

Bitmap - Used to display graphics on the screen using pixels, where each pixel is stored in a specific memory location

CAD - An acronym for Computer Aided Design. Process of designing objects using computer technology where the designer uses a computer terminal as a window to access data and design tools.

dpi - Dots-per-inch. Desktop laser printers commonly print at 300 dpi; professional laser printers start at 1200 dpi and go to 2400 dpi or beyond. Screen resolution can also be measured in dpi.

Fill patterns - A "fill" is a pattern used to fill up an area, to distinguish it. For example, in a bar chart, the bars may be filled with different patterns to distinguish them from one another.

Folios - Page numbers.

GIF - A file format containing graphical images.

IMG - A file format containing graphical images used by the GEM operating environment (e.g., the GEM version of Ventura Publisher.)

PCX - A popular file format containing graphical images originally invented by makers of PC Paintbrush, a paint program.

PostScript - A page-description language used to send fonts and graphics from a computer to a printer (or other display or output device) in a manner that allows the printer to print the image at the highest quality of which it is capable.

Scanner - An electronic device used to transfer original printed or handwritten pages into a computer file. Particularly useful in putting pictures into a computer.

Serif - Ornamental extensions on the top and bottom of letters such as the letter "T". One purpose of the serif is to help the reader's eye stay on a line of type.

Spot-color - In publishing, simple colors applied to areas of the page; you might use spot color to highlight a picture. Spot color doesn't require color separations and so it is cheaper.

Style-sheet tag - In desktop publishing or word processing, a style sheet is a list of styles created by the user and collected under individual names. For example, your style sheet may contain the BODYCOPY style; when this style is applied to a paragraph in your document, it may make the text italicized, 12 point Palatino (a type of font).

Text wrap - The way in which text automatically moves, or "wraps" to the next line when it reaches the margin limits of each line.

Toolboxes - A box on a desktop publishing application that is always visible on the screen and which allows a user to access text and graphics tools by selecting them with a mouse.

WYSIWYG - An acronym for "What You See Is What You Get". The term refers to the status of the printout of a screen image. If a program is said to be WYSIWYG, it means that whatever is seen on the screen will look exactly the same when printed out.

APPENDIX B

Reviewer Biographies and Dates of Publication

The **word processing** product comparison was developed by Jeff Eckert and Steve Irvin, Test Center; John Lombardi, Contributing Editor; Michael J. Miller, Editor-in-Chief; Gregory S. Smith, Test Development Specialist; and Serge Timacheff, Associate Reviews Editor. Our word processing reviewer, John Lombardi, is provost of a major university and author of five books. He has been working with computers since 1967. and reviewing word processing processors for InfoWorld for nearly a decade.

The **spreadsheets** product comparison was developed by Sebastian Rupley, Associate Reviews Editor; Michael J. Miller, Editor-in-Chief; Gregory S. Smith, Test Development Specialist; John Walkenbach, Review Board; and Tracey Capen and John Richey, Test Center. John Walkenbach, our spreadsheet reviewer, is consumer research manager for a large savings and loan association in Southern California.

The **desktop publishing** product comparisons were developed by Galen Gruman and Barbara Assadi, Review Board; Mark Houts, Art Director; Michael J. Miller, Editor-in-Chief; and Serge Timacheff, Associate Reviews Editor. Our PC desktop publishing reviewer, Galen Gruman, has set up an electronic publishing system for a bimonthly trade magazine and a quarterly national association newsletter. Barbara Assadi, our Macintosh desktop publishing reviewer, is manager of employee communications for a major financial services company. She also lectures and consults independently on desktop publishing.

The **database** product comparison was developed by Nicholas Petreley, Contributing Editor (author of the DataEase, DataFlex, R:BASE, and Smartware II reviews); Judy Duncan, Review Board (author of the dBXL review); Zoreh Banapour and Linda Slovick, Test Center technicians; Carla Mathews, Associate Reviews Editor; and Michael McCarthy, Executive Editor/Reviews. Database reviewer Nicholas Petreley spent five years developing database systems for business; he is now a contributing editor and test development specialist for *InfoWorld*. Database reviewer Judy Duncan owns Duncan Engineering, a California consulting firm specializing in custom multiuser databases.

Our Windows review was designed by Gregory S. Smith, Test Development Specialist; Michael J. Miller, Editor-in-Chief; and Serge Timacheff, Associate Reviews Editor. Graphics reviewer Michael Heck is a project manager for Unisys Corp.

Dates of Publication

Original dates of publication in *InfoWorld* of the reviews and product comparisons in this volume (all 1990):

Word Processing: January 29
Spreadsheets: January 22
Desktop Publishing for Professional Results: January 1
PageMaker 4 review: July 16
Affordable Desktop Publishing: June 18
Relational Databases: January 8, and June 25; the dBASE version 1.1 writeup is adapted from the review published August 20.
Windows 3: June 4

Prices, features, system requirements, and other facts are as of date of publication. Technical support calls were made during the month prior to publication date and may have improved (or declined) since then. All prices mentioned are list prices; actual retail prices are generally much lower.

Software Index

More from the New World of Computer Books...
IDG Books Worldwide

Other Valuable Guides from the New World of Computer Books...IDG Books Worldwide

Finally--a practical guide to portable computing!

Portable Computing Official Laptop Field Manual

▲ A complete, take-it-with-you-on-the-road-manual:
   with printer codes, software keystroke references,
   on-line access phone numbers, individual hardware
   references, DOS summaries, and more

▲ Leave your manuals at home--everything you need is in this one handy-sized book!

▲ From Portable Computing Magazine--the mobile professional's monthly bible

$14.95

by Sebastian Rupley, with a foreword by Jim McBrian, Publisher,
Portable Computing Magazine
1-878058-10-X, 224 pp., 5 1/2 x 8 1/2"

The powerful programming tool you need for Paradox 3.5!

PC World Paradox 3.5 Breakthrough Power Programming

▲With hundreds of programming tips and techniques not found in any other book

▲ Definitive coverage of the Paradox engine, PAL, and SQL Link

▲ Includes one 3 1/2" disk of valuable software, including a ready-to-run accounting system, an advanced program editor, and utility scripts-- fully customizable and worth $$ hundreds!

$39.95, includes one 3 1/2"disk with over 2 Mb of program code,
condensed onto a 1.44Mb disk
by Greg Salcedo & Martin Rudy, with a foreword by Richard Swartz, Borland International
1-878058-02-9, 750 pp., 7 3/8 x 9 1/4"

Available at your local bookstore or computer/software store.
Or call (800) 28BOOKS.
(That's (800) 282-6657)

IDG Books Worldwide Registration Card - InfoWorld Test Center Buyer's Guide

Please take the time to fill this out—and you'll be sure to hear about updates to this book and new information about other IDG Books Worldwide products. Thanks!

Name _____

Company/Title _____

Address _____

City/State/Zip _____

What is the single most important reason you bought this book? _____

Where did you buy this book?
- ❑ Bookstore (Name _____)
- ❑ Electronics/Software Store (Name _____)
- ❑ Advertisement (If magazine, which?_____)
- ❑ Mail Order
- ❑ Other:

How did you hear about this book?
- ❑ Book review in: _____
- ❑ Advertisement in: _____
- ❑ Catalog
- ❑ Found in store
- ❑ Other: _____

How many computer books do you purchase a year?
- ❑ 1
- ❑ 2-5
- ❑ 6-10
- ❑ More than 10

How would you rate the overall content of this book?
- ❑ Very good
- ❑ Good
- ❑ Satisfactory
- ❑ Poor

Why? _____

What chapters did you find most valuable? _____

What did you find least useful? _____

What type of computer are you using or do you intend to buy? _____

What kind of chapter or topic would you add to future editions of this book?

_____

Please give us any additional comments. _____

_____

Thank you for your help.

❑ I liked this book! By checking this box, I give you permission to use my name and quote me in future IDG Books Worldwide promotional materials.

FOLD HERE

IDG Books Worldwide, Inc.
155 Bovet Road, Ste. 730
San Mateo, CA 94402

Attn: Reader Response